Praise for *The Berman Murders*

"The 1986 murders of Barry and Louise Berman in the Mojave Desert remains unsolved. Countless theories, including alien abduction, have been mentioned in the speculation as to what happened to the couple, who were in the area on a camping trip. Attorney and journalist Kari, in his first book, presents a theory that could help solve the case once and for all. He probes whether an encounter with former U.S. Marine Corps captain Michael Pepe on the same day they went missing led to the Bermans' deaths. Readers will learn more about that chance meeting, the link between Pepe and a Cambodian sex-trafficking ring. Readers should expect graphic descriptions of the crimes. For true-crime fans who want to be taken through the details, the theories, and every piece of evidence of the Berman murders case."

—*Library Journal*

"Attorney and journalist Kari debuts with a stirring account of his nine-year quest to crack an unsolved double murder in California's Mojave Desert. In 1986, Barry Berman, heir to the Kahlua liquer fortune, and his much older wife, Louise, went missing from their campground during a romantic getaway at the Mojave hot springs. Although police suspected foul play, and the Bermans' remains were discovered in a makeshift grave three years after their disappearance, the case never led to any arrests. Kari, who learned about the murders as a young conservationist studying the desert, became interested again as a journalist decades later. His investigation put him on the trail of Marine Corps captain Mike Pepe, who encountered the Bermans at the campground the same day they disappeared. Years later, Pepe moved to Cambodia and engaged in underage sex trafficking, for which he was eventually expelled from the country, tried in the U.S., and sentenced to 210 years in prison. Through deep research, including interviews with Pepe's close contacts and the discovery that he was a key suspect early in the investigation, Kari mounts a convincing case that Pepe may have murdered the Bermans, possibly after soliciting them for sex. Dogged reporting and expert pacing make this a good bet for true crime fans."

—*Publishers Weekly*

"In the early days of January, 1986, Inyo County, California, law agencies were alerted to the disappearance of Barry and Louise Berman. The couple's pickup truck was found near a hot springs in Saline Valley, a tourist destination. Covering a large swath of desert and mountains, the valley can be an unforgiving and dangerous place. With each passing day, the possibility of rescue dwindled. Although police found that the Bermans had interacted with a few other visitors at the springs, they had no firm suspects. A lack of evidence led to the case going stale until 1988, when a park visitor discovered the Bermans' remains. Investigators zeroed in on a possible suspect, a former marine named Michael Pepe. They would be in for a rude awakening in uncovering the extent of Pepe's depravity. Kari deftly explores this cold case set in the expansive Mojave Desert, meticulously breaking down the ins and outs of the investigation while providing biographical sketches of the victims and the cruel forces of fate that brought them to their ends."

—*Booklist*

"The twists and turns in The Berman Murders will have you on the edge of your seat. The story begins in a Mojave Desert valley, where a hippie couple on a camping trip vanishes from a hot springs oasis after bathing with naked strangers. By delving into the backgrounds of the people at the scene, the author presents a theory about how deviant sexual dynamics may have led to the double murder. The story follows the path of the chief suspect across the world to Cambodia, where behind the walls of an upscale villa he rapes and tortures underage girls—never guessing that someday they'll confront him in open court."

—**Freida Lee Mock**, Academy Award-winning filmmaker, director, screenwriter, and producer

"It's hard to believe this story is actually real – it's fascinating, creepy, and ultimately inspiring. *The Berman Murders* starts with a counterculture couple (one being a reluctant heir) who mysteriously disappear in a remote desert valley and ends with girls who were sex trafficked in Asia. The author ties these two worlds together in such a compelling way that it's hard to put the book down. I love that the book features so many strong women: the federal court judge; the two lead prosecutors; and brave young women who cross the ocean from Cambodia to confront the alleged perpetrator."

—**Starr Parodi**, Grammy-winning producer, artist & composer, and former president of The Alliance For Women Film Composers

"The Berman murders tells the story of a heinous cold case that became hot again and was finally solved, thanks to a dogged sheriff and attorney/author, Doug Kari. The reader is taken on a roller coaster ride that begins in a remote California desert valley, then takes you to a villa of repeated child sex abuse in Cambodia, a conviction, an overturned conviction and then finally justice. Captivating and extremely well-written. Kudos to the author for his persistence and for putting this gripping saga on paper for all to read."

—**Gerry Renert**, TV series creator/executive producer, 3x EMMY nominee, President of SupperTime Entertainment

"The Berman Murders is a gripping story about an unsolved double homicide. The depth of Doug's nine-year investigation into the perplexing case is impressive. The result is a book that takes you from a hot springs oasis in Death Valley, where two campers mysteriously vanished, to the slums of Phnom Penh, where underage children are trafficked for sex. The book follows the case's path to wherever it leads."

—**John Hueston**, called "the best lawyer of his generation," former federal prosecutor and co-founder of the litigation powerhouse Hueston Hennigan

"A married couple goes for a hike in the desert. In that remote, eerie and beautiful landscape they have a random encounter with a criminal deviant and are never seen alive again. It's the stuff of nightmares. Though *The Berman Murders* is an absorbing read, it's hardly a comfortable one. The book can't deliver justice for the Bermans, but at least they are not forgotten."

—*California Review of Books*

"Kari's book is a lightning-fast read. It's a compact 250 or so pages that while heavy on the details never feels overly dense. His time as an alt-weekly writer serves him well here, as he applies those endangered publications' style to his book. There's a mic drop before every break, a grabby hook that keeps even folks whose Apple Watch are telling them to stand up sitting down and turning pages."

—*Reality Blurred*

THE BERMAN MURDERS

Unraveling the Mojave Desert's Most Mysterious Unsolved Crime

DOUG KARI

ROWMAN & LITTLEFIELD
Lanham • Boulder • New York • London

Rowman & Littlefield
Bloomsbury Publishing Inc, 1359 Broadway, New York, NY 10018, USA
Bloomsbury Publishing Plc, 50 Bedford Square, London, WC1B 3DP, UK
Bloomsbury Publishing Ireland, 29 Earlsfort Terrace, Dublin 2, D02 AY28, Ireland
www.bloomsbury.com

First published in the United States of America 2024
Paperback edition published 2026

British Library Cataloguing in Publication Information available

Library of Congress Cataloging-in-Publication Data
  Names: Kari, Doug, author.
  Title: The Berman murders : unraveling the Mojave Desert's most mysterious
    unsolved crime / Doug Kari.
  Description: Lanham : Rowman & Littlefield, [2024] | Includes
    bibliographical references and index.
  Identifiers: LCCN 2023034256 (print) | LCCN 2023034257 (ebook) | ISBN
    9781538186381 (cloth) | ISBN 9781538186398 (ebook) | ISBN 9798216392224 (paper)
  Subjects: LCSH: Murder--Investigation--Mojave Desert--Case studies. |
    Berman, Barry (Barry Alan), -1985? | Berman, Louise (Louise Rhoda), 1932
    or 1933-1985?
  Classification: LCC HV8079.H6 K374 2024 (print) | LCC HV8079.H6 (ebook) |
    DDC 363.25/95230979495--dc23/eng/20231113
LC record available at https://lccn.loc.gov/2023034256
LC ebook record available at https://lccn.loc.gov/2023034257

For product safety related questions contact productsafety@bloomsbury.com.

Dedication

To Jane

Contents

Contents

Preface

At daybreak on January 6, 1986, a couple on a camping trip in the Mojave Desert set out for a stroll and never returned. The local sheriff's office eventually discovered that Barry and Louise Berman had been murdered.

As years passed and the double homicide remained unsolved, the Berman case spawned speculation and conjecture. Was it a robbery gone bad? Did someone kidnap the Bermans and then kill them?

Despite extensive investigation by local and federal authorities, to date there hasn't been an arrest in the case—let alone a conviction. But this doesn't mean there's no plausible theory.

The mysteries of the Mojave Desert have been one of my lifelong passions, instilled by my grandmother, Dale King. After Grandpa died, she moved into a cabin in a lonely desert valley and spent her days roaming the backcountry. Along the way, she met old timers who told stories about vanished travelers and hidden treasures.

As a teenager, I began following in Grandma's footsteps, exploring places like Death Valley and Joshua Tree. I listened to her tales and became an avid reader of *Desert Magazine*, which recounted many of the Mojave's legends and mysteries.

In the 1980s, I became involved in desert conservation and cofounded the wilderness group Desert Survivors. One of the places I cherished the most, and worked hard to protect, is a pristine and enchanting locale called Saline Valley.

After the Bermans disappeared from a primitive campsite at Saline Valley's clothing-optional hot springs, the case became a subject of speculation and conjecture among desert aficionados—and over the years, it gnawed at me. As I pursued a career as an attorney, learning how to interview witnesses and gather evidence, the mystery lingered in the back of my mind.

Nearly three decades after the Bermans vanished, I decided to delve into the case. The project stretched over nine years and involved multiple crime scene visits and dozens of interviews—plus records requests, online research, and all the other digging that comes with investigative journalism.

Along the way, I published articles about the case, including an *LA Weekly* cover story that helped raise awareness and stir up new information. But until now, the full story of what's been uncovered about the Berman murders has never been told.

Doug Kari

November 2023

ADVISORY

This book includes graphic accounts of alleged murder, rape, sex trafficking, torture, and child abuse. Some readers may find these subjects disturbing.

ACKNOWLEDGMENTS

Thank you to everyone who helped bring this book to life, with special thanks to Michael Westerman, for providing invaluable information and images; friends of the Bermans who agreed to be interviewed, especially Eleanor Snow, Arthur Korb, Mary Sullivan, Anne Sullivan, and Dr. Larry Koplin; Inyo County officials who cooperated, notably Deputy Leon Boyer (Ret.), Sheriff Bill Lutze (Ret.), and District Attorney Tom Hardy; Tom Ganner, for sharing his knowledge about Saline Valley; the brilliant editor Marilyn Moyer, for helping me rethink the story; Liz Stahler and Gerry Renert, for redlining my query letter; literary agent Linda Langton, for championing the manuscript; Desiree Duffy, Dave Duffy, and the Black Chateau team, for building my author platform; my wife Jane Zhang and children Lauren Seawright, Jon Kari, Will Kari, and Hui Bao, for their steadfast support; Jim Morrison, Morgan Irby, Jim Cope, Jon Blaufarb, Don Falk, and Stuart Jeffries, for having my back in the desert and in life; Starr Parodi, Gianna Marino, and Leslie Diller Zollo, for showing what it means to be committed to art; Bob Freitas, for being a mentor in the law; my mom Dale Kari, dad Bill Kari, and sisters Kathy Makus and Karen Jarrell, for a childhood where reading came first; former English teacher Norman Dessler, for making me learn the basics; Jill Stewart and *LA Weekly*, for printing my cover story; Peter Johnson, Carri Geer Thevenot, and the *Las Vegas Review-Journal*, for supporting my work as an investigative journalist; Jeremiah Dobruck and the *Long Beach Post*, and Terrance Vestal and the *Inyo Register*, for running my articles; Susan Bien, for helping me navigate the publishing process; Paul Bonin, for locating witnesses and sources; Matt Webb, for material about Cambodia; Andrew Jacobs and Joe Vasile, for well-timed encouragement; and editor Paul Dinas, for exposing my first draft as hopelessly flawed.

CHAPTER ONE

A Search for Two Lovers Leads to Silence

ONE OF THE MOST BAFFLING MURDER MYSTERIES IN THE MODERN-DAY Wild West began with a routine call to the police.

A two-way radio at the sheriff's headquarters in Inyo County crackled to life shortly before lunchtime on Friday, January 10, 1986. Leon Boyer, the deputy working dispatch, recognized the caller as Robert Pollard, known locally as "Chili Bob."

A sunbeaten thirty-nine-year-old and avid consumer of canned beer, Chili Bob served as campground host at the hot springs in Saline Valley. The valley, hidden amid tall mountains about two hundred miles north of Los Angeles, was among the most remote locations in the western United States.[1]

Chili Bob was calling to report an abandoned pickup truck at one of the primitive campsites adjacent to the hot springs. The owners of the pickup, a man and woman, had disappeared earlier in the week. Deputy Boyer said he'd send someone to investigate.

Boyer, then forty-three, was a tall man with muscular hands and piercing blue eyes. He was a rancher by trade, with a down-to-earth manner and an instinct for truth—what people in cowboy country sometimes call "horse sense."

To Boyer's way of thinking, the call from Chili Bob wasn't cause for alarm. Maybe the missing couple went backpacking into the wilderness, or they hitched a ride into town to buy more supplies. Although the call warranted follow-up, it seemed no different from the various minor incidents that the sheriff's office regularly handled.

From this benign beginning, the case of Barry and Louise Berman would become a yearslong saga of near misses and dead ends that confounded Deputy Boyer and other law enforcement officials and tormented the missing couple's family and friends. How did Barry, the heir apparent to the Kahlúa liqueur fortune, and Louise, a 1960s wild child turned spiritual seeker, end up dead in the desert—murdered while on a romantic getaway?

The case's circuitous path, stretching over three decades, would lead investigators to far-flung places: the Berman mansion in Beverly Hills, where Barry came of age amid fabulous wealth but a frigid family life; the headquarters of a Marine Corps base in the California desert, where investigators interrogated a captain they considered their primary suspect; a maximum security federal prison in Arizona, where jailhouse informants claimed to know exactly how the murders occurred; and the slums of Phnom Penh, where the rape and torture of underage girls by the suspect in the Berman case dovetailed with Deputy Boyer's theory years earlier that sexual predation led to the Berman murders.

Not until the 2020s, after law enforcement officials spent millions of dollars in their dogged pursuit of the murder suspect turned child molester, would the events chronicled in this book culminate in a series of ferocious courtroom battles where the young women confronted the predator who assaulted them. Meanwhile, family and friends of the Bermans watched from the sidelines, hoping the outcome would bring a sense of closure.

***

When Deputy Boyer fielded a radio call about an abandoned pickup and two missing campers, he was stationed at sheriff's headquarters in Independence, the Inyo County seat, population around six hundred.[2] After signing off with Chili Bob, Boyer radioed another deputy, Larry Freshour, thirty-nine, who lived and worked in Olancha, about forty miles to the south. Olancha, a ranching settlement and roadside stop, was populated by a couple of hundred people and ten times as many cattle.

Deputy Boyer asked Freshour to drive into Saline Valley, check out the abandoned vehicle, and try to locate its owners. Because the winter sun wouldn't set for another six hours and no storms were in the forecast, Boyer assumed that Freshour would get going right away.

But Freshour delayed his journey—the first of what would become a colossal assembly of lapses, mistakes, miscues, and derelictions, at multiple levels of officialdom. But in fairness to Freshour, his procrastination may have said less about him personally and more about the frontier culture of the sheriff's office and Inyo County as a whole.

The county was a world apart from the rest of California—isolated by the Sierra Nevada rising to the west like a massive wall, and the desolate Mojave Desert stretching to the east. Although driving to Inyo County from Los Angeles took less than four hours, the county's handful of small towns and one incorporated city, Bishop, population 3,500, had more in common with places like Whitefish, Montana, or Sheridan, Wyoming, than with urban California.

A sizeable number of residents kept horses, and almost everyone owned at least one dog. Springtime meant trout fishing in the streams off the Sierra. In the fall deer hunting season opened. The best known spot in Bishop, a bakery called Schat's, was famous for "sheepherder bread." The biggest event of the year was the Mule Days parade, featuring covered wagons, stagecoaches, and other vestiges of the Wild West.

Inyo County embraced its western heritage and all that came with it. Hundreds of cowboy movies and TV shows had been filmed in the Alabama Hills outside the town of Lone Pine, with the snow-capped Sierra Nevada as the backdrop.

The county's actual frontier history had been all too authentic, culminating in a bloody slaughter that locals called the Indian War.[3] In 1866, after the conflict ended and Inyo became a county, the sheriff's office had struggled to bring order to a region rife with thievery, shootings, drunkenness, and brawls. At least two of the early sheriffs had been murdered.

In a region this wild, citizens sometimes took matters into their own hands. The sheriff's office website recounts a story from the early days, about men caught stealing horses. When the horse thieves ended up hanging from telegraph poles, the sheriff "assumed the men committed suicide" and let the matter lie.[4]

By 1986, some 120 years after its founding, Inyo County was of course much tamer. But in a county the size of Massachusetts, with a population of fewer than eighteen thousand souls, there were limits to what the sheriff's office could accomplish. The office only employed about fifty deputies and reserves, along with three lieutenants and four sergeants, to police an area of ten thousand square miles.

This was still the frontier, steeped in the values of individualism and self-reliance. People were expected to watch out for themselves—especially in the backcountry.[5]

Because Deputy Freshour passed away in 1991, we don't have his account of why, after being assigned the call by Deputy Boyer at midday on a Friday, Freshour didn't head to Saline Valley that afternoon or first thing next morning. Maybe he assumed the owners would return to their pickup over the weekend. Maybe he was too busy thinking about the NFL conference championship games scheduled to be played on Sunday.[6]

Saline Valley's status as one of Inyo County's remotest locations probably factored into Freshour's thinking. Put simply: Getting into Saline Valley wasn't easy. When measured in a straight line, only twenty-five miles separated Chili Bob's trailer in Saline Valley from the sheriff's office in Independence, but the intervening Inyo Mountains formed a barrier that required hours of challenging off-highway driving to circumvent.

This daunting geography had been spawned by the massive energy of plate tectonics. Over the span of geologic time, colliding plates of Earth's crust created a series of tall mountain ranges, and in between, deep valleys. Mount Whitney, at an elevation of 14,505 feet, the highest point in the forty-eight contiguous states, stands along Inyo County's western edge, while ninety miles away, Badwater Basin in Death Valley is the lowest point in North America.

Amid the tall mountains and deep valleys are more geologic obstacles: ancient lava flows, towering rock spires, and crumbling volcanic domes. Many of the access roads were unpaved, which created another set of challenges.

Whether delayed by imposing geography, weekend plans, or some other excuse, Freshour didn't start the drive into Saline Valley until Boyer radioed him again the following Monday, January 13. Frustrated by Freshour's unresponsiveness, Boyer ordered the recalcitrant deputy to get on it.

Inyo County sheriff's investigator Dan Williams, in an interview for this book on April 22, 2018, defended Freshour by saying the late deputy's Ford Crown Victoria wasn't fit for the arduous trip—especially in winter when the south road into Saline Valley was in bad shape. Instead, Freshour needed to use the department's four-wheel-drive Bronco.

"He would've had to trade cars," said Williams.

Trading cars required Freshour to drive twenty-five miles to the substation where it was stored, and another forty miles to reach the Saline Valley turnoff. At that point he'd begin the real journey: a fifty-mile, dirt-road drive that might take another two to four hours, depending on conditions.

But Leon Boyer, who retired from the sheriff's office years ago, dismissed Williams's explanation as revisionist history. "Bullshit," said the former deputy. "He could've gotten there in his Vic."[7]

***

Deputy Freshour headed east through the desert on a two-lane strip of asphalt, bound for hot springs where strangers bathed naked. Miles away from the nearest town, at a windswept plateau, he reached a junction marked by a small wooden sign: Saline Valley Road.

Freshour jounced along the dirt road across the open desert, over boulder-strewn hills, and into a shallow valley that hosted the Mojave Desert's version of a forest: Joshua trees, thousands of them, coloring the valley a dusky shade of green. Named by nineteenth-century Mormon pioneers who thought the upraised limbs evoked the biblical Joshua, the so-called trees are succulents—akin to giant cacti.

The road climbed a spur of the Inyo Mountains, which was the mountain range that Freshour needed to cross on his way into Saline

Valley. The dirt surface turned rocky as it ascended a volcanic slope, and there were snow patches from an earlier storm. Then came wind-stunted pinyon pines, along with more snow and pools of mud.

The road traversed a steep mountainside, then turned sharply and descended into a canyon heading down toward Saline Valley's southern end. Freshour followed the rough route through miles of dips and twists, until he reached a place where the canyon sides gave way and the road led onto a rocky slope.

Here, the full length of Saline Valley came into view—one of the most sublime and hauntingly beautiful vistas on the North American continent.[8] A visitor could see mountains on both sides, towering above waves of sand dunes and at the deepest point, a silvery saltwater lake. The valley looked like a remnant from the end of the last ice age—suspended in time, profoundly still, and untouched by civilization.[9]

Although breathtaking to behold, Saline Valley wasn't a place where someone would want to go astray. Every local knew the stories about travelers who perished in this inhospitable region of California. After all, nearby Death Valley got its name in the 1800s when a group of pioneers took a wrong turn, became stranded, one of them died, and the others feared they, too, would perish.

In the 1960s, a father and his teenage son, along with a companion, ventured into Saline Valley to explore an abandoned mine. After their vehicle got stuck, they tried to walk to safety. Personnel from the sheriff's office found their sun-blackened bodies lying along the road, one after the other. In 1986, somewhere out in the distance, was another vehicle that had been left behind. The owners hadn't yet been identified, let alone been located.

Deputy Freshour continued down the rocky slope to the valley floor. Bearing northward, he kept a lookout for Bat Rock—a boulder painted with a psychedelic rendition of a bat.[10] This marked the turnoff to the hot springs and the unique encampment that surrounded them.

By 1986, the hot springs in Saline Valley had become the site of a cultural phenomenon—at times appearing like a scene from the movie *Mad Max* or foreshadowing of Burning Man.[11] At one of the camps you might find a "magic bus" full of flower children, in another a group of firefighters on a weekend retreat. Saliners shared a love of the valley's ethereal beauty and seductive aura of wide-open freedom.

Although the soaking pools at the hot springs were denoted as "clothing optional," the reality was that most bathers got naked. Nudity was also acceptable around the campground—it was commonplace to see people wearing nothing but sandals and their birthday suits, perhaps accessorized with sunglasses or a broad-brimmed hat.

But the ubiquitous nudity didn't mean the springs were a hotbed of licentiousness. There was an unwritten code: no leering at strangers, no unwanted touching, and no hitting on someone unless doing so was clearly invited.

Saline Valley was more about getting back to nature than getting busy with other campers.

The hot springs were a byproduct of the region's relentless tectonic energy. From deep beneath the earth, heated groundwater percolated upward and through fissures in the rocky crust, breaching the surface and creating ponds. The largest set was the Lower Warm Springs, which was a bit of a misnomer: The pond water averaged a temperature of 107 degrees.

Backcountry adventurers had started exploring the area in the 1940s and 1950s, around the time that the last members of the Timbisha Shoshone in Saline Valley were driven out by poverty and a fight over water rights.[12] For the inbound Saline Valley aficionados, the mesquite trees and Lower Warm Springs made for a welcoming oasis.[13]

In the 1930s, the Civilian Conservation Corps installed a metal tub with plumbing connecting it to one of the hot springs.[14] It became a favorite spot to soak in hot mineral water and bask in the views of the Inyo Mountains' dramatic eastern escarpment—a ten-thousand-foot mountainside rivaling the Grand Canyon in breathtaking precipitousness.[15]

But some campers during those formative years regarded the hot springs as a venue for rowdy partying—the sort of place where beer cans get tossed in the air and blasted with six-shooters. Over time the area became trashed.

In the mid-1960s, a man called Preacher Don envisioned the hot springs as something grander than a rough-and-tumble hangout.

According to valley lore, he wintered at Lower Warm Springs intending to write a religious book. It's unknown if Preacher Don ever finished his tome, but he and his wife buried the scattered garbage and spearheaded the construction of Sunrise Pool, the first concrete soaking pool. Preacher Don also proselytized to visitors about protecting the hot springs.[16]

This marked the spiritual beginning of an ad hoc movement by explorers, artists, hippies, Beat Generation castoffs, and assorted desert rats to transform Lower Warm Springs into a free-spirited oasis. Besides building soaking pools where people could lounge and imbibe, these Saline Valley "regulars," as they called themselves, built outhouses and constructed a community fire pit.

During the 1960s and 1970s, Lower Warm Springs evolved into a haven of irrigated gardens, open-air showers, and whimsical touches like an outdoor library. Regulars built campsites in the shade of mesquite trees, or out in the open desert with boundaries of stone.

On a cinder cone overlooking the hot springs, a regular called "Sunshine" rearranged rocks to create a huge peace sign.[17] West of the hot springs, daring aviators cleared a landing strip where rising terrain allowed little leeway for an errant pilot to pull up and go around. They dubbed the makeshift airfield "Chicken Strip."

In keeping with Inyo County's frontier culture, no one asked for government permission or applied for a building permit. Development of the hot springs was a result of peaceful anarchy, with like-minded folks banding together in pursuit of common goals.

"They maintain a sense of order out there without government interference," said one Inyo County official at the time.[18]

Because it was public land, open for visitors to use but the property of the federal government, in theory, the Bureau of Land Management (BLM), part of the U.S. Department of Interior, administered Saline Valley. But the BLM had razor-thin resources to oversee the millions of acres under its jurisdiction, so the agency took a hands-off approach. Within the agency, however, debate raged about whether what was taking place there was getting out of hand.

In a bid to assert some measure of control, the BLM anointed Chili Bob as campground host.[19] This gave him nominal power to maintain order, and it was a practical solution because Bob owned a two-way radio—the same radio he used on January 10 to call the sheriff's office in Independence and report an abandoned pickup and two missing campers.[20]

***

When Deputy Freshour stepped out of his vehicle and onto the ground at Lower Warm Springs, he unwittingly marked the beginning of what would become the most massive search and rescue effort in Inyo County history.

Freshour started by meeting with Chili Bob, who lived at the campground year-round. Bob's home was a tiny travel trailer, tucked under mesquite trees, surrounded by junk and cases of beer.

It's fair to assume that Chili Bob repeated to the deputy what little he knew about the missing couple. He likely told Freshour that their pickup could be found at nearby Palm Spring (which bore no relation to the resort city of Palm Springs hundreds of miles away).[21] Palm Spring in Saline Valley was a smaller, less developed set of hot springs about three-quarters of a mile uphill from Lower Warm Springs.

Palm Spring was located around two concrete soaking pools: an above-ground tub shaped like a miniature crater and aptly called Volcano Tub, and an in-ground pool, beautifully crafted with coping of stone, called Wizard Pool in honor of Walter Baumann, aka "Wizard," the well-known regular who spearheaded its construction.

When Freshour rolled into Palm Spring, he spotted the abandoned truck: a 1982 Datsun King Cab four-wheel drive, factory-painted in Blue Mist, and equipped with a white camper shell. The doors were locked, and there was camping gear and clothing inside, along with what looked like food and supplies.

Two bathing suits—a man's and a woman's—hung from the steering wheel. A pair of towels had been draped over nearby bushes.

Freshour jotted down the make, model, and license number of the pickup, then looked around for clues. According to Deputy Boyer, Freshour didn't see a note on the dashboard or any other obvious explanation for what happened to the owners. Boyer also recalled that

Freshour spoke with a few visitors, but no one reported seeing any recent activity in the vicinity of the pickup.

Around the same time Freshour was out in Saline Valley, back at the sheriff's headquarters Deputy Boyer fielded a phone call from Pauline Colbert of Santa Barbara, California. Until now, Boyer hadn't worried much about the abandoned pickup despite Freshour's dilatory response. But Deputy Boyer's outlook changed after Colbert told him what she knew.

Colbert said her friends Barry and Louise Berman left home on Friday, January 3, for a camping trip to the Death Valley region. They'd been scheduled to return on Tuesday, January 7, and retrieve their two dogs from a kennel—the date was circled on a calendar in Barry's workshop.

This meant that Barry and Louise were six days overdue—a dangerously long time to be lost in the desert. But Deputy Boyer kept a cool head, thinking there must be some reasonable explanation for the couple's tardiness. "I figured they'd gotten overly ambitious," he said during an interview for this book on May 21, 2014.

When Freshour radioed into headquarters with the abandoned pickup's license plate number, the registration information dovetailed with Colbert's account. The truck was owned by Barry Alan Berman, thirty-five, who lived with his wife Louise Rhoda Berman, fifty-two, in Goleta, a town along the California coast west of Santa Barbara.

Deputy Boyer also learned background information about the missing campers, and it didn't fit the profile of most visitors to Saline Valley. Turned out that Barry and Louise, despite driving an economy pickup truck and camping in the backcountry, lived in a mountaintop home adjacent to Rancho del Cielo, the famous coastal ranch of President Ronald Reagan. Barry's father, Jules Berman, a liquor magnate known as "Mr. Kahlua," was one of Southern California's most prominent businessmen.

As news of the missing travelers and their VIP pedigree spread through the sheriff's office, any lingering laissez-faire attitude quickly evaporated. A core part of the office's mission was to help folks in peril; Barry and Louise might be in serious trouble. Most people can't survive more than a few days in the desert without water, and with nighttime temperatures in the thirties, hypothermia presented another grave threat.

On another front, unless the Bermans were quickly located, the incident could prove awkward for Sheriff Don Dorsey. The sheriff, who'd been secretly stealing cash that was supposed to be used for snaring drug dealers, would be up for reelection in a few months. If people started asking pointed questions about his handling of the Berman case, how would he explain the three-day delay between Chili Bob's radio call and the lackadaisical follow-up by Deputy Freshour?

Sheriff Dorsey's response was to summon one of his office's most capable men, Sergeant Dan Lucas, and place him in charge of finding the missing couple.[22] Well regarded by his peers and physically fit, Lucas, then forty-one, would later be elected sheriff of Inyo County, after Dorsey was voted out of office and indicted on corruption charges.[23]

Along with a confident manner and an easy sense of humor, Lucas had an analytical mind and wrote well-reasoned reports.[24] He also possessed strong outdoor skills, and in 1986 served as sergeant in charge of Inyo County's search and rescue (SAR) team.

The SAR team was a volunteer group with oversight provided by the sheriff's office. Drawn from Inyo County's robust community of climbers, skiers, and outdoor adventurers, SAR team members could scale rock and ice, rappel down cliffs, and route-find in high mountains and remote deserts.

The next morning, well before sunrise, Sergeant Lucas and five SAR team members gathered at the sheriff's substation in Bishop.[25] After a short briefing, they climbed into their vehicles and headed out, bound for the rugged northern route into Saline Valley, the opposite end from where Freshour ventured in.

After driving through mud and snow to cross the Inyo Mountains, and enduring a rocky descent into northern Saline Valley followed by miles of washboard dirt road, Sergeant Lucas and the SAR team finally rolled into the hot springs around 9:30 a.m.[26]

Lucas met with Chili Bob, who explained he'd been away from the valley for a few days during the prior week. On his return, he learned about the abandoned pickup truck and radioed the sheriff's office. Bob's best estimate was that the owners had been gone for six or seven days.

At this juncture, Sergeant Lucas's mission was solely search and rescue; he wasn't yet thinking in terms of a crime scene. Lucas ordered a pair of two-man teams to look for footprints around Palm Spring, a process called "sign-cutting." He assigned BLM Ranger Bruce Albert to drive along a remote route that was, in effect, a backroad to the hot springs—the only way a vehicle could get in or out without using Saline Valley Road.[27]

Albert, a lanky outdoorsman with an angular face, knew the region as well as anyone, and he'd driven the backroad before. The backroad was a jeep trail consisting of wheel tracks formed by years of off-highway vehicle use. Designated by the BLM as the "Saline-Eureka Corridor," and called by Saline Valley regulars the "Corridor" for short, the jeep trail began at Palm Spring campground and ascended the northeast extension of Saline Valley.

Fifteen torturous miles above Palm Spring, the Corridor crossed over a pass at the intersection of the Saline Range and Last Chance Range—the mountain ranges defining the north-to-east side of Saline Valley. From there the Corridor descended into a narrow gorge leading to Eureka Valley, home to some of the tallest sand dunes in North America.[28]

As Albert navigated up the Corridor in his four-wheel-drive truck, driving through dry washes and climbing over cutbanks, he scanned the area with an expert eye looking for unexpected movement, a spot of color, or anything else that might be a sign of a human, dead or alive.[29] A seasoned ranger and avid adventurer, he'd spent many days exploring Saline Valley and hiking in the surrounding mountains.

About two miles above Palm Spring, Albert stopped at Upper Warm Springs, a thickly vegetated oasis that remained undeveloped. A trained tracker, Albert examined the ground closely, looking for fresh footprints.

Albert continued driving up the Corridor, slowly making his way along the rocky route. Here and there he stopped to look for footprints, survey the surroundings with binoculars, and listen for any sounds. There was nothing but resounding silence and miles of open desert.

CHAPTER TWO

Desperate and Heartbreaking Mission

BACK AT PALM SPRING CAMPGROUND, SERGEANT LUCAS WAS HOPING for a quick break in the case. Maybe something inside the abandoned vehicle would help him figure out what happened to the missing owners?

Lucas used a length of wire to jimmy the pickup's door.[1] Inside the truck he found food, clothing, cookware, and cowboy boots, along with the bathing suits that Deputy Freshour had seen draped over the steering wheel.

In the back, under the camper shell, was a nest of sleeping bags, blankets, and foam pads. This suggested that the Bermans planned to sleep in their vehicle and didn't set out on an overnight hike.

No wallets turned up, but Lucas did find Louise's temporary driver's license. His most interesting discovery: two cameras loaded with film.[2] Besides whatever clues the photos might hold, the fact Barry and Louise left their cameras behind indicated they hadn't planned to be away for very long.

Lucas also found maps in the cab, including one with Saline Valley Road underscored. The turnoff to the hot springs had been marked with a circle, and a margin note indicated a right turn at Bat Rock. But the sergeant didn't see any hint of where the missing couple might have gone after they arrived at Palm Spring.

The pair of tracking teams spent a long day scouring the desert around the campground, but they didn't find a single clue. More disappointment came when Albert returned from his foray up the Corridor and reported to Lucas that he hadn't observed anything interesting or unusual.

With a full day of searching gone by and no leads to pursue, Sergeant Lucas stared out at the vast desert wilderness and knew he faced a Herculean task: finding two missing campers amid a maze of dry washes, mesquite thickets, sand dunes, a saline lake, and some of Inyo County's least-explored mountain ranges. Realizing his team was outmatched, Lucas radioed into the sheriff's office and asked for more help.

That evening the winter air turned bitingly cold, and it seemed unlikely Barry and Louise could still be alive after a week in the wilds under such trying conditions. But dawn on Wednesday, January 15—day two of the search—brought renewed hope as the dead quiet of a chilly desert night gave way to the hushed voices of early risers, the clink of breakfast dishes, and the crackle of morning campfires.

Shortly after sunrise, a distant *thump-thump* grew into a roar as two Bell AH-1 Cobra helicopters flew into Saline Valley and circled down for a landing. The Cobras, which had been sent by China Lake Naval Weapons Center, an air base about eighty air miles to the south, gave Sergeant Lucas's search and rescue effort a huge boost—especially because this was sparsely vegetated terrain where people could likely be spotted from the air.

Then China Lake Mountain Rescue Group, a volunteer group of trained civilians who worked at the weapons center, showed up in force, joining a team from Indian Wells Valley who'd arrived the night before.[3] Lucas now had two helicopters and more than thirty ground searchers at his command—sufficient resources to cover all the terrain lying within a day's walking distance of the Bermans' truck.

The Cobras, with a pilot in the rear and an observer in front, started flying grid patterns about a hundred feet above the desert floor. The ground teams began searching by walking in tandem, evenly spaced in a long line. These techniques made for tedious work, serving as a methodical process of elimination. But if Barry and Louise were anywhere near the hot springs, Sergeant Lucas was determined to find them.

By lunchtime, the searchers were right back where they'd started, without a single lead. For Lucas, it was a bewildering situation. Did the two missing campers run off somewhere? Did they leave the valley in someone else's vehicle?

Lucas decided to send one of the helicopters to the Bishop airport so rolls of film from the missing couple's cameras could be shuttled by police cruiser to Dwayne's Friendly Pharmacy and developed.[4] A few hours later, after the Cobra returned, he scoured the photos for clues.

In some of the photos, Barry and Louise could be seen wearing Nikes, but the sneakers hadn't turned up inside their truck—only cowboy boots. Convinced the Bermans must have been wearing the Nikes when they left camp, Lucas radioed into the sheriff's office for forensic help. Soon he got back information about what shoeprint pattern matched the Nikes.

Armed with this new information, Lucas reached out to every agency that might be willing to join in the hunt. The following morning—day 3 of the search—it became apparent his pleas had been heeded. Saline Valley transitioned from a serene desert wilderness into something akin to a war zone.

Crews arrived from adjacent Mono and Kern counties, supplementing the SAR teams from Inyo County, Indian Wells Valley, and China Lake, and bringing the total number of searchers to more than fifty.[5] The California Highway Patrol (CHP) sent in a pair of helicopters, and the army flew down a Bell UH-1 "Huey" helicopter from Sacramento, California. The most dramatic development was the deafening arrival of a massive, twin-blade Boeing CH-47 "Chinook" helicopter commanded by a National Guard crew.

A possible break came when searchers spotted tracks resembling the Nike shoeprints leading toward the Saline Range, which rose from the desert north of the hot springs. Maybe Barry and Louise hiked into the hills and got lost?

Sergeant Lucas bet big on this lead. The Chinook lifted off in a swirl of dust and shuttled two dozen men to the top of a high ridge. The searchers fanned out, some heading down the Saline Range's meandering canyons, others scouring the rocky southeastern slopes. But when this exhausting effort didn't produce any results, many of the searchers decided to call it quits.

By now, Sergeant Lucas suspected that Barry and Louise might be crime victims. To the veteran sergeant, it didn't make sense that a pair of able-bodied adults would vanish without a trace. He gave orders to have the abandoned pickup loaded into the Chinook and flown to Bishop so it could be examined by forensics experts.[6]

"Foul play was in the back of my mind, especially when two people disappear," Lucas recalled when interviewed for this book on May 20, 2014.

Still, it seemed implausible to Lucas that a perpetrator would be lurking in a peaceful desert valley, far off the beaten path. Without hard evidence that a crime took place, the case remained a search and rescue operation. It was still possible that the missing couple wandered off, got lost or hurt, and hunkered down. Not sure where else to look, Sergeant Lucas decided that he'd focus again on the Corridor the next day.

**

Meanwhile, at the Berman family mansion in Beverly Hills, a situation that initially seemed insignificant—a grown son a few days overdue returning from vacation—had turned into a crisis more serious than anything Jules Berman had ever faced.

The first sign of trouble came when Pauline Colbert phoned seventy-five-year-old Jules to deliver the news that Barry and Louise were missing. Although Colbert already feared that something terrible might have happened, Barry's mother Ruth Berman, a sixty-six-year-old high society matron, decided not to cancel her afternoon mah-jongg game.

"People like us don't get murdered," she said.

But after three days of intense searching in Saline Valley failed to produce any sign of the missing couple, Jules and Ruth were worried sick. Determined to do whatever it took to locate his son, Jules arranged for a private plane to fly him to Inyo County so he could meet face-to-face with sheriff's officials.

On Friday morning, January 17—day four of the search—the airplane carrying Jules and his entourage landed at the Bishop airport. By this time Sheriff Dorsey and pretty much everyone else in Inyo County officialdom knew that the elder Berman was a Beverly Hills tycoon, legendary in the business world, and politically well-connected. Out in Saline Valley, Sergeant Lucas received orders to helicopter back to Bishop so he could join in the meeting.

Jules's entourage included Colbert, who'd called the Inyo County Sheriff's Office a few days earlier to file the missing person report. She'd been the last person among Barry and Louise's circle of friends to see them; she'd hosted the couple for dinner on January 2, the evening before they left for the desert.

Since filing the missing person report, Colbert proved to be an invaluable resource for the sheriff's office, providing information about the couple's backgrounds, personalities, and habits. "Pauline had lots of details about the Bermans," said Deputy Boyer years later. "She really filled us in."

Jules also brought along Char Margolis, a psychic who'd been involved in other high-profile missing person cases. Because Char had scored some notable successes and been a guest on Regis Philbin's television show *AM Los Angeles*, she was something of a local celebrity. Ruth Berman knew about Char and enlisted her help.

At the meeting in Bishop, Sergeant Lucas talked about the hot springs in Saline Valley, the discovery of Barry and Louise's truck, the massive search and rescue effort, and the absence of any clues. The veteran lawman explained that by all rights, if the missing couple had gotten lost anywhere within walking distance of the hot springs, by now they would have been located.

"That area is so easy to search that we should have found them if they were still there," sheriff's spokesperson Lieutenant Jack Goodrich said at the time. "With all the personnel and air cover, we should have found something by now."[7]

Besides the confounding question of what happened to Barry and Louise, which was prompting all manner of speculation, there was an elephant in the room: How long would the search continue?

Already the effort had consumed enormous resources in a rural county with a limited budget—a huge investment in hopes of finding two travelers who might've left the area voluntarily or been kidnapped and spirited away. But as the meeting ended, Sheriff Dorsey instructed Sergeant Lucas to return to the valley and continue the hunt.

The following morning—coincidentally his forty-second birthday—Lucas was back in the field, this time with eleven searchers and a pair of helicopters from CHP. Lucas focused most of his attention on a decrepit miner's cabin situated near the Corridor but hidden from view at the edge of a wash.[8] Saliners avoided the place because it was known as the haunt of Richard Watkins, aka "Wolfman," who had a reputation for being snarly.[9]

Lucas's search of the cabin was another indication that his theory about the case had shifted. While other searchers were still operating on the premise that Barry and Louise might have gotten lost, Lucas was scouting for evidence of something more sinister.

"The possibility of some type of criminal action, kidnap, murder, removal from the area, is the . . . most likely scenario," he wrote in his report.

Near the cabin, Sergeant Lucas turned up a stone slab with dried blood and clumps of hair—a find that might have excited a rookie. But the veteran sergeant, although not a homicide investigator, sized up the slab as a chopping block for butchering jackrabbits, and the state DOJ's lab later confirmed his supposition.[10] Eventually, investigators eliminated Wolfman as a suspect, as Leon Boyer explained thirty years later.

"Wolfman had an airtight alibi," said the retired deputy. "At the time Barry and Louise disappeared he was incarcerated in Nevada."

While Sergeant Lucas searched around the decrepit cabin, a CHP helicopter ferried Char into the valley. Although some of Barry and Louise's friends doubted Char, saying later they thought she was a fraud, it's common in missing person cases to enlist the aid of a psychic when conventional search methods fall short.

Deputy Boyer, who rode with Char in the helicopter, said years later that he appreciated her assistance. "We put a lot of faith in her," he recalled. "She had good clues."

Char believed that the Bermans had been murdered. She instructed the searchers to look for a shallow grave with something small sticking out—perhaps a shoelace.

"I knew they were in the desert," she said on June 17, 2014, when interviewed for this book. "I felt the energy of their spirits. They wanted to be found."

Char steered the searchers toward a stone hut located near the Corridor, about a mile north of Palm Spring, and called by Saline Valley regulars the "Hogan." The Hogan was dome-shaped—similar in style to the traditional wood-and-mud structures built by the Navaho, but the name made little sense in the context of Saline Valley because this was ancestral land of the Timbisha Shoshone, not the Navaho who lived hundreds of miles away. Even so, because the structure looked like something that could have been built by Native Americans, it was a popular day hike destination for campers at the hot springs.[11]

Char also suggested that the searchers look again around the volcanic rock peace sign overlooking the hot springs. The Peace Sign, which some conservative Inyo County lawmen derisively dubbed the "chicken foot," was another popular destination for visitors on a day hike.

On January 19—day six of the hunt—some of the searchers continued to work with Char. Although it seemed unlikely that she would find Barry and Louise, given how exhaustive the search had already been, the sheriff's office was willing to keep following her suggestions—especially if doing so would bring some measure of comfort to Jules.

"I remember how devastated the father was," Char recalled. "My heart was breaking for him."

Other searchers combed the Last Chance Range, an imposing chain of mountains dividing Saline Valley from northern Death Valley. With peaks rising nearly eight thousand feet above the valley floor, buttressed by steep and rocky slopes, the Last Chance Range was as remote as its evocative name suggested. In fact, the range was so labyrinthine that maps of the region didn't agree on where it started and ended.

One search team probed the canyons along the base of the Last Chance Range, where dry waterfalls, polished by eons of intermittent flash floods, made exploration hazardous. Maybe Barry and Louise slipped and fell? Two other teams were airlifted to the top of the range, and from there split up and descended by different routes.

"We worked and worked and worked," said Lucas.

But the herculean effort came up empty. That evening, with no hope of finding Barry and Louise alive in the desert, the Inyo County Sheriff's Office called off the search.

Pauline Colbert drove Barry and Louise's pickup back to their home atop Refugio Road in Goleta. Their Christmas tree still had presents underneath. It was, she said later, "a nightmare beyond a nightmare."

But Colbert refused to give up. She organized a private search party to continue the hunt, enlisting help from more than a dozen friends and family members of the missing couple. Jules borrowed a jeep, and Ruth, who was accustomed to being waited on by servants, went shopping for supplies.

Jules's longtime private secretary Valerie Dinnes, then forty-two, accompanied her boss on the trip.[12] "Mr. Berman insisted he wanted to go look for his son," Dinnes said when interviewed for this book on September 6, 2021. "I warned him: Don't even start on that, stay with the detectives."

The unlikely group of out-of-towners managed to drive a Winnebago motor home into Saline Valley—a remarkable feat considering the rough and narrow dirt roads. By day they searched for any clue the sheriff's office might have missed.

"We all fanned out and walked around in circles," Dinnes recalled. "Running in every direction."

At night they gathered by the campfire, reminiscing about Barry and Louise while clinging to hope that the couple might yet be found alive. "Jules tried to do his best," said Dinnes. "It affected him a lot—Barry was his only child."

This desperate and heartbreaking mission spurred the Inyo County Sheriff's Office to make one last attempt. On January 27, three weeks after Barry and Louise disappeared, Sergeant Lucas and Bureau of Land Management ranger Bruce Albert spent the day helicoptering into mine, cave, and cabin sites in the far reaches of Saline Valley and up into the surrounding mountains.

Late in the day, Lucas and Albert met with Jules and the private search party. Lucas explained that if Barry and Louise were still alive, by now they would have been found. Convinced the youthful husband

and his older wife were victims of a yet-to-be-determined crime, Lucas assured their friends and family that solving the case would remain a top priority of the Inyo County Sheriff's Office.

Privately, the exhausted sergeant felt glad he was no longer in charge. "I was relieved when the case was handed over to investigators," he said years later.

Once Lucas bowed out, primary responsibility for the case shifted to investigator Robert "Randy" Nixon, at that time aged thirty-one, assisted by Deputy Leon Boyer.[13] Although not an investigator by background, Boyer had a knack for detective work, and because he'd been involved from the outset, he felt passionate about wanting to crack the case. In the months and years to come, the determined deputy would prove to be the most stalwart of all the law enforcement officials involved.

But Boyer and Nixon lacked the resources to treat Saline Valley as a crime scene and methodically sweep the area for evidence—the landscape was too vast. An attempt to utilize cadaver-sniffing canines failed when the dogs' paws became bloodied by the rough terrain.[14]

Instead, Boyer and Nixon pursued the piece-by-piece process of interviewing witnesses, building a profile of the two apparent victims, and retracing their steps from their home in Goleta to the hot springs in Saline Valley in hope that these pieces of information would eventually solve the puzzle of what happened to Barry and Louise.

CHAPTER THREE

All-Seeing Eyes Looked Deep within Him

LEGEND SAYS THAT WHEN SOMEONE DIES, THEIR LIFE PASSES BEFORE their eyes. For Barry and Louise, their final journey began with a pickup truck ride past landmarks in their lives. Although husband and wife presumably didn't see it this way, the first segment of their trip into the Mojave Desert was in effect a drive-by retrospective.

They'd started preparing for the journey around New Year's 1986. Barry, sinewy of build and with serious demeanor, took charge of packing the truck. He had experience exploring the wilds of California and Nevada with journeys taking him to remote hot springs. A self-reliant man and blacksmith by trade, he could handle himself in the outdoors and repair things in a pinch.

Louise, a shapely woman with eyes of robin's egg blue and blonde hair streaked with gray, had celebrated her fifty-second birthday a few days earlier. She glowed with excitement about the upcoming adventure, calling it a second honeymoon. Like her younger husband, Louise was familiar with roughing it, having lived for a while in a tent in the mountains of Colorado, and later in a cabin with a wood-burning stove.

Barry and Louise might have been called "hippie types," but there was far more to the couple than their bohemian appearance. Both had been shaped by childhood challenges: Louise was a survivor of sexual abuse, while Barry had grown up with parents who were preoccupied with their own affairs and relied on servants to run the house.

Barry and Louise had both gone searching for what was missing in their lives, and both eventually found their way to an Indian satguru[1]—their shared religion was how they met.

Five years into their love affair, having weathered a phase in which they almost broke up, their desert vacation was a make-up trip: a chance to share an adventure and rekindle their romance. Barry crammed supplies into the space behind the front seats of the king cab truck. Louise packed the meals, which in keeping with her and Barry's faith, were strictly vegetarian. Like their fellow disciples, Barry and Louise believed the slaying of animals gave rise to bad karma.

Unlike many travelers who venture into the desert, Barry and Louise didn't carry a gun. They had no interest in target shooting or plinking at random objects, and certainly not in hunting jackrabbits. As for the possibility of a hostile encounter, they assumed positive energy, common sense, and the love of their all-seeing master would shelter them from harm.

A few days before Barry and Louise set out on their trip, Mary Sullivan, a thoughtful, willowy woman who was a devotee of the same satguru, visited the couple at their home atop the Santa Ynez Mountains, about twenty meandering miles from the Pacific Ocean.

"As I was leaving, they were standing there together," she recalled in an interview for this book on June 2, 2014. "They said they were going to visit desert hot springs. They were excited. They seemed at peace."

On January 3, a cool and cloudy Friday morning, Barry and Louise loaded their two dogs into the pickup and closed the house and workshop. The house, built with eclectic features like wood paneling from recycled wine casks, had been a wedding present from Barry's father. The couple moved there after marrying in 1981. Since then, Louise had planted flowers, added a sun porch, and decorated the inside with Tibetan rugs.

The workshop, a standalone structure, was where Barry operated his business, Valley Forge Works. George Ziegler, a former high school classmate who became president of a steel company and one of Barry's suppliers, recalled that the talented blacksmith crafted ironwork the old-fashioned way, heating the metal to above seven hundred degrees

Fahrenheit, and then hammering, twisting, and welding it into ornamental products like garden gates and floor lamps.

"He had the build of a weightlifter," said Ziegler. "Swinging a hammer on solid steel is a tough job and hardly anyone practiced that craft in Los Angeles anymore."[2]

Three days into the new year of 1986, Barry climbed into the pickup and fired up the engine. With Louise by his side and the two dogs in back, he turned onto Refugio Road and began driving down the mountain. Soon they passed by the gate of their next-door neighbor Ronald Reagan, who at that time was president of the United States.

Since being sworn in five years earlier, Reagan had been using his 688-acre Rancho del Cielo as a working retreat for riding horses, chopping wood, signing legislation, and hosting dignitaries such as Queen Elizabeth II. Although on this day Reagan was visiting Mexico, Barry and Louise would often see armed Secret Service agents standing post along the road.[3]

Continuing downhill, Barry and Louise passed the spot where an unfortunate mishap had befallen Mike Love of the Beach Boys, who was an acquaintance of theirs.[4] While ascending the steep grade to their house, Love's 1939 Rolls Royce had overheated and dripped oil onto the exhaust system, which in turn ignited the car's wooden chassis.

But the freewheeling rock star who cowrote hits such as "California Girls" and "Good Vibrations" turned the catastrophe into a practical joke. He towed the blackened carcass of the Rolls into town and plopped it down in front of a bank.

On a darker note, farther down the mountain, the winding road crossed over Refugio Creek, the site of the most traumatic event in Louise's life. Three years earlier, during an El Niño storm that dumped nine inches of rain in under sixty hours, Laura Nold, the only child of Louise's third marriage, had climbed into a VW Fastback to visit her mom.

Nineteen-year-old Laura didn't realize that Refugio Creek, normally just a trickle, drained a large chunk of Santa Ynez terrain. By the time she turned up Refugio Road, the creek had swelled to a torrent and was raging across the roadway. Laura tried to drive through anyway.

Early next morning, searchers found her battered VW a couple of hundred yards downstream. The windows had been blown out, the roof was caved in, and the car was filled with mud.[5]

Searchers spent hours probing the stream with poles and crisscrossing the waters offshore, but they never found Laura. The prevailing theory was that her body had floated out to sea, but Louise still hoped that Laura's remains might be found someday.

After descending to the base of Refugio Road, Barry and Louise reached U.S. Highway 101, where they turned onto the ramp heading south. As they drove along the highway, with open rangeland to their left and the Pacific Ocean to their right, they passed by a ranch called El Capitan, which covered six square miles of fields and hills.[6] Barry's father Jules had purchased the ranch twenty-one years earlier, at the pinnacle of the career that made him a mogul.

Barry's mountaintop life of physical toil and transcendental meditation was a stark contrast to his father's world of mega-deals and glittering wealth. In fact, it was Jules's relentless pursuit of money that caused Barry to leave the family mansion in Beverly Hills and head in a different direction, far off the beaten path, and ultimately into remote Saline Valley.

***

During the mid-twentieth century, Jules's meteoric rise had been the talk of Beverly Hills. How did a slight Jewish boy from a middle-class background manage to amass such a huge fortune?

His was a classic American success story. In 1933, after attending The Ohio State University, Jules borrowed a thousand dollars from his father and opened a liquor store called Llords, adding the second "L" to make the name catchier. Jules chose Beverly Hills as its location because, as he said years later when he sat for his oral history, "That's where the money is."[7]

Jules was an ingenious promoter who saw how the movie industry had burgeoned into a cultural phenomenon; he wanted some of that glory to reflect on his venture. Carrying gift baskets loaded with liquor, he talked his way onto studio lots and won over big-name customers like Ginger Rogers, Jack Warner, Marlene Dietrich, and Bing Crosby.

"If I depended on the people who walked in, we would have starved to death," Jules said years later when he sat for an oral history. "It was just that I went out and got the business."

Jules built Llords into a six-store chain and sold the enterprise at a premium price—his first entrepreneurial jackpot. When World War II broke out, he joined the navy and served honorably as an officer. After the war, Jules "married well" by wooing Ruth Herskovits of New York City's Upper East Side, whose grandfather had amassed a fortune in the fur trade.

Jules landed a job as West Coast rep for Schenley Industries, a liquor distributor based in the Empire State Building.[8] His position gave him an executive title, job security, and a generous salary.

"I never knew life could be so easy," he said later.

But there was a problem: Schenley wanted him to move to New York. "I just didn't like New York," Jules explained. So he left Schenley and launched his own liquor brokerage, Jules Berman & Associates.[9]

During the war, soldiers stationed overseas had become fascinated by foreign products, from Swiss watches to British sports cars, and they brought these evolving tastes back home. Jules had a hunch that imported alcoholic beverages would likewise succeed in the U.S. market, so he began scouting for opportunities.

This led to a meeting with a Dutch brewer looking for someone to promote his family's unique-tasting beer in America. The brewer's name: Freddy Heineken.

By November 24, 1950, when Ruth gave birth to Barry Alan Berman, the couple's first and only child, forty-year-old Jules was on his way to amassing a fortune. Building on the success of Heineken, he scored a series of wins by importing foreign labels: Guinness Stout, Bass Pale Ale, Cinzano Vermouth, and J&B Scotch.

After Jules learned that Schenley wanted to divest its ownership of an obscure Mexican liqueur called Kahlua, he made a deal to pay $50,000 for the brand.[10] Jules plowed money into advertising and hustled relentlessly. Sales soared and the cash rolled in. People started calling the high-flying liquor distributor "Mr. Kahlua."[11]

From there Jules branched into real estate. In 1960, the year Barry turned ten, Jules and two business partners cut a deal to buy Lake Arrowhead, an aquatic jewel nestled in the mountains near Los Angeles. The $6.5 million purchase price included the adjoining village, a pair of hotels, and 3,200 acres of woodlands. Jules carved a golf course into the forest and began selling lots.

By the mid-1960s, as Barry passed through his teenage years, Kahlua was a global phenomenon, selling upwards of a million cases per year. Lake Arrowhead was a success too, with booming lot sales and a golf course that drew the likes of Bob Hope, Bing Crosby, and Conrad Hilton. Jules curried friendships with other notables including California governor Pat Brown and Occidental Oil tycoon Armand Hammer.

Jules used his riches to fund a flamboyant lifestyle. He moved the family into a Beverly Hills mansion, bought a yacht that he named the *Kahlua*, and stocked his garage with luxury cars: Rolls Royce, Cadillac, Maserati. His vacation properties included an estate in Acapulco, a lodge on the shores of Lake Arrowhead, and a ten-thousand-acre hunting preserve.[12]

In 1964, television talk show hostess Pamela Mason interviewed Jules in a show titled *Jules Berman, millionaire*—a title that said it all.[13] Jules had become subsumed in wealth and its trappings.

The following year, Jules made an impulsive decision to sell Kahlua to Hiram Walker, which stunned his former colleagues at Schenley, and which Jules himself later struggled to explain. He remained an executive with the Kahlua brand but focused mostly on real estate, using half of the $8 million sale proceeds to buy El Capitan.[14] Spanning 3,638 acres, with miles of open space and sweeping ocean views, the ranch was one of coastal California's premier private properties.

***

As Barry and Louise headed south along Highway 101 past the rangeland and avocado orchards of El Capitan, they reached a place that other motorists didn't know about. On the ocean side of the freeway, shielded from view by thick vegetation and rising terrain, was an isolated parcel of Jules's ranch, bounded by train tracks on one side and coastline on the other.

Barry knew this place intimately. To him the secluded parcel, roughly twelve acres in size, was more than a beautiful slice of oceanfront land. This was where the younger Berman, starting as a teenager, came to escape from his parents' Beverly Hills world.

Barry was the quintessential "poor little rich boy" who longed for something more. Although he had been born into wealth that most people can only dream about, to him it didn't seem to matter.

Barry's childhood best friend Larry Koplin, who grew up to become a well-known plastic surgeon, recalled the younger Berman as someone who possessed "his own internal compass"—a moral magnetometer that pointed him away from the material world embraced by his parents.

"He was a rich kid who didn't lead a rich kid's life," said Dr. Koplin when interviewed for this book on June 10, 2017. "He didn't behave or dress or consume like someone who grew up here."

Barry wasn't merely unimpressed by his parents' wealth; he came to despise their values and priorities. Jules was consumed by the liquor trade and real estate deals; he traveled the world on business and paid scant attention to his only son. Ruth, who as a girl had been shipped off to Les Fougères, a stern-and-proper finishing school in Switzerland, circulated among wealthy women playing mah-jongg, sipping tea, and chatting about Beverly Hills society.[15]

"She was not the 'let me bake you some cookies or make you some hot chocolate' kind of mom," Dr. Koplin explained.

With two aloof parents and no siblings for companionship, Barry became a pensive and solitary youngster. Instead of demanding expensive clothes and elaborate toys, he enjoyed exploring out back of his parents' mansion, which abutted open space surrounding Franklin Canyon Reservoir. He tinkered with Heathkit radios in a workshop above the garage and found he liked working with his hands.[16]

Meanwhile, the world outside the Beverly Hills bubble roiled with strife. By the mid-1960s, the U.S. government was shipping thousands of men to Vietnam—a war that some Americans, especially young people like Barry, considered immoral and absurd. The civil rights movement brought more dissension as television news stations broadcast images of police tear-gassing protestors and beating them with nightsticks.

The conflicts often cleaved families along generational lines, with parents decrying the unrest while their children demanded change—a phenomenon dubbed the "generation gap."[17] For Barry, the gap grew into a chasm, exacerbated by the swirling controversies that Jules all too often incited.

The Sierra Club opposed Jules when he razed a forest to build the golf course at Lake Arrowhead. He angered people in the entertainment industry when he bought Runyon Canyon in the Hollywood Hills, leveled the San Patrizio mansion that had hosted Errol Flynn and Janet Gaynor, and announced plans to build a 157-home "Tiffany development."[18]

Jules launched a clever but controversial advertising campaign to promote Kahlua by exploiting pre-Columbian burial effigies looted from shaft tombs in western Mexico. The ads ran in trendy magazines like *Playboy*, *Glamour*, and *Ebony*, showing the burial effigies arranged in mocking scenes with cartoon-like quips.[19]

As a member of the California Athletic Commission, Jules voted to deny a boxing license for Muhammad Ali, who was under indictment for refusing to enter the draft. UPI quoted Jules as saying, "We all have religion and I have a religion, but my country comes first."[20]

If Jules ever harbored second thoughts about these choices, they weren't evident in his public pronouncements or oral history. By all indications he relished the life of a Beverly Hills mogul: dealmaker on a global scale, traveling by private plane, connected in the art world, a donor to worthy causes, respected in boardrooms and country clubs, with a well-bred wife, a European secretary, and a mansion staffed with servants.

But like many young people during the 1960s, Barry gravitated toward the counterculture of "sex, drugs, and rock 'n' roll."[21] Although it appears hookups weren't part of Barry's teenage experience, he often smoked weed in the hills behind his house, and he sometimes experimented with mushrooms and LSD. Popular music resonated with Barry: Jimi Hendrix, Janis Joplin, The Rolling Stones, the Grateful Dead.

After Jules bought El Capitan, the ranch became an ideal getaway for Barry and his friends to hang out, party, and surf. They'd drive out from Beverly Hills and bunk in a trio of rundown cottages—old prefab military dwellings—on the oceanfront parcel of land. Barry seemed to thrive in the rustic location, far from the stifling luxury of the Berman family mansion.

Following graduation from Beverly Hills High School in 1968, Barry enrolled at Cal Poly (California Polytechnic University) in San Luis Obispo, a state university situated a couple of hours north from El Capitan.[22] The school had a casual atmosphere, so Barry could have dabbled in coursework and still had time to party and surf. But when he realized academia wasn't his calling, he decided to quit school.

Jules hoped his only son would join the family business, but Barry wanted nothing to do with his father's world. Brent Lieberman, a surfing buddy of Barry's who later became an outdoor photographer, said that Barry "didn't want his life to be ruled by the almighty dollar—he wanted to go the other way."

Barry set out on a long trip—what might be called a walkabout or seeker's journey—looking for answers to the questions that plagued him. Viewed through a certain lens, Barry's sojourn could be dismissed as a spoiled kid trying to "find himself" instead of buckling down. But in fairness, as heir apparent to the Berman family fortune, Barry could have been far more self-indulgent.

"He had material options that could have given him an extremely comfortable, predictable, safe life," said Dr. Koplin. "He eschewed that."

Barry headed to the Far East, venturing overland into India. Toward the end of his journey Barry crossed into Punjab Province, where the Beas River flows down from the Himalaya. Alone and carrying a backpack, he walked into an ashram the size of a town, and the center of the spiritual practice Radha Soami Satsang Beas.

From the moment Barry entered the ashram, his life would never be the same. Although an Indian religion with stringent rules might have seemed a radical prescription for a wealthy teenager from Beverly Hills—a stoner who liked to surf—Radha Soami turned out to be exactly what Barry was seeking.

A few years after Barry's fateful first trip to Punjab Province, several friends and fellow devotees took up residence in the trio of oceanfront cottages on the seaside edge of El Capitan. Mary Sullivan, who in 1986 practiced polarity therapy, and later became a licensed acupuncturist, was one of them.[23] So was jewelry-maker Arthur Korb, who'd sponsored Barry for initiation into Radha Soami.

The evolution of El Capitan into a hamlet for members of a Far Eastern faith began when Barry dropped out of college and went on his across-the-globe trip. The youthful seeker didn't need to travel the world to find religion—he had many choices close to home, including his family's traditional Judaism. But for Barry and many other young people of that era, the generation gap included a rejection of conventional faiths.

After the Beatles flew to India to study transcendental meditation under Maharishi Mahesh Yogi, with an entourage including actress Mia Farrow and Mike Love of the Beach Boys, Eastern religions soared in popularity.[24] Suddenly, it seemed everyone, from college students to movie stars, wanted to find their "third eye center" and seek a higher plane.[25]

Radha Soami, which had arisen in the 1800s, was one of those trending religions. The faith incorporated Hindu beliefs that the soul travels through multiple lifetimes, carrying good and bad karma. But unlike Hinduism, Radha Soami embraced upward mobility and regarded all caste members as worthy comers.

Leadership of the sect was a family affair, and in 1951, Charan Singh became Radha Soami's fourth satguru, a position he held until his death in 1990 at age seventy-three. During his lifetime, his disciples regarded him as godlike, on par with Jesus Christ, and even now he's still revered by those who call him Master or "Baba Ji."[26]

When Barry visited the dera circa 1970, the satguru's staff provided him with free food and a place to sleep. Every morning he attended satsang, translated from Sanskrit as "truth group," where devotees gather for inspiration and fellowship.

Satsangs at the dera gave Barry a chance to see Charan Singh in person and listen as his words in Punjabi were translated into English. A vigorous middle-aged man at the height of his mortal powers, the charismatic satguru boasted millions of followers worldwide.

At one point, the guru turned his gaze on the young traveler, and Barry felt the all-seeing eyes of Charan Singh look deep within him. Another awe-striking moment came when Barry departed from the dera. He was invited to return but told, "Next time don't bring the drugs." Although Barry hadn't gotten high at the dera, he'd stashed some hashish in his backpack, and it seemed to Barry that the omniscient satguru knew this.

After returning to California, Barry began attending local satsangs, and he vowed to follow the four rules comprising "the Path" toward spiritual enlightenment:

1. Adhere to a vegetarian diet.

2. Behave ethically.

3. Abstain from drugs and alcohol.

4. Meditate for two-and-a-half hours every day.

Even though these mandates weren't easy to follow—especially the required daily meditation—Barry embraced the Path with fervor. He moved to Garberville, a rustic town in Northern California, and began building his trade as a blacksmith.

Although the forested setting seemed an ideal venue for a life of craftsmanship and contemplation, it wasn't long before the young satsangi left redwood country and relocated to El Capitan's oceanfront edge. Barry's move coincided with a stunning setback for Jules—one of the rare occasions the elder Berman suffered defeat as a businessman.

When the younger Berman relocated from Garberville to El Capitan, and even in January 1986 when he and Louise drove by on their way to Saline Valley, the ranch remained pretty much the same as it had been for the past hundred years. This wasn't what Jules had intended when he bought the land, and he never got over feeling bitter about the outcome.

When Jules purchased El Capitan he regarded the ranch as a golden business opportunity. Jules wanted to develop the property into an upscale community of 1,500 homes and condos, tennis courts, and an equestrian center. With his typical fondness for hyperbole and grand gestures, Jules shipped in Lipizzaner horses and hired a trainer from Austria.[27]

"See, I wanted to draw attention to the ranch," Jules explained in his oral history. "I knew I needed something unusual."

After pushing his proposal through the planning commission and wooing Santa Barbara County supervisors, Jules won final approval. But two local housewives spearheaded a movement to stop the project—one of them being Selma Rubin, who later became known as "Mother to Earth Day."

Rubin and her colleague rallied students from nearby UC Santa Barbara and gathered enough signatures to qualify for an antidevelopment initiative for the November 1970 ballot. After Jules's last-ditch lawsuit to derail the initiative cratered in court, his development plan lost by a landslide vote.[28]

With the development of El Capitan dead in the water, Barry invited Arthur Korb to move into one of the oceanfront cottages. Korb, at that time aged twenty-nine and an older brother figure to Barry, was a product of the counterculture who'd been shaped by 1960s-style experiences.

Raised by his single mother, a concert cellist, Korb spent his boyhood in Sierra Madre Canyon northeast of Los Angeles—a mecca for artists, musicians, and beatniks.[29] In 1962, the year Korb turned twenty-one, he took a journey deep into Mexico.

"I first ate peyote in Zihuantanejo," Korb recalled years later in an interview for this book on May 31, 2014. "Timothy Leary gurued me through the trip. At that time, he was still a Harvard professor."[30]

Korb attended the legendary Monterey International Pop Festival in 1967, where The Who concluded their set by smashing drums and kicking amps. The next performer to take the stage, who wasn't yet well-known, pushed the boundary even farther.

"I saw Jimi Hendrix burn his guitar," said Korb. "It was like he was holding his penis."[31]

During this era, Korb reveled in dropping acid and exploring desert ghost towns. "The earlier cultures left behind residual stuff. I started assembling junk sculpture." Soon he graduated to crafting custom jewelry, and this became his profession.

Korb, handsome and charismatic, found his way to Radha Soami through one of his romantic involvements. "I got into it because I had an affair with a manic-depressive woman. Then she changed and became calm and centered. I wanted the same. She said, 'Come to satsang.'"

Korb gave up dropping acid and committed himself to the Path. "LSD gave me access, a brief elevator ride, an experience of a bigger existence," he explained later. "But to get there you have to earn your way by doing daily spiritual pushups."

After Korb and his then-wife Barbara moved to El Capitan, Barry decided to leave Garberville and join them. Later, Barbara's sister Mary Sullivan moved into the third cottage.

With this group of young satsangis in residence—Barry in the cottage closest to the ocean, Arthur Korb and his wife in the middle cottage, and Mary Sullivan and her family in the cottage farthest back—El Capitan glowed with the love-and-sharing aura of a commune.

"We were all a bunch of hippies," said Sullivan.

Barry's role as facilitator of the El Capitan hamlet, along with his work ethic and devotion to his master, earned him respect from his satsangi peers. "He was humble and helpful and very frugal," Sullivan recalled. "You'd never know he had any money." Ordained-by-mail as a minister, Barry occasionally officiated a wedding, including one of Korb's marriages.[32]

Barry also hosted a regional satsang that drew Radha Soami devotees far and wide to El Capitan's oceanfront edge. "Naria was conceived the night of the Bhandara," Sullivan recollected. Nine months later, when Sullivan gave birth to Naria in the bedroom of her cottage, she invited Barry to attend.

Sullivan said that Barry "lived like a monk, contemplative and reflective. He was really into his master and meditated 2-1/2 hours per day. He did his ironwork, sometimes went to Renaissance Faire. He was a caffeine person, he loved chai tea. He smoked Baba cigarettes and chewed the Indian stuff that turns your lips red."[33]

Although Barry lived for years at El Capitan without a woman in his life, he did fall in love at least once before he met Louise—with Mary's younger sister Anne Sullivan.

"We were innocent and open-hearted," Anne recalled when interviewed for this book on December 13, 2017. "I knew he was in love, but it was a difficult time for me. I was in my twenties, following the Path, trying to be celibate. I felt bad that I couldn't give him what he wanted."

In a letter Barry wrote to Anne in 1976, he talked about returning from Los Angeles and "feeling a bit dizzy from the city energy. I don't exist too awful well in cities in case you hadn't guessed."

Barry invited Anne to visit him at El Capitan. He even floated the idea of them moving together to Hawaii and buying a place on the beach.

"I think about you too darn much," he said. "Will you tell your astral body to please stay away from this brain between 3–7 a.m. Pacific Standard Time, as I must concentrate at the eye center and think up wrought iron designs at this time."

But Anne began drifting away from the Path and its rigorous daily meditation. "I liked rock-and-roll too much." She last saw Barry in 1980, when he stayed at her apartment in Maryland.

"We had a bit of an argument," Anne recalled. "He wanted to be my boyfriend. I set a boundary. He knew it was a lost cause."

That same year, Barry met Louise at a satsang in Santa Barbara. She was a forty-six-year-old beauty with blonde hair, a warm smile, and blue eyes full of light and promise. He was twenty-nine years old, shaggy-haired, with a body well-muscled from all the ironwork.

Louise told Barry she needed a place to live, so he rented her a room in his seaside cottage. Korb said he thought Louise was just a boarder, until one day he strolled into Barry's cottage unannounced.

"They didn't know I was looking. I saw Louise touching Barry in an intimate way."

CHAPTER FOUR

All but Broke, in Jail, and about to Turn Forty

LOUISE'S AGE BRACKET AND CHECKERED PAST RAISED EYEBROWS WITH Barry's family. By the time she reached El Capitan and the arms of her younger husband-to-be, she'd been through three failed marriages, various love affairs, countless drug trips, and a humiliating stint in jail.

Despite all this, Louise sparkled with positive energy and girlish enthusiasm. She was optimistic by nature, and as a believer in the teachings of Charan Singh, she felt boundless hope for an everlasting future.

"My mother shined a light on this other side of thinking," said Michael Westerman, her eldest son, in an interview for this book on May 17, 2014.

In January 1986, as Louise and Barry continued past El Capitan on their journey to Saline Valley, the highway turned inland, and the coast vanished from view. About ten miles down the coast from El Capitan, they passed through the town of Goleta—the last place Louise resided before moving into Barry's cottage. The life journey that brought her there had been long and challenging.

※※※

Born Virginia Rhoda Wiltshire in 1933, she was the only offspring of a marriage between Evelyn Forsyth, a Canadian immigrant who was pathologically self-absorbed, and John Wiltshire, one of a series of men who cycled through her mother's life.

Because of her mother's narcissistic personality and tumultuous sex life, Louise's childhood was fraught with instability, and the two of them never bonded. After one of the men molested Louise, her mother farmed her out to live with other people.

The traumas of not bonding with her mother, being molested by an older man, and then being banished from the house as if the assault were her fault, left Louise with deep emotional wounds.

"Women never get over them," said her childhood best friend Eleanor "Ellie" Snow, a retired real estate agent, when interviewed for this book, on February 26, 2017. "She was a troubled little child—always searching, searching, searching."

Louise never revealed to her family which of the men molested her—except she said that the culprit wasn't her birth father. Around the time Evelyn married Lowell Robertson in 1946, the abuser was gone from her mother's life, and Louise moved back in.

But Evelyn remained selfish and controlling, and she felt jealous of Louise's good looks. Louise in turn was a strong-willed girl and unafraid to talk back.

Even though mother and daughter clashed, Louise enjoyed a relatively stable home life thanks to her new stepfather, who worked as a plumber.

"Lowell was a lovely man, quiet as a church mouse," said Snow. "He was Steady Eddie."

The family lived in a working-class neighborhood in East Hollywood, in a little house that Lowell kept in good repair, and with ample food in the fridge. Ellie lived a few blocks away, in a crowded Catholic household with her birth mom, siblings, and an immigrant stepfather with old-country ways.

The two friends, perhaps drawn together by challenges they faced on the home front, became inseparable. "She called me her guiding light," said Snow.

Ellie, a pixyish blonde with a mischievous manner, and Louise, who had an engaging personality and statuesque figure, made for a dazzling duo. On weekday mornings, the girls rode to Belmont High on the No.

44 city bus.[1] On weekends they danced at the gym, skated at the Roller Bowl, or watched first-run movies at Hollywood theaters.

"She was a fun girl, loved having a good time," said Snow. "We had our own little clique. Everyone knew who we were."

In 1950, the same year Barry Berman was born, Louise, at that time a high school sophomore and romantically precocious, fell for a senior named John Woodward.

"I was so upset because he was taking my best girlfriend away," said Snow. "But they were in love."

After John graduated and moved into an apartment, the young lovers hatched a plan to elope. Louise told her mother she was staying over at Ellie's house; Ellie told her mom the opposite story. The girls jumped into John's Chevy and rode through the night to Las Vegas.

Because the minimum age at that time for getting married in Nevada without parental consent was twenty-one for men and eighteen for women, Ellie had altered their IDs. The county clerk scrutinized John's draft card and Louise's driver's license, eyed the fidgety youngsters, and became suspicious.[2] She dialed the phone number on the marriage license application and Louise's mother answered.

"My daughter isn't eighteen yet, you send her home!"

John drove the two girls back to Los Angeles to face the parental wrath. "We went to my house first," said Snow. "I was forbidden to see Louise again . . . but it didn't last."

Despite the misadventure, Louise kept hounding her mother for permission, and Evelyn finally relented. "She married John to get the hell out of the house," said Snow. "I married my first husband for the same reason. Back then a girl couldn't make enough to afford her own place."

After John served a brief stint in the army, he bought a house on the GI Bill and landed a job as a plumber. Louise gave birth to two sons: first Michael and then Jim. With steady income, a starter home, and two baby boys, John and Louise were living the midcentury version of the American Dream.

But the dream didn't last. Louise hated being a housewife and longed for something more. "It all started to fall apart," said Snow. "They never really had that much in common. I think it finally dawned on her that she wasn't that madly in love."

By the mid-1950s, Louise was divorced, working as a secretary, and living in Hollywood with her two little boys.³ This was an era when being a "divorcee" was sometimes equated with being sinful and slutty. Despite the social stigma, Louise had no shortage of suitors.

"She fell in love all the time," said Snow. "She'd call me up, 'Ellie, I know what you're going to say, but this is for real!'"

By 1961, the year her future husband Barry turned eleven, Louise had matured into a slender and elegant twenty-seven-year-old with manicured nails and a radiant smile. Out of the blue, she bumped into a former junior-high classmate named Joe Gatto.

In the following decades, Gatto would become a renowned educator and founding faculty member of Los Angeles County High School for the Arts. After Gatto was mysteriously shot to death in 2013,⁴ his obituary in the *LA Times* quoted muralist Robert Vargas: "He challenged and inspired us to pull from within ourselves and not be afraid of that path of discovery, wherever that may lead us."⁵

Apparently, Gatto inspired Louise and vice-versa because they had what Snow described as a "torrid affair." In June 1961, they wed in a civil ceremony at the Los Angeles County courthouse. But a few weeks later they split up.

"His family went crazy," said Snow. "They were Italian, a good Catholic family. She was a divorced woman with two children. They absolutely came off the wall about it."

But according to Marianna Gatto, Joe's youngest daughter from a subsequent marriage, within her family there's a much different version of the story: Louise told Joe she was pregnant, and he wanted to do the right thing. When it turned out Louise wasn't pregnant the marriage ended.⁶

Whatever the reason behind the swift breakup, it's clear Louise wanted a man in her life. Soon afterward, she fell for Loth "Wes" Westerman, an L.A. firefighter with movie star looks.

Joan Roberts, an exuberant woman who later moved to rural Oregon, was a close friend of Wes and Louise's; she'd first laid eyes on Wes while still a schoolgirl, when he was in his twenties.

"He looked like the Marlboro Man," Roberts recalled when interviewed for this book on May 18, 2017. "My goal was to have sex with him when I turned eighteen."

But Louise beat Roberts to the punch. Only nine months after the breakup of her second marriage, Louise married Wes Westerman in Las Vegas.

Louise hoped the marriage would bring her restless searching to a blissful end. But instead of living happily ever after, Louise was destined for more heartache.

***

Decades after the Wes Westerman phase, as Louise and her fourth husband Barry headed toward Saline Valley, they motored down the road to Santa Barbara, the California mission city of whitewashed walls and red tile roofs. There they exited the highway and drove to a pet kennel, where they dropped off their two dogs.

After tanking up on gas, Barry and Louise headed south again, passing the community of Mussel Shoals and miles of sandy beaches. Past Ventura they turned east, following a rural highway along the Santa Clara River.[7]

To their right, over a range of craggy peaks, was a place called Box Canyon—an isolated area of sandstone formations and folded hills. Even though Louise and Barry skirted past the area, no closer than ten miles as the crow flies, for Louise it may have been too close for comfort.[8]

***

After Louise married Wes Westerman, she moved into his house in Box Canyon with her two sons Michael and Jim. Michael, who longed for stability and a normal family life, took his stepdad's last name. Soon Louise gave birth to Laura—the daughter who later died when her car was swept down Refugio Creek.

"Laura was beautiful, with long legs like her mom," said Joan Roberts. "I imagined her flying up and landing on a flower, like a princess with wings in a fairytale."

But as the passion between Louise and her third husband faded, the couple started to clash. Louise complained that Wes was a flake who started projects he never finished; she began calling him "Wes the Mess." Wes countered that Louise became someone far different from the woman he married.

"I arranged for her to go to design school; she was very gifted at making clothes," he recalled years later when interviewed for this book on May 19, 2014. "But she didn't stay with it. She got involved with friends who smoked marijuana. It was amazing how she changed."[9]

Louise indeed changed, from a coiffed 1950s secretary to a free-spirited woman of the 1960s. One reason was her restless personality, shaped by childhood traumas. Another was the unsettled era, when Barry was an alienated teenager and America reeled from civil strife and the agony of Vietnam.

Another reason was Box Canyon itself, which had become a counterculture mecca. True to his background as a firefighter and former military man, Wes remained staunchly conservative. But Louise gravitated toward the artists, musicians, and hippies who lived and partied nearby.

Wes suspected she was dealing drugs. "There were people coming and going at all hours of the night," he recalled, blaming the demise of their marriage on this troubling turn of events.

But Eleanor Snow had a different take. "I never understood the marriage to Wes. He was so controlling, and she was the last person who could be controlled. It was like releasing a starving person."

As part of the divorce settlement, Wes bought Louise her own home in Box Canyon, and she moved there with her two sons. But Wes and Louise had a bitter custody dispute about Laura. Wes convinced the judge that because of Louise's drug use and "radical ways" he should be granted sole custody.

Then Louise lost control of Jim, a troubled teen who abused alcohol. After an outburst where he knocked his mom to the kitchen floor, Jim left home and moved in with a friend.

In the wake of these midlife crises, Louise's "searching, searching, searching" became even more manic. "Things just took off," said Joan Roberts. "There would be parties, people would be dropping acid."

Michael, a serious young man who was determined to make something of himself, watched helplessly from the sidelines. "It was a counterculture environment in the canyon," he recalled. "Everybody was taking drugs up there. She was involved in all of that."

Louise hooked up with a string of lovers—including a guitar player, an architect, a former Marine, and one of the hippies who lived in a teepee on her front lawn.

"She was absolutely gorgeous," said Roberts. "Sensual body, big breasts. She moved a couple of young guys in there—good for her, good for Louise."

Around 1972, Louise sold her house in Box Canyon and hadn't yet found another place to live. One day she picked up Laura for a brief visitation but instead took the little girl and skipped town.

"The police took me down to the station," said Michael. "I didn't tell them anything."

Mom and daughter fled to Pagosa Springs, a resort community in the San Juan Mountains of Colorado.[10] They moved in with a former lover of Louise's named Jim, who back in Box Canyon was one of the tepee-dwelling hippies. But by this time Jim had met someone else.

That summer, on a break from attending college, Michael drove his VW across the western US, planning to reunite with his mom and half-sister. He found them living in a tiny room under the same roof as Jim and his new girlfriend.

"It wasn't a good situation," said Michael dryly.

Remaining in Jim's house wasn't an option and renting a place during the high season was all but impossible. Seeing no other solution, Louise and her two children pitched a tent near the San Juan River, up in the mountains above town.

Michael managed to find construction work, and after an interlude of camping out, the family moved into a one-room cabin at a nearby ranch. But the primitive structure lacked hot running water, and Louise had to cook on a wood-burning stove.

"Mom wasn't in the best state of mind," Michael recalled. "She was trying to figure out what to do next."

As a fugitive Louise couldn't apply for a job, and the cash she'd generated by selling her house in Box Canyon was running low. When friends invited Louise to move into their apartment in Canoga Park, she and Laura headed back to California.

But Wes Westerman lived near Canoga Park, and he hadn't stopped searching for his missing daughter. "It was terrible, I couldn't sleep," he recalled years later. "All I wanted was my daughter back." When Wes spotted Louise's VW bus parked outside the apartment, he called the police.

Louise ended up behind bars, her life at a low ebb. She was all but broke, in jail, about to turn forty, with a daughter she couldn't see anymore and a son, Jim, who was estranged from her and struggling with substance abuse.[11]

But she still had her son, Michael, who by this time had followed a girl to Vancouver, Washington, a wooded suburb of Portland. The relationship didn't last, but Michael stayed the course. He became manager of a shoe store, bought a house, and joined the Army Reserve.

After Louise got out of jail, she decided to leave California and move in with her eldest son. Once in Vancouver she landed a secretarial job, and at some point, she discovered Radha Soami. The daily meditation and shunning of intoxicants marked the end of Louise's wild-child ways.

Eventually, Wes took note of the change, so he granted Laura permission to move north and rejoin her mom and stepbrother. But when the winter of 1979 brought fierce snow and ice storms to the Portland region, Louise told Michael she hated the climate and wanted to head back to California. Laura and her boyfriend Brett Nold decided to tag along.

Louise and the two teenagers moved into a townhouse in Goleta. The following year, Laura and Nold got married, so Louise wanted to give the newlyweds space.[12] At a satsang in Santa Barbara, she mentioned to the other devotees that she was looking for a place to live.

CHAPTER FIVE

Blissfully Unaware of What Lay Ahead

ON THEIR JOURNEY INTO THE DESERT IN JANUARY 1986, BARRY AND Louise skirted around the jagged peaks north of Box Canyon and drove into the Tehachapi Mountains, an oak-and-chaparral landscape similar in appearance to the Santa Ynez.[1] By now the waypoints of their separate pasts were in the rearview mirror, and they'd begun their journey into what they hoped would be a bright future.

Barry and Louise turned onto a two-lane highway and descended eastward into Antelope Valley—a desert expanse named for the pronghorns that used to roam there. The wayfaring couple hadn't yet entered the wilds; the pronghorns had been hunted to extinction and the valley was being invaded by tract houses. But it was still a place of desolate beauty and long vistas, a world apart from coastal California.

As husband and wife crossed through Antelope Valley, whatever they chatted about remains a mystery. Maybe they focused on what lay ahead on their trip into the backcountry, or perhaps they discussed their five-year-long journey as a couple.

***

The unlikely pairing of Barry and Louise arose because of circumstance: She needed a place to live, so he rented her a room. Within the close quarters of Barry's cottage, the relationship evolved into something more.

Around the beginning of 1981, some six months after Louise moved into Barry's seaside abode, the two housemates became lovers. Anne

Sullivan, who until then might have been Barry's only romantic interest, said, "As far as I knew he was a virgin. I wondered, who was this Louise who broke through his solitary existence?"

On the surface, they seemed like a mismatch. Barry was a young man from a wealthy family, never married and with no children. Louise, while beautiful and charismatic, was an older woman with a troubled past and three children from two ex-husbands. What did Barry see in her?

According to Arthur Korb and Mary Sullivan, who lived in the adjacent cottages at El Capitan, the housemates became lovers partly because of the oceanfront hamlet's secluded setting.

"Barry was isolated," said Korb. "He had friends, but he didn't have romantic involvements. Louise was there and they got involved."

Louise fell hard for Barry, but the introspective young man didn't feel the same draw. "Barry wasn't as into it at first," said Sullivan. "He struggled with it."

His reaction didn't come as a surprise to those who knew Barry. For most of his adult years he'd lived a contemplative life, spending much of his time alone, deep in his own thoughts. Suddenly, he was sharing his bed and being asked to open his heart.

But because Barry focused more on spirituality than worldly matters, he was able to look past the seventeen-year age difference and see Louise as a beautiful soul rather than as a woman who, at first glance, looked old enough to be his mother.

"Barry didn't care about what anyone thought," said Sullivan. "How people looked wasn't important."

There was tenderness between Barry and Louise—they genuinely liked each other—and they began to grow together. "The relationship was sweet," said Sullivan. "They were good partners."

Michael Westerman said that for his mom, the love affair with Barry was a breakthrough. "In the past she'd picked men for all the wrong reasons. With Barry they were two souls headed in the same direction."

Once Barry and Louise became intimate, marriage was all but inevitable. The strictures of Radha Soami hold that sexual relations should only occur within the bounds of matrimony. As Arthur Korb phrased it, "You marry the person you're sleeping with."

They wed on Saturday, June 27, 1981, at a church in Solvang, a village in Central California known for its quaint Danish architecture. The ceremony was simple, with fewer than a dozen guests.

Jules and Ruth Berman didn't attend; they disapproved of the union. But Jules did gift his son the house atop Refugio Road—apparently without adding Louise's name to the deed.

After moving into their new home, Barry and Louise began hosting monthly satsangs and inviting friends to visit. Barry concentrated on building his blacksmith business, and Louise, energetic and creative, tended to the garden and tackled projects around the house.

When Laura's car got swept down Refugio Creek, and the realization set in that she was gone, Barry and Louise mourned the loss together. They also found solace in their faith, which held that one life's end is but a precursor to the next.

The following year, Barry and Louise traveled to India to visit the dera. They sat at their master's feet and listened to his discourses, along with hundreds of other devotees. Afterward, they sprawled on straw mats and shared vegetarian meals.

Louise returned to California bearing a shawl the satguru had blessed, and she often spoke about how much the trip meant to her. With decades of tumult and trauma behind her, Louise had finally found contentment—or so it seemed.

But in 1985, Barry and Louise began having marital problems. Barry withdrew and sometimes went sailing alone off the Santa Barbara coast. At one point, he talked about taking a solo voyage across the South Pacific to New Zealand—a route spanning close to seven thousand miles.

During this rocky phase in their marriage, Barry and Louise didn't formally separate, but they did stop sharing a bed. "Mom was concerned they were falling apart from each other," said Michael Westerman. "I told her these things happen, just ride it out."

Sure enough, as the year came to an end, Barry and Louise rekindled their romance. The precise alchemy remains a mystery, but perhaps the things they shared—their devotion to Charan Singh, their home atop Refugio Road, their two dogs and cat Daisy—drew them back together. Perhaps they personified the law of physics and romantic love: that opposites attract. Or perhaps, as Louise often told Michael, she and Barry were soulmates.

Louise phoned her eldest son to let him know they were going on a make-up trip. "Mom said things were better now," Michael recalled. "She called the trip a second honeymoon."

When Barry mentioned to Arthur Korb that he and Louise planned to visit Scotty's Castle in Death Valley, Korb told Barry about a hot spring oasis southwest of there, in a remote location called Saline Valley.

"I said, 'Man, you've got to check it out.'"

**

After leaving Antelope Valley and passing through the windswept town of Mojave, Barry and Louise continued north into Red Rock Canyon, a state park of multicolored cliffs. Another thirty miles and a turn to the east pointed them in the direction of Ridgecrest, a sun-faded military town adjacent to the Naval Weapons Center.

By the time the wayfaring couple stopped for gas, they'd traveled nearly 250 miles from home, and they were only a few miles south of the Inyo County line. They'd reached the unique region of California that had been sculpted by plate tectonics and parched by the rain shadow cast by the Sierra Nevada.

From the perspective of first-time visitors this was inhospitable terrain, the "land of little rain" in the words of writer Mary Austin— seemingly difficult to penetrate, and with an aura of romance and drama. It was also mostly devoid of civilization.[2] East of the Sierra, the human population dwindled, and desert wilderness began.

Where Barry and Louise spent the night on Friday, January 3, following their day-long drive from the coast, remains unknown. Because they carried camping gear, and no motel receipt turned up, it's likely they parked somewhere in the desert, sleeping under the camper shell of their blue Datsun pickup truck.

Husband and wife were now in territory where they'd never been— they were breaking new ground. From this point forward, come what may, they were in it together.

The second day of Barry and Louise's desert vacation took them deeper into Inyo County's desolate wilderness. About sixty miles north of Ridgecrest they drove through the vast high-desert basin of Panamint Valley. It hosted an impressive sand dune system along with a human population of perhaps a dozen souls.

At the northern end of Panamint Valley, Barry and Louise turned onto a dirt road leading into Wildrose Canyon, where miners in the 1870s crafted stone-and-mortar charcoal kilns resembling giant beehives. Louise, wearing jeans and a jacket, posed for a photo inside one of the blackened domes.

Where they pitched camp that evening isn't known, but the surrounding desert offered countless choices. Together under the stars, in a universe still expanding, husband and wife enjoyed a night of peacefulness and possibilities, blissfully unaware of what lay ahead.

The next day, Barry and Louise surfaced eighty miles away at Scotty's Castle, on the eastern edge of Death Valley, a few miles shy of the Nevada border. The so-called castle, a Spanish Colonial Revival mansion built in the roaring twenties, traced its roots to an unlikely friendship between Chicago millionaire Albert Johnson and prospector Walter Scott, aka "Death Valley Scotty."

Johnson poured vast sums into building a vacation retreat he called Death Valley Ranch. Scotty, who tended the place, told tall tales about the mansion being funded by gold from a secret mine. Over time, people began calling the place Scotty's Castle.

After Scotty and Johnson passed away, the National Park Service converted the mansion into a museum. Years later, as Barry and Louise took a tour, the young blacksmith snapped pictures of the wrought-iron gates, railings, and balustrades, which were famous among craftsmen of his trade.

After the tour ended, Barry and Louise bought gas and headed out of Death Valley. They retraced their route into Panamint Valley, but instead of turning south toward Ridgecrest, they continued west along Highway 190, a two-lane strip of asphalt across the arid landscape. About 120 miles out from Scotty's, at a lonely plateau, Barry and Louise reached the turnoff for Saline Valley Road.

The sun hung low in the sky and the air grew chilly as Barry and Louise navigated the same dirt road where eight days later, Deputy Larry Freshour would pass through on his way to investigate their abandoned pickup truck. Given they were in unfamiliar terrain, and with the winter afternoon waning, a less confident pair of travelers might have called a halt and made camp. But the youthful husband and his middle-aged wife pressed on, even though the route bore few markers.

By the time Barry and Louise descended into Saline Valley, the desert was draped in darkness. Only fifteen days had passed since the winter solstice, so the sun set around 5:00 p.m. on the West Coast. With the waning moon not due to rise until the wee hours, only the stars in the sky and the Datsun's high beams illuminated the lonely landscape.

Sometime after nightfall, Barry and Louise made the right turn at Bat Rock. After driving across the Saline Valley floor, they entered the realm of hot baths, casual nudity, palm trees, and Chili Bob.

When husband and wife reached Lower Warm Springs, the Datsun's headlights illuminated tents, travel trailers, and truck-bed campers, along with pickups, jeeps, and a few passenger cars. New Year's was a popular time to visit the desert, and about fifty people remained at the oasis.

Lower Warm Springs had a reputation as a lively venue, with free-flowing alcohol and conversation, along with plenty of tobacco and weed. As the two new arrivals rolled in, they would have been greeted by the sights and sounds of campers partying around the community campfire, while naked bathers reveled in the warmth of Crystal Pool, the main soaking pool in the center of camp.

No one knows whether Barry and Louise kept driving or stopped to have a look around. At some point, they left Lower Warm Springs and headed up the connecting road to Palm Spring.

As Barry and Louise pulled into Palm Spring, the Datsun's headlights reflected off the water of Wizard Pool and illuminated three men soaking in it. The motor stopped and the lights clicked off. A few minutes later the truck's doors opened, and the two newcomers stepped out under the star-cover of a moonless evening.

Wearing bathing suits, they slipped into the hot water.[3] The men checked out Louise, but under the starlight they couldn't see much, other than the shape of her body as she entered the pool. They did notice she seemed older and plumper than Barry, who was slender and well-toned.

One of the men in Wizard Pool, a thirty-something named Mike, was traveling alone. Like most visitors to the hot springs, he bathed naked, but at night the water appeared inky black, so it was hard to tell. Mike, who had a relaxed and resonant voice, told the newcomers he was in the military, and mentioned he'd gone to college in New Mexico.

The other two men, both in their twenties, introduced themselves as Brian and Greg and said they were from Modesto, a city on the western side of the Sierra. They'd spent the afternoon riding their dirt bikes in the sand dunes on the southwestern side of Saline Valley, near the base of the Inyo Mountains.

By law, the dunes were off-limits to vehicles, but Bruce Albert, the BLM ranger on duty, had a huge swath of eastern California to patrol, and he hadn't witnessed the incursion. Now the two riders, having stripped off their dusty riding outfits, were lolling in Wizard Pool and sipping White Russian cocktails—vodka, Kahlua, and cream—a recipe Jules Berman helped popularize.

Barry and Louise told the men they'd driven in from Santa Barbara. The wayfarers seemed happy to be in camp and acted comfortably around each other—it was apparent they were a couple. There was no sign of any problem or lingering tension between them.

The couple from Santa Barbara came across as hippie-types. Barry talked about wanting to visit Indian ruins, and he specifically mentioned the Hogan as a possible destination.

The five bathers basked in the pool, making small talk and gazing up at the stars. Eventually, Brian and Greg headed to bed and left the Bermans conversing with Mike.

On Monday, January 6, dawn came around 6:30 a.m. Because pre-dawn meditation is a daily routine for most Radha Soami devotees, it's likely Barry and Louise were already awake.

Sometime after daybreak, a lady from Humboldt County in Northern California, who was staying at Palm Spring with her husband and preadolescent son, reportedly saw the couple from Santa Barbara leaving on a hike. Carrying daypacks, they walked away from the campground and headed up the Corridor.

Around 8:00 a.m., the two motorcyclists, Brian and Greg, arose and got dressed, and so did their older buddy Mark, who'd gone to bed early. By then the Bermans had already left on foot, and their Datsun pickup remained parked in camp.

Meanwhile, the military man named Mike was preparing for a day trip. Dressed in a camouflage shirt, he unloaded gear from the bed of his vehicle, a Datsun pickup like the Bermans' truck, only his was a two-wheel-drive model instead of four-wheel-drive. Carrying water, extra gas, and a shovel in back—standard supplies for a backcountry journey—Mike climbed into his pickup and started driving up the Corridor, in the same direction the Bermans had gone.

After downing coffee spiked with Kahlua, the motorcycle riders rode out of Palm Spring and headed up the Corridor on their Yamaha dirt bikes—but they didn't confine themselves to the BLM-approved route. Within a mile of camp, they turned up a wash toward the Peace Sign, then doubled back. In this manner, detouring to explore washes and spur roads, the three dirt bikers worked their way up the Corridor.

While Barry and Louise, the solo traveler named Mike, and the three dirt bike riders were all away from camp, a man and woman drove into Palm Spring. Because they've asked not to be named in this book, we'll call these two travelers Dale Dunsmuir and Katy Aberdeen.[4]

Like the Bermans, they were an odd couple. Dale was a free-spirited musician and mountaineer who was well-known within the community of outdoor adventurers living in Inyo County. Katy was a fair-haired beauty, also outdoorsy and adventurous, who looked young enough to be Dale's daughter.

Around the same time that Dale and Katy arrived in camp, about eight miles up the Corridor, the three motorcycle riders stopped for lunch and snapped a few photos. Setting off again, they crossed over Steel Pass and descended the precipitous gorge into Eureka Valley.

Like the sand dunes in Saline Valley, the Eureka Dunes were off-limits to motorized play. But with nobody there to enforce the rule, the riders had free rein.

Back in camp, as daylight waned late in the afternoon, Dale and Katy noticed a pickup truck approaching down the Corridor.

"It was near sunset when the military guy returned to camp," Katy recalled when interviewed for this book on May 30, 2014. "I saw him driving his truck into camp from the direction of the undeveloped springs."

Mike parked his pickup and walked over to Dale and Katy's campsite. Katy said later that he looked dirty and sweaty.

"He was super nervous. He said he quit smoking, but he wanted a cigarette. He traded some canned peaches for a pack of cigarettes."

Katy said that as she and Mike chatted, "He started talking about threesomes. He told us he'd been in a threesome. I was upset. This was not something we were interested in. I wanted to get that guy out of there. I had a bad feeling about him."

According to Brian Casey, that evening, after he and his buddies returned from their daylong excursion, the lady from Humboldt County asked if anyone had seen the couple from Santa Barbara.

The riders said they hadn't seen anyone all day. Mike responded that he might have spotted the couple hiking up the Corridor with their backpacks. Mike also said that while he was up the Corridor, parked off to one side, he saw the three riders go by.

When dawn broke the next day, the couple from Santa Barbara still hadn't returned to camp, but no one seemed alarmed. Mike packed up to leave, and in keeping with Saline Valley tradition, offered his surplus supplies to the other campers. Brian accepted the offer and retrieved some neatly cut firewood from the back of Mike's pickup.

On Wednesday, the three motorcycle riders loaded their dirt bikes into their trailer, climbed into the Mercury Meteor, and drove home to Modesto. At some point, the family from Humboldt packed up and left, and on their way out apparently told someone down at Lower Warm Springs about the missing couple.

No one thought to notify authorities until two days later, on Friday, January 10. That's when Chili Bob returned to Saline Valley, learned there was an abandoned vehicle parked up at Palm Spring with the owners nowhere to be found, and radioed into the sheriff's office in Independence.

CHAPTER SIX

Clues Too Few and the Desert Too Vast

WITH THE SEARCH AND RESCUE EFFORT OVER, AND NO SIGN OF BARRY and Louise Berman in Saline Valley, investigator Randy Nixon and Deputy Leon Boyer felt the full weight of the case on their shoulders. At this point they had zero clues: the searchers hadn't found anything of interest, and forensic examination of the Datsun pickup had come up empty.

The absence of leads compelled Nixon and Boyer to consider a laundry list of possibilities. "We covered every angle we could think of," Boyer recalled years later.

Robbery was one possible scenario, and a hypothesis Jules embraced. After the press in Los Angeles and Santa Barbara delved into the mystery, he spoke with a reporter about his theory of the case.

"I think Barry and Louise may have been on their way to the hot springs around there to search for artifacts," said Jules. "From the lack of any kind of clues, I think they were taken out of the area and probably killed somewhere else, possibly for the little bit of cash they were carrying."[1]

But Boyer, who prided himself on having the imagination to think like a criminal, didn't believe two travelers in Saline Valley would be murdered in an opportunistic robbery. The remote valley didn't attract thieves, and besides, when Barry and Louise disappeared, they carried little of value except for travel money, Louise's few items of jewelry, and Barry's silver belt buckle. Their credit cards hadn't been used since they bought gas in Death Valley.

Given Jules's immense wealth, kidnapping for ransom was a possibility, but this, too, seemed unlikely. Only a few people knew in advance about the missing couple's trip into Saline Valley. Besides, the Berman family hadn't received a ransom demand.

Another angle centered on the adage, "Follow the money." With Barry the heir apparent to the Berman family fortune, did anyone stand to benefit by removing him from the picture? Boyer believed that Valerie Dinnes, Jules's private secretary, might gain some advantage if Barry vanished, but he soon ruled her out as a suspect.

"Valerie was a straight shooter," he said thirty years later.

Jules dismissed out of hand any suggestion that an insider was involved. "It wasn't for money; it wasn't for revenge," he told a reporter. "Nobody hated them; nobody followed them."[2]

Another angle focused on Barry and Louise's status as disciples of Charan Singh. Was there something nefarious about this Eastern religion and its charismatic leader?

It seemed a fair question, given the era in which Barry and Louise disappeared. The 1970s and 1980s had seen the rise of notorious cult leaders such as Jim Jones, instigator of the "drink the Kool-Aid" suicides at the jungle encampment called Jonestown,[3] and Bhagwan Shree Rajneesh, the guru who invaded Central Oregon with hundreds of followers.[4]

The possibility of cult involvement also hearkened back to Charles Manson and the "Helter Skelter" murders of actress Sharon Tate and seven other victims in 1969. When Manson and his so-called family committed the murders, they'd been living in a rugged canyon about sixty miles south from Saline Valley.[5] Ever since then, the Manson family's connection to Inyo County had been a celebrated part of the sheriff's office lore.

Before becoming a murderer, Manson was obsessed with finding the "Hole"—a supposed portal to a kingdom at the center of the earth. He became fascinated by the hot springs in Saline Valley, believing they might contain the hidden portal. One of his disciples, Charles "Tex" Watson, reportedly got scalded by diving into a hot spring in search of the Hole.[6]

But when Boyer interviewed friends of the missing couple who were disciples of Charan Singh, they seemed intelligent and sincere—a stark contrast to the brainwashed zombies who surrounded cult leaders like Jones or Manson.[7] There was no evidence that the satguru or his followers had anything to do with Barry and Louise's disappearance.

An even more tenuous possibility arose from the location of Barry and Louise's mountaintop home in Goleta—directly above Ronald Reagan's ranch. Could the couple's disappearance be part of a plot to get within striking distance of the sitting U.S. president? The sheriff's office quickly dismissed this theory: with Barry and Louise out of the picture, the property fell under Jules's control.

A less wild theory held that the missing couple ran off in search of a simpler life. Barry's friends told Boyer that Jules's only child despised his father's obsession with wealth. They related a story that Barry, while a college student at Cal Poly, came home once on a visit and found only ostentatious cars in the garage, so he insisted that his father rent him a Ford.

David Morse, a classmate of Barry's at Beverly Hills High School who eventually became an international real estate developer, said years later that he thought Barry might have been seeking a more ascetic existence. "It wouldn't have surprised me if Barry had dropped out and ended up in Bali, Bhutan, or some quieter part of the world."

But other friends of Barry's reported that he loved his father and tried to reconcile himself to their differences. They also noted that Barry accepted certain advantages of being Jules Berman's son: The Refugio Road home had been a wedding gift, and Barry enjoyed the sailboat Jules gave him. Besides, it wasn't in keeping with Barry and Louise's personalities to inflict heartache on their loved ones by running away.

Boyer also learned that during the prior year, Barry and Louise had struggled with marital problems—to the point where they almost split up. Maybe the couple got into an argument that escalated into murder-suicide?

At first blush this theory didn't seem outlandish, given that domestic disputes rank among the leading precipitators of deadly violence.[8] But Boyer also found out that Barry and Louise's desert vacation was a make-up trip. Besides, the missing couple believed in nonviolence—it was a core tenet of their religion.

Some spacey Saliners thought a UFO abducted Barry and Louise, but Deputy Boyer focused on a more down-to-earth scenario: someone they encountered in Saline Valley might have been the culprit. Although robbery seemed an unlikely motive, perhaps something else prompted a predator to attack.

Before long, the Inyo County Sheriff's Office identified the three motorcycle riders and tracked them down in Modesto. Brian Casey proved to be the most informative. He came across as smart, with a good recollection, and willing to answer whatever questions investigators posed. He seemed the same way decades later when interviewed for this book on December 7, 2014.

As a youngster, Casey had a knack for using hand tools and fixing bikes. When he was in the fourth grade, his dad, a Vietnam veteran who didn't come around much, showed up one day and dropped off a mini-bike. That's when the budding mechanic graduated to motorcycles.

Brian met Greg Snyder, who was the same age and likewise rode motorcycles, when they played football together at Modesto High School. Greg's dad had been killed in an auto accident, and same as Brian, he'd grown up without a father at home.

Mark Muscio, who was older than Brian and Greg, already worked as a motorcycle mechanic. He became a mentor to the two younger guys; like him they were gutsy, athletic, and loved to ride. When Brian and Greg graduated from high school in 1984, Brian was already working alongside Mark at a Yamaha shop owned by Kenny Roberts, a legendary local motorcycle racer.

Toward the end of 1985, Mark, at that point aged thirty-seven, invited his two younger buddies, both nineteen, to join him on a New Year's trip into Saline Valley. The three men left Modesto on Saturday morning, January 4, 1986, with Mark at the wheel of his 1962 Mercury Meteor, towing a trailer with three dirt bikes: two Yamaha IT 175s and a newer-model Yamaha IT 200.

A few hours before Barry and Louise arrived in Saline Valley on Sunday, January 5, the three men from Modesto rode into the sand dunes near the base of the Inyos. Mark snapped a photo of the younger guys doing jumps. That evening, back in camp, Mark went to bed early while Brian and Greg mixed White Russian cocktails and soaked in Wizard Pool.

On Monday, January 6, sometime after the Bermans and the military man named Mike left camp, Brian, Greg, and Mark headed up the Corridor on their Yamahas. Although this flagged the men as potential suspects, when questioned by investigators they seemed guileless and not the least bit nervous.

A series of photos taken by Mark, date-stamped on the back "Jan 1986," corroborated the men's accounts of what they did on January 6. The photos showed the riders' progress as they stopped for lunch up the Corridor, descended toward Eureka Valley, and returned as daylight waned.[9]

Although the men admitted they rode into places that were off limits to motorcycles, they were open about this, and came across as rambunctious guys having fun in the outdoors. There was nothing in their statements, demeanors, or contemporaneous photos to suggest they were involved in Barry and Louise's disappearance.

Nixon and Boyer failed to locate the family from Humboldt County, but by all indications they remained in camp on January 6.[10] Boyer did speak with Katy Aberdeen and Dale Dunsmuir, who were well-known in the local community. The account they gave flagged Mike as a "person of interest," meaning he was a possible suspect and needed a closer look.

Motive, means, and opportunity are pillars of a homicide investigation, and as a military man, Mike presumably had the means—either with a weapon or his bare hands. The opportunity could have presented itself after Barry and Louise hiked up the Corridor, and Mike drove his pickup in the same direction.

Katy's statement that Mike returned down the Corridor late in the day, "super-nervous" and "all dirty" as he bummed a pack of cigarettes, heightened the suspicion. But what about motive: Why would Mike want to harm Barry and Louise, a pair of friendly, live-and-let-live strangers?

Deputy Boyer focused on Katy's account that Mike, a few minutes after meeting her, and without any prompting, floated the idea of a threesome. This behavior seemed beyond inappropriate to the point where it suggested that Mike might have been driven off the rails by a sexual motivation.

The sheriff's office wanted to question Mike about what he did on January 6, but the problem was, no one knew his full name or where he could be found.

In theory, someone else in Saline Valley might have been the culprit, and one investigative report mentioned an "old man" seen hiking down the Corridor on the day the Bermans disappeared. But there were no corroborating details, and besides, why would an aging hiker want to harm Barry and Louise?

Another hypothetical possibility: an unknown perpetrator drove up the Corridor from the Eureka Valley side, kidnapped or killed the Bermans, and escaped the same way. But the gorge leading up from Eureka Valley to Steel Pass—a series of stone steps—was a challenging route that attracted serious off-road explorers, not random visitors looking for trouble.

To sheriff's investigators it seemed implausible that an off-road explorer would make the difficult passage only to waylay two strangers. Besides, anyone coming up the gorge and crossing over Steel Pass on January 6 likely would have been noticed at some point by the motorcycle riders.

Of course, with no bodies and no clues, the possibility remained that Barry and Louise ran off voluntarily. It was also possible that the missing couple got lost and perished in the desert without being spotted by Sergeant Lucas and his team.

But the search had been so exhaustive, especially from the air, that the notion of the Bermans getting hopelessly lost seemed unlikely. Saline Valley mostly consisted of terrain where hikers could be seen from a distance, and they in turn could see for miles.

Sergeant Lucas wrote in his report, "The probability that two people would become lost in that area is minimal."

***

The sheriff's office landed the first real clue six weeks after Barry and Louise disappeared, when someone reported seeing abandoned athletic shoes in the desert.[11] That same afternoon, Nixon drove into Saline Valley to investigate.[12]

When Nixon arrived at the scene, he found the shoes about two-tenths of a mile uphill from Lower Warm Springs, near the rutted road leading to Palm Spring. The shoes—two pairs of powder-blue Nikes, one size seven-and-a-half and the other size eight—matched with the shoes seen in photos of Barry and Louise. The Nikes were tucked under a bush and partially hidden from view, about twenty feet from the road.

Nixon collected the shoes and placed them in an evidence locker at the Bishop substation. According to Deputy Boyer, Louise's pubic hair was found after the shoes were analyzed by the state DOJ lab.

One possible explanation for the couple's shoes ending up near the connecting road: Barry and Louise had been kidnapped there, forced to go barefoot so they wouldn't run, then loaded into a vehicle and spirited away.

But Deputy Boyer, who'd trained himself to think like a deviant, had a different take. The Nikes turned up where the connecting road dipped into a swale; a vehicle stopped there wasn't visible from Lower Warm Springs down below, or Palm Spring up above. Boyer theorized that the culprit killed Barry and Louise while they were hiking up the Corridor, and while driving away from the crime scene, stopped to stash the shoes, either to dump the incriminating evidence or to misdirect searchers.

But after the Nikes surfaced, no other evidence turned up, and once again the trail turned cold. Deputy Boyer pushed the sheriff's office to be creative and devote more resources to the case, but he wasn't the person in charge.

The Berman investigation began to suffer from weariness and resignation—the clues were too few and the desert too vast.

Deputy Boyer resolved to push forward on his own. The rancher turned lawman had been deeply affected by the disappearance of Barry and Louise; he'd seen firsthand the suffering of their family and friends.

Convinced that the military man named Mike was the likely perpetrator, Boyer was determined to track him down. The dogged deputy told

Jules Berman, "I'm not going to rest until we have this guy in custody and have a conviction."

Based on descriptions given to him by Katy Aberdeen and Dale Dunsmuir, Deputy Boyer, a natural-born sketch artist, penned composite drawings of Mike.[13] A psychological profile obtained by the sheriff's office predicted the perpetrator would return to the crime scene, so Boyer began taking camping trips into Saline Valley on his own time, accompanied by his teenage son Jay.

The first break came four months after Barry and Louise disappeared, when Boyer met two Saline Valley regulars—a couple from central California who have asked not to be named. They remembered meeting a man named Mike whose face resembled the composite drawing.

The encounter occurred around Easter 1986, when the couple shared a pool with Mike and his girlfriend. They recalled he was a military man from Barstow, in his thirties or early forties, who was involved in logistics.

"Mike had a husky body and a shock of dark hair sticking up," they recalled when interviewed for this book on May 16, 2014. "He looked like Fred Flintstone."

They described Mike's girlfriend as "younger, medium build, dishwater blonde," and they said Mike seemed "really domineering with her." They recalled at one point lounging in a pool with Mike and his girlfriend when the "subject turned to the Bermans and he said nothing, as if he hadn't heard of it."

This alone aroused suspicion. In the spring of 1986, the Berman case was the talk of Saline Valley—a recurring topic of speculation and anxiety. When hearing this talk, Mike must have realized the missing people were the husband and wife who arrived at Palm Spring on Sunday evening, January 5, parked near his camp, and chatted with him in Wizard Pool. Why hadn't he reached out to the authorities?

Armed with information provided by the couple from central California, Deputy Boyer turned his attention to finding a military man named Mike who lived in Barstow and worked in logistics. That led to the next break in the case.

Back in the 1980s, an environmental movement was underway to protect wildlands in the California desert. Shortly after Barry and Louise disappeared, California senator Alan Cranston introduced Senate Bill 2061[14], the California Desert Protection Act. Commonly referred to as the "Desert Bill," the legislation sought to preserve vast areas of desert wilderness, elevate Death Valley National Monument to national park status, and incorporate Saline Valley into this new national park.

But the Desert Bill was an anathema to many Saline Valley regulars—they feared enhanced protection would end the hot springs way of life. People opposed to the Desert Bill posted a petition at Lower Warm Springs, and many visitors signed it.[15]

Deputy Boyer noticed the petition and began looking for signatures by men named Mike or Michael, hoping one of them might turn out to be the suspect Boyer was seeking. Six months after the Bermans disappeared, Boyer braved the summer heat and took another trip into Saline Valley. The enterprising deputy checked the petition again, looking for recent signatures, and spotted one that seemed interesting: a signature from a man named Mike Pepe who listed an address in Barstow.

By this time, Nixon had moved away from Inyo County and taken a job elsewhere. The new lead investigator on the Berman case was thirty-three-year-old Marston Mottweiler, who, despite his relative youth, already had years of experience under his belt.

Mottweiler ran the name "Mike Pepe" and discovered that Michael Joseph Pepe, thirty-two, lived on a Marine Corps logistics base in Barstow, California. Pepe's driver's license photo bore an uncanny resemblance to Boyer's composite drawings. Armed with this identifying information, Mottweiler and Boyer began delving into Pepe's background.

At one point, Pepe underwent a tape-recorded interrogation by sheriff's investigators (more about that later). Several people who knew him agreed to be interviewed for this book, including members of his family.

Pepe declined multiple requests to sit for an interview or provide written comments.[16] To date, he's never been arrested or charged in the Berman case. But he's also not wandering free. Currently, he's incarcerated in Arizona in a maximum-security federal prison in the desert south of Tucson.

CHAPTER SEVEN

"Michael Was Weird with Sexual Stuff"

ON THE SURFACE, INVESTIGATORS FOUND NOTHING AMISS IN MICHAEL Pepe's background. But investigation in connection with this book revealed, with the benefit of hindsight, that he possessed some potentially troubling personality traits.

His mother, Dorothy Ronan, was a nursing student in Massachusetts when she met his father, Joseph Pepe, a U.S. Navy-enlisted man from New Jersey. Joseph, the son of Sicilian immigrants, married Dorothy in Boston when his ship was being repaired.

Michael, their first child, was born on September 20, 1953. In the manner of old-school parents, Dorothy and Joseph were overjoyed to have a boy—and they gave him the middle name Joseph in honor of his father.

When Mike was a youngster, the Navy transferred Joseph to a base at Port Hueneme in Ventura County, California, about forty miles down the coast from Santa Barbara. The family bought a house on the south side of Oxnard, close to the Navy base.

When interviewed for this book, Joseph Pepe described the area as a bicycles and ball games sort of neighborhood, where folks waved hello and smoke from barbeques drifted over backyard fences. "My kids grew up playing in the street," he said.[1]

Joseph and Dorothy were devout Catholics who regularly attended Mass at St. Anthony's, located about a half-mile from their home. "Joe and Dot were very active in the Catholic church," recalled Joan Marvel, who lived across the street. "Joe was a deacon."

Over the span of fourteen years, the Pepe family grew to include five children. Mike was the oldest, and Brian, born in 1967, was the youngest. In between came three girls: Elaine, who was Mike's favorite, followed by Maureen and Andrea.[2]

"Norm and I loved them," said Marvel. "They were a close-knit family. Maureen was one of my daughters' best friends. Maureen was full of fun."

As a career U.S. Navy man, Joseph often shipped out to sea—sometimes for a year or two. Back in Oxnard, Dorothy worked nights as a nurse at St. John's Hospital so she could stay home during the day.

Mike's three sisters were sociable and well-known in the neighborhood. Although he was less outgoing and kept to a small circle of friends, by all indications he wasn't a loner or a weirdo.

Mike's childhood best friend Billy Joe Haigler, a big-boned guy from a family that moved to Oxnard from rural Missouri, declined to be interviewed for this book, but he did make a brief statement: "As far as I was concerned, he was the greatest guy growing up."[3]

According to people who knew Mike well, he liked being the smart one in his friend group and wanted the others to look up to him. He came across as intelligent even though he didn't always do well in school.

"He was smart," said Marvel. "Very smart."

As a child, Mike enjoyed playing with G.I. Joe action figures and watching John Wayne movies. Along with his best friend, Bill, he was active in scouts—Cub Scouts first, then Boy Scouts. He did a lot of backpacking and loved spending time outdoors.

Mike and Bill also liked target shooting near the Haigler's house. One day, Mike was walking back home when thugs pulled up next to him in a car. They grabbed Mike's .22 rifle and started driving away—but he wouldn't let go. The thugs beat him over the head as they dragged him down the street, leaving him bloodied and suffering from a concussion.

This incident underscored a personality trait of Mike's that wasn't readily apparent. Although most of the time he seemed mellow and soft-spoken, lurking underneath was a certain fierceness.

"He could explode," said his sister Maureen O'Hara, who's now a business attorney, when interviewed for this book on September 14, 2021.

Mike could also be fussy. He kept his bedroom tidy. He didn't like different types of food touching each other on the plate. He was demanding with his mom, and she catered to him when Joseph wasn't around.

Mike thought of himself as the man of the house, so when Joseph returned from overseas, father and son often clashed. Joseph was smaller than his eldest son, but he was a fiery Sicilian. When the two of them tussled, it sometimes turned physical, with furniture being knocked over and Dorothy yelling at them to stop.

Mike also didn't have a warm relationship with his little sisters. "Michael was never very kind and loving," said his sister Andrea. "Unless there was something he wanted."

When Mike got in trouble, his first reaction was denial. Even though Dorothy would say, "I'd rather have you spit in my face than lie to me," for Mike to admit guilt was, in his mind, tantamount to being weak.

Mike attended Hueneme High School in Oxnard, along with classmates of diverse backgrounds. He made the Vikings football squad as a reserve but came across as a bit awkward.

"He was not very popular," recalled former CHP officer Dan Marple, who was a star running back at Hueneme High.

Another high school classmate, Tim Shroyer, who became CTO of a satellite division of General Dynamics, remembered Mike as a decent fellow. "I never saw anything extreme. There were some guys I didn't get along with. He wasn't one of them."

Mike finished high school in 1971, the same time frame in which Barry moved to Garberville and became a blacksmith, and Louise was living wild-and-free in Box Canyon. But in contrast to their counterculture leanings, Mike enlisted in the U.S. Marine Corps. He was only seventeen years old.

Michael Pepe's foray into the service seemed a natural fit given his dad's navy career and his experiences as a Boy Scout—and it played into his latent fierceness. Still a few months shy of his eighteenth birthday, Pepe got sent to boot camp at Camp Pendleton, a sprawling Marine Corps base along the coast of northern San Diego County.[4]

There, the stocky teenager faced a punishing ordeal. For ten-plus weeks, the drill instructors goaded, berated, and screamed at Pepe and the other recruits: the classic break-and-remake style of training.

Many recruits washed out, and those who made it became hardened in attitude and physique. In the words of a Marine Corps cadence, "Mean DI's makin' fighting machines, they take boys and make them mean!"[5]

The recruits mastered the killing arts: effective use of rifles and sidearms; techniques in hand-to-hand combat; and how to kill with a KA-BAR, a fearsome style of fighting knife. They also learned about the time-honored values of duty, honor, and loyalty, and about the Marine Corps' proud history of defending America's freedom.

After graduating from boot camp, Pepe underwent training as an aviation electrical technician. He impressed his superiors as capable and smart, and the Corps decided to send him overseas. After serving as a groomsman at the wedding of his favorite sister Elaine to Richard Williams, a local lad who was aiming for a career in law enforcement, Pepe shipped out for a tour of duty in Japan.

Seen in hindsight, this event marked a turning point. Pepe was assigned to a Marine Corps air station in southern Japan, about twenty-five miles from Hiroshima.[6] He was in a foreign country, thousands of miles from St. Anthony's and his Catholic upbringing, at a location with brothels and strip clubs nearby. This was likely the first time in his life that Pepe experienced sex as a purchasable commodity.[7]

After completing his overseas tour, Sergeant Pepe became a drill instructor at Camp Pendleton in San Diego. Dennis Carpenter, a retired Ventura County sheriff's official whose family knew the Pepe's, recalled that as a drill instructor, Pepe had a reputation for being abusive toward recruits.

"I heard vicious stories about Pepe," said Carpenter when interviewed for this book on January 20, 2015. "I was shocked."[8]

Pepe fell in love with the former Carol Ann Moore of Portsmouth, Virginia, a student at the Naval Training Center in San Diego. Moore, who was five years older, had previously been married—meaning she wasn't an eligible bride in the eyes of the Catholic Church. Regardless, the young Marine sergeant proposed to her.

Pepe and Moore tied the knot at a chapel on the naval base in San Diego. Bill Haigler served as Pepe's best man; Mike's sister Elaine was Moore's matron of honor.

The bride, a petite brunette, wore a pale blue gown and carried a bouquet of forget-me-nots. In a photo printed in the local paper, Pepe could be seen standing trim in his Marine Corps dress blues.[9]

Moore didn't respond to requests for comment, but it appears her marriage to Pepe quickly disintegrated. Public records indicate she filed for divorce not long after the wedding.[10]

"Carol needed a lot of emotional support," said Pepe's sister Andrea, who spent a summer living with Carol at her parents' home in Florida. "Michael was not the type to do that for her."

Despite the marital problems, Pepe's military career was thriving: He'd been selected for "Broadened Opportunity for Officer Selection and Training" or BOOST, a college prep program. This put him on track to becoming a Marine Corps officer.

As part of the BOOST program, Pepe enrolled at the University of New Mexico and was assigned to an ROTC unit. He majored in business and earned good grades; it turned out he liked enterprise management better than aviation electronics.

Along the way, the now-divorced Michael Pepe met a classmate who caught his eye: Laura Whealy, a woman six years his junior, who'd grown up in Albuquerque. Same as Carol Moore, she was a warmhearted brunette and former high school athlete.

"He dated Laura's roommate first, and then her," said Andrea. "He was a charmer."

In May 1980, coincidentally a few weeks before Barry and Louise's wedding in Solvang, Michael Pepe and Laura Whealy got married in Albuquerque. These were heady times for the up-and-coming Marine, because that same month he earned his bachelor's degree in business administration, accepted a commission as a second lieutenant, and got sent to Quantico, the legendary base in Virginia known as the "Crossroads of the Marine Corps."

"He did so well," said his former neighbor Joan Marvel. "He came up through the ranks of the military. The family was so proud of him. This was their golden boy."

At Quantico, Pepe attended officer's school, where candidates learned what it meant to be a leader in the Marine Corps. Pepe and his classmates were taught to embrace the "warrior ethos" and to devote themselves to being 24x7 Marines, with the mental fortitude "to act in the fog of war."[11]

After completing basic officer's school, Pepe embarked on the next step in his military career: twelve weeks of training as a ground supply officer.[12] Although not a glamorous specialty, supply was viewed as crucial within the Corps, in keeping with the oft-repeated adage, sometimes attributed to Frederick the Great or Napoleon Bonaparte: "An army marches on its stomach."[13]

With his training completed, Pepe was transferred to a supply posting on the West Coast. The position carried certain privileges: officer housing on base, being addressed as "Sir" by persons of lower rank, and advancing in a profession that might someday be a stepping-stone to a lucrative civilian job.

But life as a Marine Corps officer meant dealing with internal politics, and at one point, Pepe got passed over for promotion. Years later, when questioned by Inyo County sheriff's investigators, Pepe said that the career setback happened because he got into a dispute with a superior officer.

"He wanted some stuff done supply-wise that I thought was very questionable," Pepe explained. "I got up and walked out of his office and damn that was it."

Under the USMC's "up or out" advancement system, two strikes meant you were out. Pepe knew that if he got passed over again, he might be forced out of the Corps prior to reaching the twenty-year mark, which would leave him unemployed and ineligible for a military pension.[14] Joseph and Dorothy's golden boy was starting to lose his luster.

Then Pepe got a lucky break. After excelling in a competitive selection process, he landed a position as aide de camp to Brigadier General Donald L. Humphrey, commanding officer at Marine Corps Logistics

Base Barstow. The base, founded during World War II to provide supplies to Marines in the Pacific theater, was situated in the Mojave Desert about halfway between Los Angeles and Las Vegas.

Serving as aide de camp was a plum position for an upcoming officer such as Pepe because it brought him into contact with VIPs and gave him an insider's view of high command. As part of his daily uniform, Captain Pepe now donned an aiguillette—a braided rope worn in a loop over the left shoulder, signifying his role as the one-star general's designated adjunct.[15]

Pepe started his new job with high hopes, but he soon learned that being an aide de camp could be a grind. Pepe spent his workdays shadowing General Humphrey: managing appointments, handling the general's uniforms, and juggling myriad other tasks ranging from meaningful to mundane.

"I don't get in until six o'clock and I work weekends," he complained later when sheriff's investigators questioned him. "Especially with the social events going on."

Meanwhile, on the family front, there was strain in Captain Pepe's marriage. He and his wife Laura now had two daughters: Andrea, named in honor of Pepe's youngest sister, and baby Elizabeth. On the surface, they seemed like a lovely family. But behind closed doors, things were getting creepy.

"Michael was weird with sexual stuff," said his sister Andrea. "He was kinky. A lot of women don't like that."

Pepe began wooing a civilian named Felicia, who worked on base as a clerk.[16] Felicia, a blonde-haired woman about the same age as Laura, was reportedly flattered when the Marine Corps captain turned his attention her way. Soon it became an open secret around headquarters that they were sleeping together.[17]

Pepe also took solo getaway trips into the surrounding desert. Sometimes he ventured into Saline Valley and camped at the hot springs, which had a reputation among military men as a place where hippie girls shed their clothes.

Although a Marine Corps captain might have seemed an unlikely fit for a counterculture environment, Pepe enjoyed the hot springs scene.

Saline Valley's aura of unfettered freedom offered a welcome contrast to life back at base, and he wasn't put off by the ubiquitous weed and alcohol.

Shortly after New Year's 1986, Pepe decided to take another trip into Saline Valley. The base offered tents and camping gear for recreational use by USMC personnel. He packed his truck, and after bidding farewell to Laura and his two little girls, set out alone on the half-day journey to the hot springs.

After arriving at Palm Spring, Pepe parked his pickup and pitched camp. While soaking in Wizard Pool on the evening of January 5, he met Brian Casey and Greg Snyder, two motorcycle riders from Modesto. When the young men learned that Pepe was in the military, Snyder asked Pepe if he'd ever killed anyone. Pepe said that no, he never had.

Soon after this snippet of conversation, a pickup truck rolled into Palm Spring campground. The truck's doors opened and a couple wearing bathing suits slipped into the water, saying they were from the Santa Barbara area and were newcomers to Saline Valley.

***

When Pepe returned to his post at headquarters a few days later, Veronica McClintock, a civilian who served as General Humphrey's secretary and sat at a nearby desk, noticed that the general's aide de camp was acting jumpy and out of sorts.

"He seemed nervous," she recalled when interviewed for this book on September 6, 2021. "He kept taking a lot of smoke breaks, which he didn't do much of before that."

Over the next few months, Pepe returned to Saline Valley at least twice: once with a buddy who was a sergeant on base, and once with Felicia.

"He would go out camping with a young girl who worked in materials," McClintock recalled. "They were having an affair."

McClintock had grown to dislike Pepe, and she felt sorry for his long-suffering wife. "Laura was very nice," she said. "He was sloppy and kind of a braggart. He thought a lot about himself. I don't understand why he was even selected as an aide."

A few months after the Bermans disappeared, a leadership change took place at MCLB Barstow. General Humphrey announced his retirement and the command passed to Brigadier General Hollis E. Davison. General Davison, then fifty, was a square-jawed native of Ventura County who had served two tours of duty in Vietnam.

General Davison wasn't impressed by his new aide de camp. "I inherited Pepe, and it wasn't good from the start," he said when interviewed for this book on September 6, 2021. "He was pudgy, and his uniform was sloppy—he wasn't spiffy the way you'd expect a young captain to be. He bothered the young ladies with suggestive comments and seedy conduct. He wasn't the kind of person I wanted."

The general would think even less of his inherited aide de camp after Inyo County sheriff's investigators showed up and started asking questions.

CHAPTER EIGHT

Liars Tend to be Vague

A MONTH AFTER GENERAL DAVISON ASSUMED COMMAND OF THE
logistics base in Barstow, Deputy Boyer identified Captain Michael
J. Pepe as the "Mike" who was camping at Palm Spring campground
when the Bermans vanished. Because Pepe was a U.S. Marine, the Inyo
County Sheriff's Office asked for assistance from the Naval Investigative
Service (NIS), which later became known as NCIS.[1]

NIS, headquartered at Quantico, investigated crimes committed by
members of the U.S. Navy and Marine Corps. This meant Inyo County
and NIS had joint jurisdiction to work on the case.

NIS helped the sheriff's office prepare for Pepe's interview. Ten
months after the Bermans disappeared, on a warm and sunny high-desert
day in November 1986, a pair of sheriff's investigators, Marston Mottweiler and his colleague Dennis Gray, thirty-three, who'd formerly served
in the U.S. Army Criminal Investigation Division, drove through the
gates of the Marine Corps base.

General Davison didn't know they were coming. "We didn't have a
lot of advance notice," he recalled. "When I got the call, they were basi-
cally there on site."

This was a tactical decision by the Inyo County investigators.
Although Mottweiler and Gray hoped the general could be trusted to
keep the impending visit a secret, they didn't want to take the chance that
Pepe might catch wind of it.

The two sheriff's investigators, dressed in plain clothes, met with the
general in his office and briefed him about the case. Afterward, they set

up in a conference room, keen on meeting the man they formally called a "person of interest" but privately viewed as the prime suspect—although in the absence of bodies or other hard evidence, they realized he might have nothing to do with Barry and Louise's disappearance.

Captain Pepe, told that some visitors wanted to speak with him, walked into the conference room wearing his service uniform and aiguillette.

"He was surprisingly timid," said Mottweiler. "Not what you'd envision when you think of a Marine."

The investigators asked Pepe to take a seat and then turned on a cassette recorder.[2] At this point, Pepe could have "lawyered up" and refused to talk. But he went ahead with the interview, which gave Mottweiler and Gray something that criminal investigators often don't have: an opportunity to question the prime suspect and record his unscripted answers.

The investigators started off slowly, not wanting to spook Pepe into walking out. They said their purpose in coming to see him was to gather "background material" about Saline Valley and "some problems" that they had there.

"It is part of my patrol area which is like eight thousand square miles," said Gray. "I don't get there very often."

The Marine Corps captain seemed wary. But as the investigators started tossing softball questions he began to open up.

Pepe told the investigators that as a youngster he was active in the Boy Scouts. "I used to do a lot of backpacking." Now that he was stationed at the base in Barstow, he liked to explore the surrounding desert.

Pepe talked about an overlook along Highway 190 near Panamint Valley, where spectators gathered to watch fighter jets barreling down a canyon. He listed four different types of aircraft he'd spotted, including the new twin-engine F-18 Hornet.[3]

Pepe said he'd visited Racetrack Playa, a dry lakebed on the east side of the Last Chance Range, where boulders move mysteriously, leaving tracks in the baked mud.[4] He mentioned a rustic hot springs resort in Panamint Valley and recounted a conversation with the former Marine who ran the place. He talked about going to see Lippincott Mine, an abandoned lead and silver mine accessible via a white-knuckle road ascending from Saline Valley into the Last Chance Range.

The investigators asked Pepe if he did much off-road driving in Saline Valley. Pepe joked, "I'm not going to get busted for anything I say, right?" Then he said, "I chased some jackasses once," and launched into a story.

***

The interrogation took a more serious turn after the investigators asked Pepe what type of vehicle he drove when exploring the desert. The Marine captain responded, "I've got a Nissan 4x4; it's a damn fine pickup."

Further questioning uncovered a curious fact: this Nissan pickup wasn't the same vehicle as the Datsun pickup that Pepe was driving on January 6 when Brian Casey spotted him leaving camp and heading up the Corridor, and Katy Aberdeen noticed him in returning late in the afternoon.

It turned out that not long afterward, Pepe sold his Datsun and bought a Nissan, which was a newer version of the same brand.[5]

The investigators figured that if the Datsun truck had some connection to the Bermans' fate—for example if Pepe had been speeding down the Corridor and ran them over—then common sense dictated he might want to ditch the vehicle. With this possibility in mind, they questioned Pepe about why he sold his Datsun.

Pepe said the Datsun was a two-wheel-drive model, which he decided to sell after getting into an accident on an icy desert road. The investigators already knew the truck had been the subject of an insurance claim they'd checked Pepe's vehicle records—but they didn't know the backstory.

As the Marine captain described the location of the accident, the investigators realized he was talking about Saline Valley Road, where the route leaves the ridgetop and heads down a canyon toward the south end of Saline Valley.

Pepe said that he descended into the canyon "a little too fast." When he hit the brakes, "it turns out that I was on ice," and the truck started to slide. Pepe said he saw a drop-off ahead, so he took his foot off the brake and tried down-shifting, but "it wasn't doing any good" so he "steered the thing . . . into the mountain."

To the investigators, it sounded implausible that Pepe deliberately crashed his truck, and they asked him to provide more details. The Marine captain said that the accident happened this past winter and he was alone at the time. This meant he was talking about the same trip where he encountered Brian Casey, Greg Snyder, and Katy Aberdeen, yet none of them had reported seeing any damage to Pepe's pickup. The investigators made a mental note to follow up.

***

When the investigators asked Pepe how often he visited Saline Valley, he said he'd been there "maybe six times in two years." He talked about hiking to the Peace Sign, visiting a petroglyph site, and searching for the Hogan. He obviously knew the valley well.

They asked Pepe where he usually stayed when camping in Saline Valley. "I like hot springs," Pepe replied. "There's an upper and the lower hot springs."

Pepe also told the investigators he felt comfortable being in the clothing-optional environment. "Nudity doesn't bother me at all. I'm not the least bit shy."

When asked if his wife Laura ever accompanied him on the trips, Pepe said that she didn't like camping. He also said that with three kids in the house—Andrea, a preschooler, along with one-year-old Elizabeth and his newborn son Jason—he and Laura were under a lot of stress.

"We've been going down to see a counselor," said Pepe.

The Marine Corps captain admitted he sometimes "screwed around" with other women. He acknowledged that he'd been having an affair with a civilian clerk named Felicia who worked on base.

Pepe said that Felicia sometimes accompanied him to the hot springs. On one trip they drove up the Corridor, crossed over the pass, and went partway down the other side toward Eureka Valley.

When the investigators asked Pepe about his most recent visit to Saline Valley, he said he'd traveled there in June 1986. But when they started asking Pepe about trips he took earlier in the year, the Marine Corps captain seemed to have trouble remembering.

When Pepe's answers turned vague, the Inyo County sheriff's investigators took note. Until this point, he'd shared specifics about his trips into the desert, but suddenly he was claiming lack of recollection.

"He was evasive and ambiguous," said Mottweiler in an interview for this book on December 29, 2015.

Although the two investigators were in their thirties, they had already spent years honing their craft. Both men understood there's no surefire way to tell if a suspect is lying. Behaviors that might seem like a dead giveaway—fidgeting, squirming, shifting eyes—could be natural reactions for someone who was nervous but nonetheless truthful.

But the lawmen knew to watch for certain clues. Research had shown that lying was cognitively challenging, so people tended to engage in avoidance behavior. In plain English: Because it's hard to think up fake answers while someone is staring at you, liars tend to be vague about the details and feign lack of recall.[6]

The investigators also knew that lying is emotionally taxing—it causes anxiety in almost everyone, the exception being sociopaths who truly believe their own falsehoods. Most people avoid situations requiring them to lie, and if faced with a direct question, a common reaction is to dodge and weave rather than give a direct answer.

***

The investigators asked Pepe if he took a trip into Saline Valley during the spring of 1986, the time frame when he visited the hot springs with Felicia. The Marine captain gave a vague answer, so the lawmen tried to pin him down.

"Would you have been there before or after March?"

"Maybe, maybe March," Pepe replied.

They asked Pepe about the trip prior to that one—the visit to Saline Valley he took during the past winter, when he crashed his truck. They already knew that Pepe had taken leave in early January, and he'd been positively identified as the "Mike" who camped at Palm Spring. But the investigators wanted to hear what Pepe would say without being prompted, so they asked the Marine captain, "Were you there around December of '85?"

Pepe responded that he "took leave around Christmas time" and visited Saline Valley "for a day or two."

When they asked Pepe if he was back home for New Year's, Pepe replied, "I think I was."

As the lawmen continued to press the point, Pepe amended his answer to say he "guessed" he visited Saline Valley "sometime around New Year's and after New Year's." Finally, the Marine Corps captain said "it would have to be after New Year's Day," which placed him at the scene in early January 1986, the same time frame when Barry and Louise Berman disappeared.

***

When the investigators questioned Pepe about his January 1986 trip into Saline Valley, he continued to give noncommittal answers. They asked if he camped at Lower Warm Springs or at Palm Spring; Pepe said he didn't remember. They asked if he was alone on the trip. Pepe replied, "I think I was."

The investigators asked Captain Pepe how he spent his time during the trip. "I probably spent it in the hot springs all the time reading a book," he replied.

They asked Pepe if he had contact with any couples while on the trip. "There's couples up there all the time," Pepe responded. But he did mention Katy Aberdeen and Dale Dunsmuir, although not by name:

Pepe: There was a couple up there that I was talking to most of the time we traded; I traded a can of peaches for a pack of smokes or something like that.

Gray: Had you ever seen that couple there before?

Pepe: No . . . they were local.

Gray: They were a young couple, an old couple?

Mike: They weren't young. They were older.

Gray: Both about the same age, different?

Pepe: She was younger than he was.

Mottweiler asked Pepe whether during this trip he heard talk about "some of the people missing." Pepe related a conversation that took place in camp:

Pepe: Some motorcycle guys had gone up and they hadn't come back that night and they were speculating what they were doing.
Gray: Did some of them disappear?
Pepe: No, well, somebody has speculated that these people who had taken off hadn't come back.

The investigators asked Pepe if he talked with other campers at Palm Spring about engaging in a threesome. "A threesome being . . . three people involved in some type of sex act."

Pepe replied, "I don't recall specifically . . . but I do recall conversations like that coming up." The lawmen asked Pepe if he mentioned a threesome when talking with Katy Aberdeen:

Gray: The reason is when Investigator Mottweiler here had talked to an individual, that individual had said that you had brought the conversation up about a threesome.
Pepe: I did?
Gray: That's what [she] told him. . . . Do you recall something like that?
Pepe: No.
Gray: Not at all?
Pepe: No.
Mott: You've never mentioned anything like that to anyone out there?
Pepe: I may have, but if you ask them specifically if I did it this time or at any other specific time I can't tell you no, but it's likely.

Conversations between friends or other couples around here often jokingly . . . I mean in that light it is very possible.

Meanwhile, Pepe kept trying to change the subject. At one point he said there were "some guys who were parked not too far away . . . they had upset somebody else up there because they were shooting." Pepe also veered into a story about men dressed in camouflage who had "semiautomatic weapons with them" and "just started shooting up the place like crazy."

The investigators allowed Pepe to ramble, but they didn't get sidetracked by these stories. When they questioned Pepe about his own weapons, the Marine captain acknowledged he carried a gun on the January 1986 trip into Saline Valley:

Pepe: Every time I'm by myself I am always armed.

Mott: So you probably had a handgun or a sidearm on this trip?

Pepe: Yeah, yeah, it's like always, when I'm by myself I'm armed.

But they didn't ask Pepe if he'd ever fired his gun while in Saline Valley, and if so, where and when. They also didn't ask if he carried any other weapon such as a KA-BAR fighting knife.

About halfway through the interrogation, the lawmen let drop that they were working on a missing person case. They explained to Pepe that they were "contacting everyone we could find." Investigator Mottweiler said, "You're at the bottom of the list, the last one we could find who was there around that time."

Pepe responded, "These must have been some pretty important people to be spending all these resources on." Then he asked, "How was I identified as being there? I'm curious about that. I'll be happy to tell you everything I know about it but how the hell was I identified as being there?"

The investigators said they found his name on the Desert Bill petition at Lower Warm Springs and told Pepe they had reason to believe he'd interacted with the missing couple.

Pepe: Oh really.

Gray: Well, you know. . . . We don't know . . . the names were Barry and Louise Berman.

Pepe: Barry, Barry and Louise?

Gray: She's around oh fiftyish and he's around thirtyish . . . and information has it that you had talked with them maybe in passing or just as a social content . . . in the hot springs themselves, in a pool.

Pepe: That's possible.

Shortly after this exchange, Pepe asked for a coffee break. As he walked out of the conference room, the two Inyo County sheriff's investigators couldn't help but wonder whether he'd return.

But Pepe didn't run away. Instead, he poured a cup of coffee at the headquarters offices adjacent to the conference room, where Valerie McClintock kept a pot brewing. Afterward, he returned to the room and sat back down.

"I think he only talked to us because the commandant ordered him to," said Mottweiler years later.

With the cassette recorder running again, the sheriff's investigators showed Pepe photos of Barry and Louise and asked if he recognized them:

Pepe: He looks slightly familiar. . . . Would she maybe be fatter or something?

Mott: No, that picture was taken the day before they disappeared, so that would be a reasonably accurate representation of her weight at the time.

Pepe: The guy looks somewhat familiar.

Mott: You think you may have seen him out there?

Pepe: He looks familiar, it may have been them, I don't know.

Gray asked Pepe if he had contact with the Bermans in a pool at the campground. Pepe replied, "I don't know," which prompted Mottweiler to follow up:

Mott: Louise is fifty-three years old. Barry is thirty-five. Wouldn't a couple that was mismatched like that have struck you as something to remember?

Pepe: Not in California.

Gray asked Pepe if he remembered meeting any motorcycle riders at the campground. Pepe replied: "I think that was the trip that I saw the guys on the motorcycles." At this point Mottweiler zeroed in:

Mott: We have a witness who told us that on Sunday night when these people arrived at the springs and set up their camp you had already been there a couple of days and had a camp set up. That the five of you, two young men, this couple and yourself were in the pool together.

Pepe: That's possible. Was this day or night?

Mott: Night.

Pepe: It's possible.

After this exchange, the lawmen asked Pepe if he recalled what discussion took place in the pool on the evening of January 5 among him, the two motorcycle riders, and the couple who'd just arrived:

Gray: Well, we'd sort of like to know what led to their disappearance.

Mott: Particularly if they said anything or had you know some indication in their conversation about where they were going, what their plans were.

Pepe: Well, they told me they had a boat and they told me they were into astrology.

Mott: What kind of astrology?

Gray: Astronomy.

Pepe: Astronomy, he's a navigator.

***

When the investigators turned their attention to January 6, 1986, the day that the Bermans disappeared, Pepe said: "I was out of camp." Previously he'd suggested that he stayed in camp reading a book, but this time he gave a different account.

Pepe said he went on a long hike, and after he returned, something seemed amiss. He asked Aberdeen and Dunsmuir "if they had seen anybody messing around with my truck."

Pepe: Now it must have been a nine-mile hike back and forth, you know I'm a Marine . . . but the reason why I'd asked about the truck is because like one of my gas cans was empty. . . . Um, the truck seemed to have been moved . . . if I remember right the truck seemed to be moved out of position.

Mott: So, somebody else drove your truck.

Pepe: No, I'm not saying that. I'm saying that I recall that there was some problem that I talked to this other couple about, and the problem being that it appeared some of my gas was missing and the truck appeared to be out of position.

To the two sheriff's investigators, this account seemed like an attempt by Pepe to disassociate himself from his Datsun pickup truck. But the story didn't fit with Brian Casey's statement that Pepe drove his truck up the Corridor on the morning of January 6, and back in camp in the evening, Pepe said he might have spotted the couple from Santa Barbara hiking with their backpacks.

With these points in mind, investigator Mottweiler asked a series of follow-up questions:

Mott: You never told anyone that you had seen this couple, um, a couple of miles up the road?

Pepe: I may have. I don't know.

Mott: Did you ever say that you had seen any couple up the road walking?

Pepe: That's possible. I don't specifically recall.

But the investigators didn't drop the point. Instead, they asked Pepe if he told the motorcycle riders that he'd seen the Bermans hiking. Suddenly, the Marine captain changed the subject:

Pepe: You did jog something . . . somebody told me that there was a cabin somewhere up there and on one of the trips, possibly this one, I went and looked at the cabin.

This was the third account by Pepe about what he might have done on January 6: stayed in camp and read a book; gone on a nine-mile hike; or visited the rundown mining cabin frequented by Wolfman. Mottweiler tried to pin him down:

Mott: When you went to the shack or mine cabin or claim up there, did you drive up there, or did you walk from the springs?

Pepe: I think I drove.

But Pepe also allowed for the possibility that the cabin visit took place on a different trip, and to the lawmen it seemed he wanted to keep his options open. "He was resistive," said Mottweiler years later. "Not forthcoming."

Yet Mottweiler and Gray didn't drill down as much as they could have. Regarding the Bermans' hike up the Corridor on January 6, the investigators never transitioned from, "Did you *say* you saw the couple hiking," to asking Pepe, "Did you *see* the couple hiking."

Nor did they delve into the curious statement Pepe reportedly made on the evening of January 6: While he was up the Corridor, parked off to the side in his pickup, he'd seen the motorcycle riders go by. This statement warranted follow-up questions, as in where did he park, and what was he doing there? But Mottweiler and Gray never asked.

***

Late in the two-and-a-half--hour interrogation, the investigators spread out a U.S. Geological Survey topographic map[7] on the conference room table and asked Pepe to pinpoint where he went on January 6:

> Mott: When you were on this hike and when you came back and the truck seemed to be moved, where can, you can show us where you went?
>
> Pepe: I think I went to the um, oh hell, I might have gone up to the Peace that day.
>
> Gray: Okay, can you show me on that map where the Peace Sign is for me, and mark it by the pin, roughly.
>
> Mike: I think.
>
> Gray: And that would have been on foot? Correct?
>
> Mike: Yeah. That would have been on foot.
>
> Gray: Where would you have parked your vehicle? Or had you walked totally from the campground up there?
>
> Pepe: Okay, I would of . . . walked from the campground, oh, wait a minute. . . . Okay, I would have walked from the campground or I would have taken a vehicle down to this one right here.
>
> Mott: Well if you drove the vehicle around to here, and then walked up, you wouldn't have come back to camp and said my gas can is empty and the truck is moved.
>
> Pepe: If it had been that trip, yeah.

It seemed the more they asked the Marine Corps captain to provide specifics, the more nebulous his story became. In the end, the investigators never did get a clear answer from Pepe about what he did on the day the Bermans disappeared:

Mott: You don't know what you did that day?

Pepe: Well, I think I went off um checking up whatever area it was.

Mott: On foot?

Mike: I don't know, I may have been in the truck. I don't know.

***

Toward the end of the interrogation, investigator Gray asked Pepe point-blank whether he was responsible for Barry and Louise's disappearance:

Gray: Did you have anything to do with the disappearance of the Bermans?

Pepe: No, I didn't.

Gray: At all?

Pepe: At all.

Gray: By accident or on purpose?

Pepe: By accident or on purpose.

After this exchange, Pepe called for another coffee break. When he returned to the conference room, the Marine captain indicated he wanted to wrap up the questioning.

"I'm feeling more and more stressful all the longer we talk, taking away from my job and all this stuff," said Pepe. But investigator Gray pushed back:

Gray: Ah, you've exhibited stress but you're telling me it's from another source, other than the death of the Bermans.

Pepe: There's a number of things that cause me stress.

Gray: And you're telling me you did not have any part of this disappearance of the Bermans?

Pepe: Correct.

Gray expressed skepticism, telling Pepe, "You have good recall except for the day we need to know what's happening and that's the day you seem to have a little less recall." After some back-and-forth, Pepe said, "Um, sorry for being nervous and for not having a better memory."

Pepe asked, "Is there anything specifically you want me to do?" The lawmen handed Pepe their business cards, and Mottweiler said, "If you could nail down the dates that would be helpful."

But Pepe never followed up on Mottweiler's request, nor did the investigators try to get in touch with him again.

Figure 1. "Louise was a fun girl, loved having a good time," said her childhood best friend Ellie Snow.
COURTESY OF MICHAEL WESTERMAN

Figure 2. When Louise met Barry she was a 46-year-old beauty with a warm smile and blue eyes full of light and promise.
COURTESY OF MICHAEL WESTERMAN

Figure 3. Barry and Louise traveled to India in 1984 to visit the Dera and sit at their master's feet.
COURTESY OF MICHAEL WESTERMAN

Figure 4. Barry was in unfamiliar terrain as he navigated the rough dirt road into Saline Valley.
COURTESY OF MICHAEL WESTERMAN

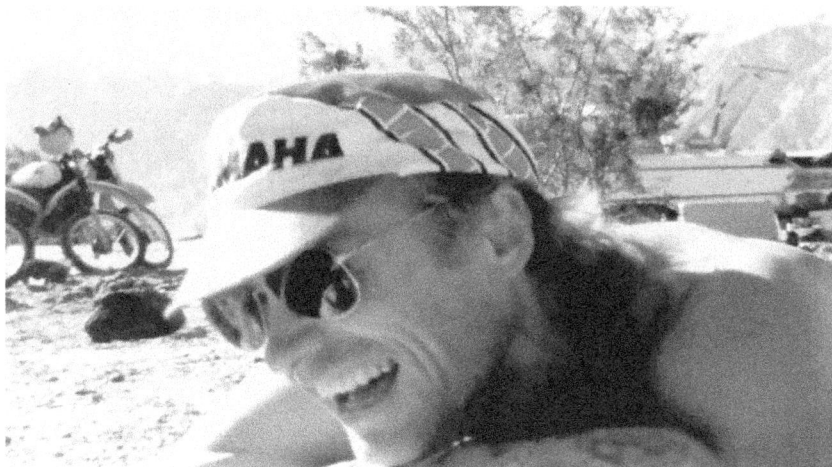

Figure 5. Motorcycle rider Mark Muscio (pictured) and his buddies Brian Casey and Greg Snyder came across as rambunctious guys having fun in Saline Valley.
COURTESY OF MARK MUSCIO

DON DORSEY
Sheriff

SHERIFF'S DEPARTMENT
COUNTY OF INYO
P. O. BOX 5
INDEPENDENCE, CALIFORNIA 93526
TELEPHONE (619) 878-2441

MISSING PERSONS

FOUL PLAY SUSPECTED

INFORMATION WANTED

ON JANUARY 6, 1986, A HUSBAND AND WIFE, DISAPPEARED FROM THEIR REMOTE DESERT CAMPSITE, IN INYO COUNTY, CALIFORNIA. ADDITIONAL INFORMATION AND EVIDENCE INDICATES FOUL PLAY IS INVOLVED.

IDENTITY SOUGHT

THE LAST PERSON TO HAVE CONTACT WITH THE VICTIMS, IS PICTURED BELOW AND THE DEPARTMENT IS ATTEMPTING TO IDENTIFY AND LOCATE THIS SUBJECT.

"MIKE"

W M A 25 - 30 YEARS, 68" - 70", 170 - 180 LBS., SHORT DARK HAIR, STOCKY BUILD, LIGHT OLIVE COLORED SKIN.

VEHICLE: NEWER MODEL DATSUN/TOYOTA, 2 WD PICKUP, SILVER TO LIGHT SKY BLUE IN COLOR

PLEASE FORWARD ANY SUBJECT INFORMATION TO THE INYO COUNTY SHERIFF'S OFFICE (619) 872-7561, ATTENTION: INVESTIGATOR RANDY NIXON OR LT. JACK GOODRICH.

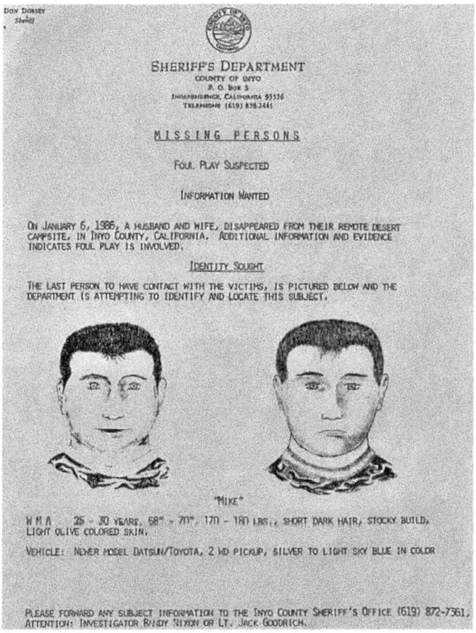

Figure 6. Deputy Leon Boyer, a natural-born sketch artist, penned composite drawings of the solo traveler named Mike
COURTESY OF LEON BOYER AND INYO COUNTY SHERIFF'S OFFICE

Figure 7. When Tom Ganner aka "Major Tom" looked into the distance something shiny caught his eye - a human skull.
PHOTO BY TOM GANNER

Figure 8. As Investigator Mottweiler looked on, Dan Lucas dropped to his knees for a closer look, peered between gaps in the rocks, and spotted bones.
PHOTO BY TOM GANNER

Figure 9. Palm Spring campground centered around an in-ground tub, beautifully crafted with coping of stone, called Wizard Pool.
PHOTO BY DOUG KARI

Figure 10. After Michael Pepe appeared in a Cambodian court to hear the charges read against him, two police officers led him away.
PHOTO BY HENG SINITH, ASSOCIATED PRESS

CHAPTER NINE

Peered beneath the Gaps and Saw Bones

THE TWO INYO COUNTY SHERIFF'S INVESTIGATORS TRADED THOUGHTS about the interview of Michael Pepe as they drove away from the logistics base in Barstow. Both lawmen reached the same conclusion.

"We were pretty sure he was the guy," said Mottweiler.

They tracked down the Datsun pickup, which Pepe had taken to a body shop in Barstow and subsequently resold. But a forensic sweep didn't turn up any evidence, such as bloodstains or strands of hair.

The sheriff's investigators questioned the two women in Pepe's life: his wife Laura Pepe and girlfriend Felicia. Both seemed frightened and didn't have much to say.

They also questioned a buddy of Pepe's—the Marine Corps sergeant who accompanied Pepe on a trip into Saline Valley. But the sergeant didn't offer any details that might help the sheriff's office locate Barry and Louise.

"He said Mike did all the driving—he didn't know where they went or anything," recalled Mottweiler. "There could've been a code of silence."

The investigators ran a DROS search, which revealed that Pepe owned firearms.[1] Although there wasn't sufficient evidence against Pepe to support a search warrant, the NIS arrived at an alternative plan. Because Pepe was a US Marine and lived on base, the commander had the authority to seize his weapons and turn them over to NIS for test-firing.

"Pepe had an absolute fit about it," General Davison recalled. "He contacted an attorney."

But one of Pepe's guns wasn't available for testing. He claimed it had been stolen. This only heightened the suspicion that the Marine captain had something to hide.

"There was no doubt in my mind that he was the culprit," General Davison said years later.

Within weeks of his interrogation by Mottweiler and Gray, Pepe was relieved of his duties as the general's aide de camp and reassigned to work as a ground supply officer.

"The fact he was possibly involved in that situation—the general didn't like the appearance that gave the command," said the general's former secretary Valerie McClintock.[2]

***

Meanwhile, the disappearance of two campers in a remote desert wilderness continued to attract media attention. Jules Berman's wealth and prominence, and the connection with President Reagan's ranch, made the mysterious case especially intriguing.

Another dramatic element arose from the Mojave Desert's reputation as the "Bermuda Triangle" of the West. Tales abounded of immigrants vanishing like mirages during the wagon-train days. About a year before the Bermans disappeared, a Saline Valley regular called "Caveman Mike" reportedly dashed away from Lower Warm Springs one night, ranting and raving, and disappeared into the desert.[3]

"It's not that unusual for people to take off into the desert and never come back," said Deputy Boyer.

In December 1986, the *LA Times* ran a feature story about the Berman case written by staff writer Ann Japenga.[4] The article profiled the two victims, outlined theories being weighed by the sheriff's office, and said Jules and Ruth were so distraught they took a long cruise so they wouldn't have to face the holiday season at home without their son.

"Thanksgiving means nothing; Christmas means nothing," Jules told Japenga.

At the behest of Inyo County investigators, in January 1987, the first anniversary of Barry and Louise's disappearance, CHP flew a fixed-wing aircraft over Saline Valley and looked for Pepe's Nissan pickup. "We thought maybe he'd go back," said Mottweiler.

Leon Boyer believed that the sheriff's office should be doing even more, and he complained about being excluded from the investigation. The dogged deputy had sketched a series of drawings that depicted Barry's silver belt buckle along with jewelry Louise was wearing when she disappeared: a lavender quartz crystal on a gold chain; a freshwater pearl necklace; an 18K gold garnet ring; and an opal ring that was a family heirloom.[5]

Deputy Boyer wanted the investigators to use these drawings to hunt for the jewelry at pawn shops and among Pepe's circle of lady friends. "The department didn't follow up like they should have," said Boyer.

Barry and Louise's friend Pauline Colbert felt angry about Inyo County's failure to work the case harder. "It was such a monumental fuckup," she said years later.

An investigation in connection with this book didn't turn up any evidence that Pepe's status as a Marine Corps officer softened Inyo County's approach to the case. Instead, budgetary constraints, a lack of leads, and a sense of resignation were the likely culprits.

"We have absolutely no motive, and we don't, in fact, have any evidence of a crime," Lieutenant Jack Goodrich, a spokesperson for the Inyo County Sheriff's Office, explained to a reporter.[6]

Jules hired a private investigator to dig into the case. He reportedly ran newspaper ads and offered a $25,000 reward, but nothing came of these efforts.

Meanwhile, Louise's eldest son, Michael Westerman, endured the trauma of his mom vanishing in the desert while his half-sister Laura, whose VW had been swept down Refugio Creek, remained missing. He told a reporter: "To have your mother, sister and stepfather disappear without so much as a trace is still something I find hard to believe."[7]

Ruth Berman suffered from the anguish and uncertainty of her son and daughter-in-law leaving on a vacation and never returning. "Here we are a year and six months later and they're still away," she lamented.

Jules Berman agonized over the fate of his missing son, saying, "I only hope we have an answer to this mystery before Ruth and I die."[8]

***

The answer came nearly three years after Barry and Louise disappeared, when a desert mountaineer set out to reach the summit of Dry Mountain.

Dry Mountain, elevation 8,675 feet, is one of the most isolated peaks in eastern California. Yet for some adventurers, inaccessibility is part of the allure. The remote setting, plus the summit's status as high point in the Last Chance Range, make it a worthy goal for folks who spend their spare time bagging desert peaks.

The normal route up Dry Mountain begins near Racetrack Playa—the place where boulders move mysteriously, leaving tracks in the mud. From there a sturdy vehicle can be driven to about 4,500 feet elevation, which is more than half the vertical distance to the summit.

This still leaves more than four thousand vertical feet to climb on foot, across miles of inhospitable, up-and-down terrain. But an ambitious and well-prepared hiker can reach the peak and return to the bottom in one day.

An elegant but even more difficult challenge is to climb Dry Mountain from Saline Valley. About seven miles up the Corridor from Palm Spring, a hiker can park their car and approach the summit via a canyon penetrating deep into the Last Chance Range. This route, while more direct, involves an elevation gain of almost six thousand feet—a daunting climb for all but the most fit of hikers.

Nearly three years after Barry and Louise disappeared, on November 12, 1988, an outdoorsman made his way down Dry Mountain on the Saline Valley side. His name has never publicly surfaced—only a photo in which he appears to be tall and lean, in his twenties, with shaggy reddish hair and a close-cropped beard.[9]

After exiting a canyon at the base of the Last Chance Range, the hiker aimed toward his car, which he could probably see in the distance, parked along the Corridor. But between the hiker and his car lay a broad alluvial fan, about two miles wide, where visitors to Saline Valley seldom ventured.

The topography of the alluvial fan had been created by flash floods. The flooding mostly happened during monsoon season—late summer and early fall—when frightening clouds would begin to build until they loomed overhead like demonic anvils.

When these thunderclouds let go of their moisture, they did so suddenly and with fury. Because there was precious little topsoil, instead of soaking into the ground the runoff would churn through the landscape, carving the dry riverbeds known as washes, bordered by the steep embankments called cutbanks.

In between the washes and cutbanks were islands of stability, with open ground covered by closely packed pebbles—a soil type called desert pavement. This pavement made for easier walking than trying to slog through the sand-filled washes.

As the hiker began navigating his way across the alluvial fan, moving from island to island, he may have lost sight of his car and strayed from a straight-line route. As he meandered, he probably saw wildflowers, rodent holes, and insect nests. If he was lucky, he might have spotted obsidian flakes or stone tools—lingering evidence of the Timbisha Shoshone who lived and hunted there before being driven from their land.

What the hiker wouldn't have expected to stumble upon, in such a lonely and remote location, was a crime scene. But atop an island of desert pavement lay a human skull.

The skull was devoid of flesh and hair and missing its jawbone, but otherwise intact. The hiker lifted the skull, placed it in his backpack, and marked the spot with a cairn of rocks. He continued the final distance to his car, and from there he descended the Corridor, drove past Palm Spring campground, and continued down the connecting road to Lower Warm Springs, looking for Major Tom.

***

Thomas Ganner, aka "Major Tom," was one of the unique characters drawn to Saline Valley in the 1980s.[10] His love affair with the valley began around the time he relocated from California to Colorado, where he owned an auto shop. For rest and recreation, Tom often journeyed to the hot springs, where he kept a trailer parked for use during these vacations.

Although unmarried, Tom had a daughter and loved spending time with her, but the mom took the little girl and moved away. Dispirited by this turn of events and exhausted from eighty-hour work weeks, Tom decided to sell his auto shop and relocate full-time to his trailer in Saline Valley.

Major Tom soon gained a reputation as someone smart and reliable, and handy at fixing broken-down vehicles or whatever else needed repair. In 1986, when Chili Bob retired as campground host and moved away from Saline Valley, the BLM appointed Tom as Bob's successor.[11]

"I likened possession of the radio to be the defining credential of campground host," Ganner later wrote in an online posting. "Much as possession of the conch shell was the mark of leadership in William Golding's Lord of the Flies."

Major Tom remained as campground host for seven years. Along the way he met his wife Carolyn, after her car broke down during a trip to the hot springs. Tom rode to her rescue, later saying, "I was her knight in naked armor."

In the early 1990s, Tom was trying to regain custody of his daughter and figured "hanging out in the desert with a bunch of naked people wouldn't present well." He moved to Ridgecrest, landed a teaching job at the middle school, and taught earth science and computer applications.

Years later, after retiring from teaching, Tom became a glacier guide and photographer in Haines, Alaska.

***

In an interview for this book on May 19, 2014, Tom recalled that he was sitting on the lawn at Lower Warm Springs on November 12, 1988, enjoying a moment of quiet. A slender young man who'd just returned from climbing Dry Mountain walked over and knelt on the grass.

"Tom, there's something I need to show you."

Major Tom sensed this might be something serious. He stood and followed the hiker to a car. The hiker popped the trunk and showed Tom the sunbaked skull.

Major Tom carried the skull to his trailer for closer inspection. All the upper teeth appeared to be present, he could tell that dental work had been done, and he didn't see any damage such as bullet holes or knife marks.

Tom used the two-way radio to call the sheriff's office, and he told the dispatcher that Sergeant Lucas needed to return to Saline Valley right away. By coincidence, Lucas had visited the hot springs earlier that same day.

The dispatcher asked Tom, "Does this have to do with the missing people?"

The next day, Sergeant Lucas and investigator Mottweiler made the long drive from Owens Valley to Lower Warm Springs and met with Major Tom and the hiker. The four men loaded into the sheriff's office Ford Bronco and started up the Corridor.

Deputy Boyer wasn't invited along despite all the time and energy he'd devoted to the case. "It pissed me off that I didn't get called to come out," he said years later.

About seven miles above the hot springs, the men parked the Bronco and started walking. Soon they reached the cairn of rocks, atop an island of desert pavement, marking the spot where the hiker found the skull.

The men spread out and began searching for more remains. They located a jawbone—unbroken and with gold fillings in some of the teeth. As the hunt continued, Major Tom stepped onto a boulder so he could gain a better vantage.

That's when something shiny in the distance caught his eye. It was another human skull.

Tom walked over and snapped some photos, and then Mottweiler and Lucas crouched down to take a closer look. As with the first skull, the jawbone was missing, but otherwise the skull appeared to be undamaged.

The hiker also reported that he'd found a larger bone, possibly a femur, up in the canyon where he'd descended from Dry Mountain. He led the group across the alluvial fan, all the way to the base of the Last Chance Range. The men entered a broad canyon, but when the hiker pointed out what he'd found, Tom and the investigators concluded they were burro remains.

The men hiked back across the alluvial fan to where the two skulls had turned up. As they searched the area methodically, they started examining the side channel of a wash—a narrow slot carved by the hydraulics of flash flooding.

The men commented on the fact that the side channel was choked with an unusual concentration of rocks that ranged in size from footballs to soccer balls. Lucas dropped to his knees for a closer look, peered between the gaps, and spotted bones.

***

The next day brought cool temperatures and gusting winds into Saline Valley—fitting weather for the grim task at hand.

Dan Lucas, Marston Mottweiler, and other sheriff's personnel gathered at the gravesite. The lawmen, solemn and serious, awaited the arrival of Leon Brune, the Inyo County coroner.

Brune, at that time age fifty-three, was a solidly built man and well-known by all. He owned a mortuary that for the past half-century had been a fixture in the rural region of California east of the Sierra and west of the Nevada border.

By the time Brune arrived, the second jawbone had turned up, along with other bones scattered over a circumference of several hundred feet. As he did a walk-through of the scene, Mottweiler and Lucas pointed out the exact locations where the skeletal remains had been found.

Brune examined the skulls with an expert's eye, estimating age based on the sagittal and coronal sutures—the jagged lines atop the skull. They fuse with age and become fully fused around the age of thirty-five to forty. Foreheads, brow ridges, and eye sockets provide clues about sex: female features are rounded while males are sharper.[12]

Brune concluded that one skull belonged to a male in his thirties, while the other appeared to be an older female. The coroner confirmed that both skulls, and the jawbones, appeared to be undamaged.

As the blustery fall afternoon waned, sheriff's personnel began excavating the grave. In the manner of archaeologists unearthing an ancient site, the men lifted away boulders and sifted through sand, placing the human remains and associated debris into body bags and paper sacks.

From the positions of the rocks and underlying bones, Mottweiler and Lucas determined that the bodies had been stacked in the narrow side channel, one atop the other, against a cutbank. Afterward, they'd been buried under rocks and dirt.

The lawmen found Barry's gold wedding band, underwire from a bra, and remnants of male underpants. As expected, they didn't find any shoes; the Nikes had turned up in February 1986, under a bush near the connecting road between Palm Spring and Lower Warm Springs.

The Bermans's clothes were also missing, along with Barry's glasses and wallet. According to Deputy Boyer, the sheriff's office later received a report that clothing had been found stuffed into a culvert near Upper Warm Springs, but this couldn't be confirmed, and no clothing was ever handed over to authorities.

All of Louise's jewelry was missing, including her opal ring, gold-and-garnet engagement ring, and two pendants. There was no sign of Barry's silver belt buckle—a unique piece handcrafted for him by Arthur Korb.

The investigators didn't find a knife, gun, bullet, or other deadly instrument—nothing to suggest how Barry and Louise met their fate. But they unearthed a crucial piece of evidence, tiny in size, yet spine-chilling in significance: a handcuff key.

Back at the mortuary in Bishop, Coroner Brune examined the skulls and jawbones again and looked closely at the teeth. The coroner's office had already obtained dental charts, so Brune was able to positively identify the remains as those of Barry Alan Berman and Louise Rhoda Berman. The coroner concluded they'd died in a double homicide.

The task of phoning Jules Berman and breaking the news fell to Leon Boyer. "The only thought that we can possibly have now is to find out who did it," Jules told a reporter. "What I want to do is find out who did it and see that they are brought to justice."[13]

But the degraded state of Barry and Louise's remains made investigating the homicides extraordinarily difficult. As noted in the autopsy report, "Received in two body bags and multiple paper sacks are multiple bones, portions of dirt, hair, clothing, and rocks as well as fragments of bones, and plant material."

The formal autopsy took place with Coroner Brune and a sheriff's official present. "The bones are separable into two, and no more than two, individuals," reported the pathologist. "One rib is fractured near the lateral margin, but it is completely uncertain whether the fracture was pre or post mortem."

The pathologist concluded that "with no clear-cut evidence of trauma or injury," the cause of death was "undetermined."[14]

Discovery of the bodies, which the sheriff's office hoped would break the case open, turned out to be another dead end. But there also wasn't much follow-up, despite Deputy Boyer's entreaties.

No attempt was made to reinterview Pepe. The remains and associated materials weren't microscopically examined for any hair that Pepe might have shed. In fact, the sheriff's office didn't even prepare a formal homicide report. At this point, Inyo County officials had all but given up.

CHAPTER TEN

Violating a Near-Universal Taboo

MICHAEL PEPE WAS FAR FROM THE CRIME SCENE WHEN THE BERMANS'S
remains were discovered in November 1988. By then, he'd been transferred from the logistics base in Barstow, California, to the Marine Corps
base in Quantico, Virginia. Meanwhile, his wife Laura took their three
kids, moved back to New Mexico, and filed for divorce.

But the murder investigation wasn't over. With the Berman case sitting cold on the shelves of the Inyo County Sheriff's Office, NIS decided
to move forward.

Why the US government got involved at this point remains opaque;
federal law enforcement authorities are notoriously tightlipped. But as
with the sheriff's office, NIS focused on Pepe as the prime suspect.

The case was assigned to Cheryl Craycraft, a NIS special agent who
grew up in Florida and had a stepfather who served as a navy commander. Beneath her attractive, well-attired exterior, Craycraft possessed
a fiery commitment to the pursuit of justice. She devoted long hours to
the investigation, poring over case files and interviewing witnesses.

"She acted like she had a dog in the fight and was going to dig into
it, whatever it took," Michael Westerman recalled. "She said she had a
strong suspicion of who did it and was watching to see if he slipped up."

The circumstantial evidence against Pepe was incriminating—especially Katy Aberdeen's account of him returning down the Corridor
on the day the Bermans disappeared, looking "all dirty" and acting
"super-nervous." Valerie McClintock's recollection that Captain Pepe
seemed jumpy and "kept taking a lot of smoke breaks" after returning

from his Saline Valley trip only heightened the suspicion. Plus, there was Pepe's missing handgun, and the fact he painted and resold his Datsun pickup.

The vague and inconsistent accounts Pepe gave to sheriff's investigators during his tape-recorded questioning could reasonably be interpreted as the behavior of someone who's guilty and feeling cornered. Pepe's demeanor stood in sharp contrast to the openness of the three motorcycle riders, who gave direct answers to investigators' questions.

Even though Pepe's interrogation occurred only ten months after the Marine captain's January 1986 visit to Saline Valley, he claimed not to remember where he camped, whether he was traveling alone, or what he did on the day the Bermans disappeared.

Did Pepe stay in camp and read a book, go on a nine-mile hike, drive up the Corridor to visit the mining cabin used by Wolfman, or walk to the Peace Sign? Or did he encounter and kill the Bermans and conceal their bodies in a cutbank grave?

With Saline Valley so isolated, only a limited number of people could have possibly committed the crime. As Deputy Boyer pointed out, "It's not like you've got twenty other guys who are potential suspects."

Because Craycraft declined to comment for this book, and the federal case files aren't open for the public (or a journalist) to review, we don't know if she discovered anything new. Given that her investigation didn't result in charges being filed, it's fair to assume the passage of time and lack of physical evidence made the case too difficult to prosecute.

Jules Berman was devastated by the loss of the son he never quite understood but cherished with all his heart. Reporter Ann Japenga from the *LA Times*, who met Jules and Ruth in late 1986, said years later in an email to the author on October 12, 2021, "The house was so luxurious, and it was clear to me that despite their wealth they'd never be happy again."

After the hiker in Saline Valley found Barry and Louise's remains, Jules declined to pay him a $25,000 reward—or any amount—saying only that the offer had expired. Jules also put an end to the hamlet at the oceanfront edge of El Capitan, serving Arthur Korb and Mary Sullivan with a notice to vacate.

When Jules sat for an oral history as part of UCLA's "Entrepreneurs of the West" project in 1994, the interviewer asked the Beverly Hills mogul about his religion. Jules responded that he used to be religious, but because his son and daughter-in-law were murdered for no apparent reason, he no longer believed in God.

"My philosophy is, if there's a God, he's not for me," said Jules. "He's for someone else."

Jules died of heart failure in 1998, a decade after the discovery of Barry and Louise's remains. He was eighty-seven years old. His obituary in the *LA Times* ended on a poignant note: "The family has asked that any memorial donations be made to the Psychological Trauma Center at Cedars-Sinai Medical Center."[1]

Ruth Berman reportedly never recovered from the loss of her only child. Perhaps a life of upper-class privilege didn't provide her with coping mechanisms for such a random and brutal outcome. Wealthy but shattered, she lived out her final years in a rest home and passed away in 2004.

Most of the Berman family fortune went to charitable beneficiaries such as the American Red Cross and the Jewish Home for the Aging. The "famed Kahlua collection" of pre-Columbian burial effigies got sold off or donated, and nowadays a piece occasionally turns up at auction.

Prior to Ruth's death, much of the open space at El Capitan was sold to a nature conservancy. As for the parcel of land and trio of cottages at the ranch's oceanfront edge, eventually another star-crossed couple, Brad Pitt and Angelina Jolie, bought the property. They installed security cameras and spotlights overlooking the beach where satsangis used to roam.[2]

Meanwhile, some disciples of Charan Singh had difficulty reconciling the notion of karma as an absolute law with the horrifying deaths of Barry and Louise—and at least one satsangi decided to abandon the Path as a result. How could it be karmically justifiable for Barry and Louise, two lovely and innocent people, to be murdered on a romantic trip and dumped in a desert grave?

"The Santa Barbara Sant Ghat was in an uproar," said a posting on the "ExSatsangi Support Group" website. "How could Charan let his disciples disappear, vanish. . . . To think that Charan would . . . just go along and let it happen, makes me nauseous."[3]

But other satsangis felt more sanguine about what happened. Mary Sullivan said, "The soul passes through multiple lifetimes, it doesn't matter how you die." She also recalled the satguru's interpretation of the killings: "Master said it was a karmic thing they had to go through."

Sullivan spoke about a moving dream she had, which came to her like a vision. Louise was in an astral realm, sitting on a picnic table in a beautiful field. She told Mary that she felt happy and said that Barry, while having a harder time of it, was going to be okay.

Jewelry-maker Arthur Korb echoed Sullivan's belief Barry and Louise's deaths arose out of karma: "It was an act that had to happen, in that way." He also said, "I believe their master took their spirits from their bodies before the murders occurred, so they wouldn't have to experience the abject horror of being slaughtered."

But Louise's son, Michael Westerman, had a different take: "I don't buy into any of that stuff. If that's what makes them feel better and helps them deal with it, okay.

"Every day when you step out that door, anything can happen. There are a lot of crazies out there. I always figured that my mom and Barry ran into a bad situation, and it looks like that's what happened."

By the early 2000s, Louise's eldest son had transcended the instability of his childhood and built a solid life for himself and his family. He worked as purchasing manager for Clark County, Washington, handling a multi-million dollar budget, and served as a captain in the Army Reserve. Although he continued to believe that Michael Pepe was the culprit in the deaths of his mom and Barry, his hopes had faded that Pepe would end up behind bars.

But believers in karma liken it to Newton's third law that every action has an equal and opposite reaction. If Pepe was responsible for the deaths of Barry and Louise, then he couldn't evade the consequences any more than he could escape from his own skin.

Yet coming events, rather than leading to Pepe being arrested in connection with the Berman murders, would instead take the case in a strange and terrible direction.

***

After the disappearance of Barry and Louise Berman in Saline Valley, Michael Pepe's life went into a long downhill slide. His military career stalled, and his efforts to reinvent himself foundered.

After Pepe was transferred from the logistics base in Barstow, he served as a supply officer at Quantico. Although he earned an MBA, he never received the hoped-for promotion to major. Yet for some reason, despite the up-or-out system of advancement for Marine Corps officers, he wasn't forced to resign.[4]

When Pepe reached the twenty-year mark in 1991, he retired from the Corps. At this point, despite his troubled past, he'd in effect been given a clean slate. He was single again, still in his thirties, well-educated, with an honorable discharge and a full pension.

But rather than building a stable life for himself, Pepe bounced around the western United States—including Sioux Falls, Colorado Springs, and his hometown of Oxnard. For a while, he ran a bed-and-breakfast. He taught at a community college. He worked at a state employment office. Nothing seemed to hold his interest and nothing he did left a discernable mark.

In the late 1990s, Pepe began a long-distance relationship with a Russian woman in her twenties named Tatiana, and he traveled overseas to visit her.[5] Eventually, he brought Tatiana to California on a fiancé visa. After the wedding they moved to Colorado, but from the outset it was a troubled union.

"Tatiana said Michael was sexually deviant," said Pepe's sister O'Hara. "He hurt her." Tatiana fled the marriage and all but disappeared.

O'Hara later told a jury that her brother "was always very selfish. It was all about him, about his lifestyle and what he wanted to do. If he left . . . people behind or left a path of self-destruction, that was just too bad and he would move on from place to place."[6]

In 2003, Pepe took a trip to Asia—a region he recalled from having been stationed there as a young Marine. Maybe he was looking for a lower cost of living, or as O'Hara suggested, fleeing from his troubles.

Pepe ended up in Phnom Penh, where he stayed for six months. After returning to the United States for a few weeks, he went back to Cambodia and remained for three more months. In 2004, after another brief return to the states, Pepe traveled again to Phnom Penh.

What kept him coming back?

Cambodia was far different from anywhere else Pepe had ever lived—California, Virginia, Colorado, or even Japan. The country's latitude, about 12 degrees north of the equator, produced a climate of stifling humidity. The low-lying terrain, formed by alluvium of the Mekong Delta, was often drenched by tropical rains.

Some regions of Cambodia were remote and scenic, but the capital city of Phnom Penh was crowded in the early 2000s, with a population of more than one million people. There were horns honking, people chattering, and music blaring. At times the sky would be fouled by smog, and at night the insects would appear.

Although Cambodia was once the center of the Khmer Empire, a kingdom covering much of Southeast Asia, in the 1970s, this country of proud and ancient heritage became the site of one of mankind's most horrific scourges. The Khmer Rouge, under Marxist leader Pol Pot, purged anyone perceived as a threat. An estimated two million Cambodians were executed and buried in mass graves of the "killing fields," or perished from starvation and disease.

The aftereffects of this genocide extended into the early 2000s, rendering Cambodia a country of wretched poverty, rampant corruption, and a justice system based more on bribery than the rule of law. Phnom Penh was often compared to the Wild West, replete with dusty streets, seedy bars, crooked characters, and shady deals.[7]

The pervasive unruliness tended to discourage mainstream tourism. Even so, some travelers enjoyed the raw vibe of Phnom Penh, finding it an interesting contrast to more polished capital cities.[8] Other people came to launch businesses or provide charitable services such as medical care.

But for some visitors, the dystopia itself was the attraction. "We've had some real nasties come through here over the years, particularly foreigners who treat Cambodia as a playground," said Australian journalist Luke Hunt when interviewed for this book on August 14, 2018.

Hunt, whose articles about Cambodia have appeared in publications such as *The Economist* and the *New York Times*, explained that the "anything goes" atmosphere drew a laundry list of unsavory characters.

"You had a combination of white-collar criminals, drunks and drug addicts, pedophiles, bank robbers, murderers. It was one of those places where, in the aftermath of war, it was a freewheeling town where you could do whatever you liked."

Early on during Pepe's visits to Phnom Penh, he found his way to Sharkey's, a bar well-known among westerners for lively music, crowded pool tables, and freelance sex workers. "I have never seen so many prostitutes in all my life," read a contemporaneous posting from a sex-tourism forum. "And it is unbelievably cheap."

Pepe began sleeping with a Vietnamese sex worker named Choeung Thisan, aka "Sang" or "Basang."[9] Besides going to bed with Pepe, Sang served as his translator and guide.

Although Sang was half Pepe's age, and strikingly beautiful, apparently this wasn't enough to satisfy his urges. In the wide-open environment of Cambodia in the early 2000s, he began pursuing girls who were even younger than Sang—including some who hadn't yet reached their teens.

***

In Cambodia, the rampant sex trafficking of children at the time Pepe moved there arose from desperate poverty and systemic discrimination.

A prime example of this was the village of Svay Pak, situated along the banks of the Tonle Sap River north of the confluence with the Mekong River, and sometimes referred to as "Kilo 11" because of its location eleven kilometers outside Phnom Penh's city center. When Pepe began visiting Svay Pak, the village of dirt streets, crumbling concrete, and corrugated tin shanties was home to about thirteen thousand people of Vietnamese descent.

The squalid conditions of Svay Pak were rooted in the Khmer Rouge's long-standing resentment of Vietnam, which had colonized Cambodia in the nineteenth century. In the 1970s, the Khmer Rouge channeled this simmering resentment by slaughtering thousands of ethnic Vietnamese. Even decades after the downfall of the Khmer Rouge and the death of its bloodthirsty leader Pol Pot, ethnic Vietnamese remained outcasts in Cambodia.[10]

Selling a child into the sex trade was one of the few ways a family in Svay Pak could earn enough money to feed itself. "We love safe sex, so please wear condoms," read a large sign at the entrance to the village, but this was a venue for trafficking in forbidden fruit, and HIV ran rampant.

Karaoke bars and brothels lined the village's rutted main street. Many of the girls who stood by the metal doors of these establishments, waving hello and blowing kisses to men passing by, were younger than Cambodia's age of lawful consent, which was fifteen. Shacks out back housed children even more tender—some barely tall enough to reach the waists of the men they serviced.

In exchange for a few dollars, a customer could obtain "yum-yum," meaning oral sex, or "boom-boom," meaning intercourse, from underage girls or boys, depending on preference. This income, albeit meager, might be the main source of income for the child's family.[11]

Some of the men who frequented these underage brothels were Cambodians who viewed sleeping with youngsters as a way of mitigating the risk of being infected with STDs. Other customers hailed from Western nations such as England, Australia, and the United States.

The foreigners included convicted child molesters and other confirmed pedophiles, drawn to a locale where they could satisfy their perversions with little fear of legal retribution. Others could be called "situational pedophiles" who thought their behavior, despite violating a near-universal taboo, conformed to local customs and practices.[12]

Perhaps Pepe fit the "when in Rome" category of abuser, because no evidence has turned up of him preying on children in the United States. Whatever the case, after Pepe began frequenting the underage brothels of Svay Pak, the retired Marine Corps captain embraced pedophilia with fearsome zeal.[13]

Pepe moved to Cambodia full time following a series of visits total-ing more than a year spent in-country. According to people involved in the fight against sex trafficking, this fact alone raised a red flag.

"What we've seen when there's an American retiring to Cambodia, sadly, many are involved with raping young girls," said Don Brewster, a pastor from California, when interviewed for this book on August 6, 2018. Don and his wife Bridget Brewster founded Agape International Missions; a nongovernmental organization (NGO) devoted to sheltering underage victims.

In a place so disadvantaged as Cambodia in the early 2000s, Pepe's MBA and US military background stood out. His annual income of about $48,000 from his Marine Corps pension, compared to less than $1,000 for the average Cambodian household, ranked him as a well-to-do man.

Pepe leased a furnished villa in the Toul Kork district, one of Phnom Penh's upscale neighborhoods.[14] He bought a Jeep SUV, and assisted by Sang, hired a housekeeper, cook, and gate-guard nicknamed "Lucky."

Pepe took a part-time job as a professor teaching management at Pannasastra University, a private school offering classes taught in English. The retired Marine captain donned the mantle of gentleman professor and told people he ran a charity distributing school supplies to impoverished children.

Pepe's supposed charity, a one-man NGO he dubbed "Socrates," wasn't officially registered with the Cambodian government but did engage in charitable giving. Pepe joined forces with Un Son, a priest at St. Joseph Catholic Church, and together they toured impoverished districts of Phnom Penh and the surrounding countryside. The part-time professor handed out books, pencils, cookies, and candy, while snapping pictures of children on his Minolta digital camera.

Besides continuing to see Sang, Pepe became involved with a Cam-bodian woman in her early twenties named Chanry Bith, aka "Nary." For a few months Nary lived with him as his spouse, although it appears they never legally married.

Nary helped Pepe cloak himself in legitimacy. Because her sister was married to Sander De Montero, a well-connected former deputy in the royalist political party FUNCINPEC, Pepe was able to forge friendships with Cambodian elites.[15]

After settling into a life of power and privilege, Pepe began trafficking underage girls—bringing them to his Toul Kork villa so he could rape and abuse them. "Pepe had a plan," said Vansak Suos when interviewed for this book on August 10, 2018. Vansak, a Cambodian, formerly worked as a Foreign Service National[16] in the American embassy in Phnom Penh, investigating underage sex trafficking.

"He made friends with senior politicians," said Vansak. "He created an NGO. He went out to distribute school materials in order to make friends with the kids."

CHAPTER ELEVEN

Fighting Spirit of a Brave Little Girl

A DOZEN YEARS BEFORE PEPE RELOCATED TO CAMBODIA, A GIRL WE'LL call Lim Kanya, a pseudonym to protect her identity, had been born to a mother who lived in the slums of Phnom Penh. Fast forward to the early 2000s and the family was still living in the slums—Kanya along with her mother, grandmother, and a younger brother.

To help support the family, Kanya's mother worked on and off as a seamstress in a garment factory, or sometimes peddled food in the streets. Kanya attended school occasionally but mostly tended to her little brother while her mother tried to eke out a living.

Kanya's family was so impoverished that they sometimes found themselves homeless and wandering—sleeping on the street in neighborhoods rife with crime and heroin addiction. Even when they did have a roof over their heads it was scant improvement.

"No space for everybody to sleep," Kanya later told a jury. "Really poor and no bathroom. No toilet."

How twelve-year-old Kanya came to Pepe's attention isn't clear, but at some point, Sang made a deal to purchase Kanya's services on his behalf. As an added incentive, Pepe promised to feed and clothe the little girl and send her to the Newton Thilay School, a private school around the corner from his villa in Toul Kork.

"Basang give my mom some money," Kanya explained years later. "And I was supposed to go live with Michael Pepe so I can do housekeeping and do whatever he asked me to do."

Sang shuttled Kanya to Pepe's villa on the back of a motorbike. Lucky drew open the gates of the tree-shaded compound, and Kanya was awestruck by what she later described as a "nice fancy home."

Inside the spacious villa, Kanya noticed photos of Pepe with famous people such Ung Huot, a Cambodian senator and former prime minister. There was even a picture of Pepe being greeted by the king of Cambodia.[1]

"I thought he was really powerful," said Kanya. "He was someone really important and close to, like, the prime minister in Cambodia."

Sang led Kanya upstairs, where Pepe had an office with a door that opened onto a large balcony—right down the hall from his bedroom and a separate massage room. Also upstairs was a bedroom stocked with stuffed animals and toys. Sang told Kanya she'd be sleeping in this room along with other girls her age.

***

The little girl we'll call Somally Rotha, and her older sister Somally Sita, grew up together in a shack built on pilings over one of the waterways of the Mekong Delta. Besides Sita and Rotha, the family included two younger brothers and an older half-brother. While their mother tended to the kids, their father tried to support the family by repairing bicycles and driving a moto taxi.

After a fire gutted their meager home, the family was relegated to living in a tent. Eventually, they managed to rent a shanty, but it was in an area of Phnom Penh that was notoriously dangerous for youngsters.

"It's considered one of the worst neighborhood slums and it still is—a lot of drugs and prostitution," Rotha told a jury years later.

In this desperate environment, underage girls like Rotha and Sita were viewed as marketable commodities. "My next-door neighbor daughters, they were all sold for sex," said Rotha. "You just assume and expect that your turn will be next."

Rotha and Sita's half-brother had a girlfriend who worked as a prostitute, and she knew about Michael Pepe and his upscale villa. The girlfriend talked to Rotha's mother, and a deal was struck for Rotha to visit the villa overnight.

"Imagine you're a nine-year-old girl and your mother brings you to this American," said pastor Don Brewster.

Pepe took a shine to the cheerful child and nicknamed her "Smiley." After Rotha mastered the technique of giving Pepe oral sex, the part-time professor offered to have her and Sita, who at age ten was a year older than Rotha, move in with him on a long-term basis.

"I remember I was sat down and talk about the opportunity of going to school and able to have food and all those things," Rotha said later. "I remember then we were expected to be given $30 when I go and live with Michael."

***

Another little girl who stayed over at Pepe's villa had been born in Cambodia but was of Vietnamese ancestry—we'll call her Ngu Tai Duyen to protect her identity. Along with her mother, who was widowed, Duyen lived in an overcrowded building with siblings, aunts, uncles, and a grandfather.

Ethnic Vietnamese in Cambodia were in effect stateless people, often lacking birth certificates or official identification, and routinely subjected to discrimination and abuse.[2] Duyen's mother tried to earn a living as a fortune teller; others in the family took whatever work they could find.

One day, Duyen and her mother were out shopping for food when Sang approached them. "That lady met with my mom at the market and they were talking with each other," Duyen later told a jury. "My mother told me to go with her and said that I would be helping her out."

***

At least five underage girls moved in with Pepe, full-time or for extended visits, during late 2005 and early 2006. He sent an email to Scottish friend Graham McCallum, aka "Mack," who was later jailed on child pornography charges: "The sweet things I have with me have the most perfect little bodies and attitudes."[3]

It also became apparent that Pepe had a "type." All the girls he trafficked were prepubescent, tiny and thin, and physically weak. "These girls were much smaller than the average nine- to twelve-year-old in the US," said Brewster.

Nary had moved out of Pepe's villa in fall 2005. To help Pepe foster the image of living a conventional life, Sang posed as his wife replete with faux wedding portraits. The Jeep SUV parked in the driveway of the villa, with a stick-on sign bearing the name of Pepe's one-man NGO called "Socrates," also helped provide cover.

Most afternoons, Sang would drop by the villa and brew Vietnamese coffee, a potent blend mixed with sweetened condensed milk and served over ice. She and Pepe would sit on the elevated balcony facing the street and chat in the manner of a well-to-do American expat and his attractive younger spouse. Even though there were little girls playing outside, the facade presented by Pepe and Sang disguised the awful reality of what occurred inside.

The daily routine inside Pepe's villa was at once mundane and horrifying. Each morning, before the girls went off to school, one of them would bring breakfast to Pepe. Then he'd check their school uniforms and make sure they had their books and homework.

"I would get a little cheek kiss and off they went," he later wrote in a letter sent home to his family in the United States. "This was all a very comfortable peaceful routine."

Pepe would usually head back to bed, and around noon the girls would return from school and wake him up. Sang taught the girls how to give him a rubdown and satisfy him with oral sex. In a letter back home to his family, Pepe claimed it was a "normal everyday thing" in Cambodia for "the younger, esp. female, to massage the older."

Following coffee with Sang out on the balcony, Pepe would head off for another nap. In the evening, he'd spend more time with the girls—including one-on-one sessions in the confines of his bedchamber.

Even if these encounters had involved consenting adults instead of tiny children, Pepe's behavior behind closed doors was outside the bounds of what most people would consider erotic pleasure.

"The pretense many pedophiles bring is that they're in love—their treatment is not purposefully torturous," said pastor Don Brewster. "But in Pepe's case it was."

***

The awful details would emerge later, after law enforcement began investigating.

Prior to Pepe's first session with twelve-year-old Kanya, he and Sang slipped a sedative into her soda, hoping to calm her down. Pepe tied Kanya with rope and raped her, but despite the sedative she began to scream—so he beat her. In one of the letters back home, Pepe tried to justify his behavior.

"Sang told me to tie [Kanya] up," he wrote. "I asked the girl if it was OK. She said yes. So I did. Sang told me to slap her face. I asked her if it was OK. She said yes. Once & easy. Sang said it had something to do with 'saving face' and [Kanya] would feel better emotionally."

***

Pepe tied ten-year-old Sita spread-eagle atop his bed, but apparently decided she was too small to rape. Instead, he put his mouth on her vagina, then switched positions and forced her to lick his anus. Afterward, he rewarded her with a dollar bill.

"Because my family is poor, I save it for them," Sita later explained to a jury. "So they can have money to spend."

Sang advised Sita that Pepe planned to have intercourse with her soon. "She say in one month I will be having sex with him and two months [Rotha] will be having sex with him."

Nine-year-old Rotha was also compelled to participate in the naked massage sessions and oral sex, and to her it felt shameful. She later explained to a jury: "In my culture, when you work in the sex industry, even if it's not by choice, you still considered trash."

***

Duyen, the ethnic Vietnamese girl who was eleven years old when she was brought to Pepe's villa, loved to play jump rope outside. But when Pepe brought her to his bedroom, the rope he used wasn't for play.

Pepe bound the little girl, right hand to right leg, left hand to left leg. As Pepe raped Duyen, she struggled and shrieked, so he slapped her until she stopped. After Pepe finished, he left her bleeding on the bed.

During subsequent sessions, Duyen kept quiet and didn't fight back. Pepe sent an email to his buddy Mack: "The first time was a bit of a bother, but after we had a break-through, everything was fine."

***

A law enforcement investigation would reveal that Pepe's conduct with other underage girls likewise involved battery and rape. The common elements included tying the victims' hands and legs, gagging them with cloth or tape, slapping the girls when they screamed, and afterward leaving them injured and sometimes bleeding.

Pepe later tried to blame Sang. "I just kept going along with whatever was happening," he said in one of his letters to his family. "I seemed not to care or resist. I just felt easy and peaceful all the time."

But Pepe wasn't peaceful and easy with Hua Thang, a ten-year-old ethnic Vietnamese girl who dreamed of becoming a singer. Like the other girls, she'd grown up in the slums—Thang's father sold ice cream. Even though Thang and her family desperately needed the money, when Sang ordered Thang to give oral sex to Pepe, the scared child ran outside.

Sang ordered Thang to get back into the bedroom and satisfy Pepe. But instead of giving the American what he wanted, the little girl bit his penis.

Before bringing Thang into Pepe's bedroom for a follow-on session, Sang forced her to take a sedative. Although the drug made Thang feel drowsy, she resisted when Pepe tried to rape her.

"At that time he wanted to sleep with me, but I wouldn't let him," Thang later told a jury. "He tied my feet and my hands, and then I remember me yelling."

Thang weighed only sixty pounds. When Pepe, who weighed four times as much, forced himself on her, she passed out. Thang awoke a few minutes later to find blood all over the sheets.

"At that time I was so dizzy, but I couldn't walk," she recalled. "I tried to drag myself into the bathroom to shower."

After another session where Pepe raped Thang and she wouldn't stop screaming, Pepe threw her out of the house. "There have been some problems with a fresh one," he wrote in an email to his Scottish friend Mack. Thang later gave jurors an account of what happened. "I was crying a lot and I ran out to the lawn. I ran outside and I prayed to God."

Sang shuttled the little girl back to the impoverished neighborhood she called home. An investigator from the International Justice Mission, an antitrafficking organization based in Washington, DC, spotted Thang as she climbed off a motorbike, broken and bleeding. After Sang drove away, the investigator walked over and asked the little girl what had happened to her.[4]

***

Whether it was an act of God, the law of karma, or the fighting spirit of a brave little girl, the incident with Thang set the wheels of justice in motion.

The International Justice Mission and World Hope International, another antitrafficking NGO, alerted US Immigration and Customs Enforcement (ICE) about an American living in Phnom Penh who was abusing underage girls. Because part of ICE's mission is to fight human trafficking, its agents sometimes work as attachés in US embassies, assigned to cases that may involve Americans, or that violate US law, such as human trafficking or drug smuggling.[5]

Despite Cambodia's reputation as the Wild West of Asia, the appalling conduct described by the two NGOs drew the interest of the Cambodian National Police. Cambodian and US officials initiated parallel investigations.

Cambodian authorities concluded it was the worst case of child abuse they'd ever encountered. Michael Pepe, who'd previously dodged two murder investigations—one by Leon Boyer and Inyo County sheriff's investigators, the other by Cheryl Craycraft and NIS—was again in legal peril.

On the US side, Gary Phillips, a veteran special agent, took charge of the case, assisted by Paul Carbone, his partner, and Eddy Wang, a colleague from the Ventura office. Vansak Suos was brought in because of his local knowledge and because he spoke Khmer, the Cambodian language. Vansak, who'd lost two sisters and a brother during the Khmer Rouge regime, had taken a job with ICE because he wanted to help protect vulnerable children.[6]

Information from the US State Department confirmed the suspect as Michael Joseph Pepe, an American citizen who listed a US address in Oxnard, California. In Cambodia, Pepe's neighbors in the Toul Kork district reported seeing young girls living at his villa.

The Municipal Court in Phnom Penh issued an arrest warrant charging Pepe with rape and "debauchery," which in Cambodian legalese means sex with an underage person. The Cambodian National Police began surveilling Pepe, waiting for the right moment to make a move.

On a sweltering Saturday in June 2006, the police trailed Pepe's Jeep SUV as he drove into downtown Phnom Penh. When Pepe parked near a post office and stepped out of his car, the police swooped down. According to Vansak, the former Marine resisted, cutting his hand in the process.

The police hauled Pepe back to his villa; Cambodian law entitled him to be present while they executed a search warrant. Inside the villa they found Kanya, terrified and confused. Rotha and Sita were off at school, and the other girls were either home visiting their families or no longer lived with Pepe.

As Phillips and Vansak looked on, Cambodian police rifled through the rooms, gathering a wealth of incriminating evidence: lengths of rope with the ends tied into slipknots; K-Y Jelly and generic Viagra; stuffed animals and children's toys; newspaper clippings about pedophiles.[7]

When the police inventoried Pepe's stash of drugs, they found sedatives including Valium, Xanax, morphine, codeine, and the date-rape drug Rohypnol. These medications could be purchased in Cambodia without a prescription.

The most damning evidence was a massive collection of child pornography. In one set of photos, Kanya could be seen sitting on a chair in Pepe's bedroom, naked with her legs spread. Other photos showed underage girls striking provocative poses in Pepe's shower or on his bed.

Pepe's photo collection had been meticulously cataloged into computer files, ranging from family shots named "Wedding 082705," which matched the date of his daughter Andrea's wedding, to photos of children in files titled "Valentine Girls" and "Home Girls 112605." These child sex abuse materials, stored on CDs, a USB drive, floppy disks, and the hard drive of his HP desktop, held hundreds of explicit images.

Digital forensic experts working in the US embassy in Singapore later recovered deleted photos in which Pepe was seen naked with Kanya. In a letter back home, Pepe admitted that Sang snapped these pictures of him, but said, "I soon realized I did not care for this, so I wiped the files on my computer."[8]

Cambodian police hauled Pepe to the station and interrogated him, but he didn't admit to anything. They carted him to Prey Sar, the largest prison in Cambodia, about fifteen kilometers southeast of downtown Phnom Penh.

If someone set out to build hell on earth, the result would likely resemble Prey Sar circa 2006. Thousands of prisoners crowded into buildings designed for hundreds. They talked, smoked, cooked, and slept on concrete floors, with allotted space per man of about eighteen square feet. The stench of sweat, food, and cigarettes filled the air. Inside the bathrooms, raw sewage collected on the ground.[9]

On hot days, the temperature climbed above 110 degrees Fahrenheit but felt higher because of the humidity. When monsoon rains fell, water streamed through holes in the tin roofing. During the day, when someone started cooking, clouds of black flies appeared. At night, as the men tried to sleep, swarms of mosquitoes descended.[10]

Signal-jamming radio waves, meant to disable cell phone reception, caused some prisoners to get throbbing headaches. On top of this was the nonstop noise of boom boxes. One Westerner who languished for two years in Prey Sar wrote in a blog, "Imagine the ten worst non-English language songs. . . . Turn it up really loud. . . . Continue for 730 days."[11]

After Pepe appeared in Municipal Court to hear the charges read against him, two white-shirted police led him away. An AP photographer snapped a photo of Pepe with his head hanging, lips pursed, and hands cuffed in front of his protruding belly.[12]

With Pepe in custody, locating and protecting his underage victims became a matter of urgent importance. Without witnesses there would be no case, and it was likely the girls would get trafficked again. After all, their own families sold them into the sex trade to begin with.

By interviewing Thang and Kanya, and examining photos recovered from Pepe's computer, the police located a total of seven victims. These included Thang, Kanya, Rotha, Sita, and Duyen, along with two others: Suong, age eleven, whose mother worked selling fruit, and Chavy, age thirteen, who Pepe purchased for himself as a private Valentine's Day treat.

Police also arrested four family members, but none were ever convicted. The police failed to find other victims, and this haunted pastor Don Brewster.

"There were photos of many girls beyond the seven," he said.

In Cambodia, if evidence showed a rescued child had been sold by her family into sexual servitude, an NGO could shelter the child and become her legal guardian. Brewster and his wife Bridget, under the auspices of Agape International Missions, their NGO, sheltered five of Pepe's victims. Another NGO, Hagar International, took in two other victims.

This aftercare provided the girls with hot food, warm beds, classroom sessions and counseling, plus plenty of toys and playtime. It also marked the beginning of a long healing process.

"The emotional and psychological trauma these kids suffered is beyond our imagination," said Brewster.

ICE special agent Gary Phillips and Foreign Service national Vansak Sous went to Prey Sar to question the erstwhile English professor three weeks after the raid on Pepe's villa hoping that Pepe, after being jailed under such awful conditions, might come clean. Pepe gave the investigators his name, date of birth, social security number, and his US and Cambodian addresses. But after receiving a Miranda warning, he invoked his US constitutional right to remain silent.

When NIS special agent Cheryl Craycraft received word that Pepe was in custody, she flew to Cambodia in hopes he'd be willing to talk about what happened in Saline Valley. Maybe he'd discuss the Berman case if doing so would get him out of Prey Sar's hellish conditions and into US custody?

Vansak drove Craycraft to Prey Sar and accompanied her to the interview room. But after Pepe learned why she was there, he refused to answer questions.

"He shut down, didn't say much at all," Vansak later recalled. Craycraft reported to Louise's son Michael Westerman, "He said he wasn't ready to talk . . . yet."

A report prepared by ICE special agent Eddy Wang described Pepe as a white male, 5'10" tall, 240 pounds, with blue eyes and black-and-silver hair. Investigators' notes from an interview with Rotha provided more intimate details: "Fat with a big belly . . . strawberry nose . . . a little bit of hair on his arms, minimal chest hair (if any), he sometimes wore glasses . . . clean shaven, is a heavy smoker, has bad breath, is dirty, and sometimes he is very angry and crazy."

Despite being charged with raping underage girls, Pepe continued to enjoy the support of his elite friends, including former Cambodian prime minister Ung Huot. The *Cambodia Daily* later reported that Ung "had known Pepe for three or four years and had dined with him the night before his arrest," and quoted the well-known politician as saying Pepe was "a good man."[13]

Such favoritism came as no surprise to US officials, given Cambodia's reputation as one of the most corrupt countries in Southeast Asia. The justice system was notoriously porous, with judges, police, and witnesses susceptible to being bribed.

Because of the rampant corruption, and in light of Pepe's high-level connections, Phillips, Vansak, Brewster, and others involved in the case, worried he might be set free.[14] The American side began urging the Cambodian government to deport Pepe so he could be brought back to the United States and charged under federal law.

Normally, US law only applied within the fifty states, and not within the boundaries of other sovereign nations such as Cambodia. But a few years before Pepe was arrested, widely publicized incidents of American men committing sexual assaults against children overseas had prompted Congress to intervene.

When Senator Orrin Hatch (R-UT) and then-Congressman Mike Pence (R-IN) introduced the PROTECT Act, the proposed law was aimed in part at Americans "who travel to foreign countries and engage in illicit sexual relations with minors."[15] Enacted by Congress on a near-unanimous vote, and signed into law by President George W. Bush, the PROTECT Act provided a legal basis for bringing criminal charges in the United States against Americans accused of molesting children overseas.

While Pepe remained in Prey Sar, the US government filed a criminal complaint against him in federal district court in Los Angeles. Even though there's no formal extradition treaty between Cambodia and the United States, the Cambodian government eventually agreed to hand Pepe over.

Eight months after Pepe's arrest, the kingdom of Cambodia expelled him from the country. Special Agent Wang, assisted by two other ICE agents, arrested Pepe, read him a Miranda warning, and escorted him onto an airplane.

CHAPTER TWELVE

Marshals Led Him in to Hear the Verdict Read

THE JETLINER CARRYING PEPE AND THE ICE AGENTS CROSSED THE globe in an arc over the Pacific Ocean and down the coast of California toward L.A. In a sense, the case came full circle, because along the way, the plane passed by Barry and Louise's former cottage at El Capitan.

After the plane landed at LAX, federal law enforcement authorities transported Pepe to a prison downtown.[1] Named the Metropolitan Detention Center and known by its initials "MDC," the 272,000 square-foot complex was a model of contemporary penal system best practices: Its cells were called "rooms," and they had wooden doors instead of metal bars. But make no mistake, MDC was still a prison, albeit it far better than Prey Sar.[2]

Patricia Donahue, representing the government, was an assistant US attorney with a tough-as-nails demeanor who took charge of prosecuting Pepe. He was hauled before a federal magistrate and arraigned on charges under the PROTECT Act, namely violation of 18 USC 2423(c), entitled "Engaging in Illicit Sexual Conduct in Foreign Places."[3]

Pepe filed an affidavit claiming he lacked the ability to fund his own defense. Based on this, he was assigned an attorney to represent him at no charge. Charles Brown, an experienced public defender built like a football player, with a calming voice and affable personality that made him well-liked by judges and jurors, was assigned to Pepe's case.

As the case against Pepe progressed toward trial, both sides enlisted reinforcements. On the government side, Donahue gained the assistance of John Lulejian, a prosecutor with experience in child molestation cases. On the defense side, Brown was paired with Carlton Gunn, one of Southern California's premier public defenders, whose rumpled appearance gave little clue that he was a battle-hardened advocate.

As the government grappled with the logistics of gathering evidence and information from overseas, they sparred with the defense over whether such evidence would be admissible in a US courtroom. The government also faced challenges in communicating with the victims: little girls living in shelters on the other side of the world, some who spoke Khmer, and others whose primary language was Vietnamese.

Pepe later claimed the government offered him a twenty-year plea deal, but he declined. Instead, he and his supposed brother-in-law Sander De Montero, the husband of Nary's sister Borat, embarked on a plan to eviscerate the government's case by making the victims unavailable to testify.

De Montero, former vice chair of the Cambodian Human Rights committee, lived in Australia but had high-level connections back home.[4] In phone calls and letters from MDC, which authorities later pieced together, De Montero and Pepe conspired to get the victims out of the shelters and reunited with their families—figuring they'd disappear into the slums of Phnom Penh or move to the outlying provinces.

In a letter to De Montero later seized by law enforcement, Pepe characterized his plan: "Suppose they gave a war and no one came." He told De Montero that silencing the victims "would be the best and quickest way to settle this problem."

With Pepe providing financing by funneling tens of thousands of dollars through Nary, De Montero succeeded in getting family members of the victims released from Prey Sar—including the mothers of Kanya, Sita, and Rotha. The next step was to find a Cambodian judge willing to order the NGOs to hand over the girls to their families.

Pepe wrote in a letter to De Montero, "I think it will not be difficult to find the court orders . . . to return them to their parents."

But on the prosecution side, the case against Pepe kept building as ICE and Cambodian National Police interviewed Pepe's victims. Ten months after Pepe was arrested and returned to the United States, Donahue obtained a superseding grand jury indictment charging him with seven counts of violating the PROTECT Act—one count for each of the identified victims.

As the trial date approached, ICE agents and guardians from the NGOs scrambled to assemble the paperwork needed to bring the seven girls to Los Angeles. Meanwhile, Donahue traveled to Phnom Penh so she could take the deposition of Sang, who'd been convicted on trafficking charges and sentenced to twenty-seven years in Prey Sar.

Because Sang didn't speak fluent English, Donahue brought along Ann Luong Spiratos, a court-approved Vietnamese interpreter. As Spiratos translated, Sang testified under oath about the deals she'd brokered to procure underage girls for Pepe.

At this juncture there was no apparent sign that Spiratos herself would end up becoming a controversial figure in the case.

After the seven victims landed on US soil, the government team readied them to appear in court. Donahue and her "second chair" colleague John Lulejian staged a mock trial so the girls could practice testifying. During free time, Phillips and other ICE agents, accompanied by Spiratos, escorted the girls on an excursion to Disneyland.

On the defense side, Pepe's trial team of Charles Brown and Carlton Gunn approached the case with the doggedness of lawyers committed to America's system of justice—where even the most damnable defendant is entitled to vigorous advocacy. They sought to portray Pepe as a professor and philanthropist caught in a corrupt Cambodian investigation, spurred by ICE agents who manipulated evidence and programmed the girls to say what prosecutors wanted to hear.

In crafting this defense, Pepe's attorneys had in mind the infamous McMartin preschool case, a 1980s sex-crimes saga involving teachers at a preschool in Manhattan Beach, California. In the McMartin case, which was eventually exposed as a modern-day witch hunt, zealous police and therapists—using leading questions and an anatomically correct doll—manipulated children into inventing wild accusations about teachers engaging in sodomy, ritual sacrifices, and other horrifying behavior that nowadays experts believe never happened.[5]

Unlike McMartin, in Pepe's case the little girls' accounts of being raped and tortured were corroborated by physical evidence such as ropes, K-Y Jelly, and Rohypnol, along with dozens of pornographic photos. But other factors weighed in Pepe's favor: the events took place in a faraway country; the victims didn't speak English; and Cambodian authorities of questionable integrity spearheaded the investigation.

Pepe also benefited from the US criminal law system's standard of proof beyond a reasonable doubt. The part-time professor didn't need to prove he was innocent; by law his innocence was presumed. He could win acquittal merely by casting shadows over the government's case.

Gunn had an impressive record of weaving shreds of doubt into a trial-winning defense. Although his shaggy mustache, longish hair, and wire-rimmed glasses gave him the visage of a friendly professor, he waged fierce fights on behalf of defendants who seemed cornered and outmatched. Could he and Charles Brown raise enough questions and uncertainties to win acquittal from the federal court jury?

The case of *USA v. Pepe* was assigned to US district judge Dale S. Fischer,[6] who'd been nominated to the bench by President George W. Bush. Judge Fischer, who was in her mid-fifties, at that time occupied a courtroom in a Los Angeles federal building bearing the name of Edward R. Roybal, a former Latino congressman and champion of minority rights.

The trial began on May 7, 2008, a cool and cloudy Southern California spring morning. Because the case required a panel of twelve jurors and six alternates, Judge Fischer asked the clerk's office to send sixty people to her courtroom so she could begin jury selection—in essence a weeding-out process.

The judge asked a series of questions designed to elicit information about whether the prospective jurors harbored any bias, or if serving on a jury posed a hardship. People who tried to exploit these excuses faced a tough grilling, and Judge Fischer only let a few off the hook.

After the judge finished with her questions, the lawyers began a high-stakes chess game weighing who to keep on the jury and who to strike. Each side had an allotted number of "peremptory challenges," meaning a prospective juror could be booted off the case summarily, with six of these challenges given to the prosecution and ten to the defense.

This led to some fascinating skirmishes. Defense attorney Carlton Gunn exercised a peremptory challenge on a single woman who worked at an import business and taught Sunday school at a Jewish temple. He also struck her replacement: a theoretical physicist with a master's degree from Stanford whose father had once been charged with child molestation.

Prosecutor Patricia Donahue challenged a divorced woman with no children who worked as a flight attendant. She also struck a married woman with a PhD in psychology who worked as a professor and taught a class on human sexuality.

Neither side challenged the single woman from Venice Beach in seat #8, who was certified to practice Ayuverdic medicine, a form of Indian holistic healing. But seat #1 saw eight prospective jurors come and go before the ninth was allowed to stay.

The sparring continued late into Thursday afternoon. After Donahue exhausted the prosecution's six strikes, and the defense used up most of theirs, only three of the original twelve jurors had survived the intensive selection process.

The trial began in earnest on Friday, May 9, but only after Juror #9, a longshoreman from San Pedro, begged off sick and was replaced by one of the alternates, a single woman who was studying to become a nurse. The twelve jurors—seven men and five women, plus the five remaining alternates—listened as Judge Fischer read pretrial instructions about keeping an open mind and listening to all the evidence before making their decision.

When prosecutor Patricia Donahue stepped to the podium to give the government's opening statement, she got straight to the point: "The evidence at this trial is going to show that that man, the defendant, Michael Pepe, tied up, drugged, beat, gagged, and then raped little girls."

Pepe's counsel Carlton Gunn took a more cerebral approach, urging jurors to set aside their emotions and take a hard look at the government's case. "The NGOs and law enforcement had their minds made up and they wanted to get the answers that they needed," he said. "Convict someone they thought was guilty.

"It's not necessarily that these girls are evil, malicious people setting up Mr. Pepe. Maybe they were abused. . . . But they weren't abused by Mr. Pepe."

Donahue called the government's first witness, Dr. Laura Watson, a British physician who worked at a clinic in Phnom Penh. Dr. Watson said her examination revealed that Thang suffered tearing and bleeding "consistent with vaginal trauma," while three other victims showed signs of forced penetration. But on cross-examination, defense attorney Brown, a handsome Black man who cut an imposing figure in the courtroom, established that Watson didn't take pictures of the injuries and didn't include DNA results in her report.

Donahue and her second-chair colleague John Lulejian followed by calling other experts to the witness stand, including an FBI behavioral analyst who outlined grooming techniques used by child molesters, and a DEA chemist who presented test results on the drugs found in Pepe's house. Then Donahue called the lead case agent, Gary Phillips, and he testified about the search of Pepe's villa and the evidence seized inside.

On cross-examination by Carlton Gunn, Phillips admitted that Thang, when first interviewed by ICE, failed to identify Pepe as the perpetrator. Gunn also questioned the handling of evidence by Cambodian police, asking Phillips, "That evidence wasn't in American custody during the whole time after it was seized, was it?"

Although lawyers for the prosecution and defense fought hard while questioning professionals who'd worked on the case, they knew this wasn't the main event. The conviction or acquittal of Michael Pepe would likely depend on testimony by the victims—and it turned out Sita felt too scared to take the witness stand. This meant the retired Marine captain's fate rested in the hands of half-a-dozen other scared little girls.

Even for litigants with every advantage—such as executives, professionals, or people who are wealthy or famous—a federal courthouse is an intimidating place. The spaces are vast and the ceilings high. Uniformed marshals patrol the hallways. Inside the courtroom, a black-robed judge sits perched above the proceedings in an oversized chair.

For a small child from a foreign country, especially a child steeped in the submission and degradation of the sex trade, few challenges could be as daunting as being placed in the front of a federal courtroom filled with somber adults. But this is what the US justice system demanded of Pepe's victims, and moreover, the alleged abuser would be there, staring from the defense table, exercising his constitutional right to confront his accusers.

***

Donahue began calling Pepe's victims to the witness stand on the fourth day of trial. This was a slow process because the girls spoke in their native tongues. Each question and answer needed to be translated by Moryvann Paigne, the Khmer language interpreter, or Ann Spiratos, the interpreter for Vietnamese.

The victims' testimony captivated the courtroom despite these language barriers. As a reporter from the *LA Times* jotted notes, Kanya recounted the months she'd spent living at Pepe's villa, including the first session inside his bedchamber.

"At first he came and he took off my clothes," said Kanya in a soft voice. "After he took off my clothes, he tied me. . . . And then he lift up my legs and then he raped me."

Donahue asked, "Was that the only time that Michael raped you?"

"No," replied Kanya. "Many times."

To help corroborate Kanya's account, the prosecution introduced into evidence one of the letters Pepe sent back home to his family. This enabled the jury to read Pepe's words about his relationship with Kanya.

"Sang told me that [Kanya's] mother was giving her to me to act in a status somewhere between wife and girlfriend," Pepe had written in his own hand.

On cross-examination, Gunn elicited testimony from Kanya about living conditions at Agape International Missions compared to the slums of Phnom Penh. His questions suggested she told authorities what they wanted to hear so she'd be allowed to stay in the shelter:

Q. You wouldn't get to stay at Agape if you said it wasn't true that you were abused by Michael, would you?

A. I don't know.

Q. Well, isn't it true that you know that you only get to stay—that girls only get to stay there if they are people who have been abused by someone or in some other way victimized?

A. Yes.

Duyen, who testified in Vietnamese, gave a similar account of Pepe's rape and abuse during the week she spent inside his villa. "He used rope to tie my hands and legs. He used tape to cover my mouth. He hit me. He used a pillow and push on my face. And then he take his penis, put it inside my vagina."

Patricia Donahue asked Duyen if she remembered how many times Pepe raped her. "I don't know how many times," replied the little girl. "I know it was many times." But on cross-examination, Brown suggested that some other man may have been the one who raped Duyen:

Q. Has anyone . . . has anyone else put a penis in your vagina?

A. Yes.

Thang, also testifying in Vietnamese, told the jurors how Pepe hog-tied and blindfolded her, stuffed a piece of cloth into her mouth, and raped her. Brown's cross-examination suggested she didn't act like an abuse victim, and instead appeared to enjoy living in Pepe's house. Brown showed Thang a picture where she could be seen playing with the two sisters, Rotha and Sita:

Q. And you're . . . it looks like you're having fun there.

A. I was playing with these sisters. I did not know that he was taking pictures.

Rotha, the little girl Pepe called "Smiley," took the witness stand on the day before her twelfth birthday. Rotha told the hushed courtroom she was nine years old when she moved into the Toul Kork villa. She testified about providing naked massages and oral sex to Pepe, saying he never put his penis in her vagina but sometimes touched her with his tongue:

Q. Where were you when he did that?

A. In his bedroom.

Q. What were you wearing?

A. Nothing.

Q. What did he do?

A. I sat on him and he licked me.

Realizing the devastating impact of this testimony, Gunn subjected Rotha to grueling cross-examination. But the 4'3" witness, the youngest of Pepe's victims to testify, fought back:

Q. During the interview, the agent and the interpreter encouraged you to say things that would help, didn't they?

A. What do you mean?

Q. Well, for example . . . there was a place where the agent was trying to get you to say Michael's eyes were a lighter blue, right?

A. No. He did not encourage.

Gunn also questioned whether Rotha, when she was first inter-viewed by investigators in Cambodia, behaved like someone who'd been victimized. But the tiny girl who dreamed of becoming a secretary stood toe-to-toe against a lawyer with more than twenty-five years of court-room experience:

Q. And you were laughing and you were giggling, weren't you?

A. You understand, I was so embarrassed, I didn't want to speak.

Q. You were laughing and giggling, weren't you?

A. Yes. I did.

Q. About this terrible thing you said happened?

A. Terrible things happened.

After the girls finished testifying, Donahue and Lulejian brought in a computer expert to lay the foundation for admitting Pepe's pornographic photos into evidence. When Judge Fischer allowed the photos to come in, this meant the jurors could examine the images of underage girls in Pepe's bedroom—including the photos he'd tried to delete, where he could be seen naked with Kanya.

On the eighth day of the trial, the government rested. Now the defense had an opportunity to present Pepe's case, which meant Brown and Gunn still had a chance to salvage reasonable doubt and avoid a verdict of guilty.

Pepe's defense focused on two main themes: He had a legitimate interest in helping vulnerable children, which was why he had little girls living in his villa, and the girls had been manipulated by investigators into making untruthful statements.

Carlton Gunn called Mao Chan Thorn to the stand—a former teacher at Newton Thilay school. Mao testified about visiting Pepe's villa three times per week to tutor Kanya, Rotha, and Sita, and said the girls seemed "very happy." Gunn asked Mao:

Q. Did the girls act like they were afraid of Mr. Pepe?

A. No. They behave and act treating Mr. Pepe like a father.

Q. Did they act like he made them unhappy in any way?

A. No. I think they were just happy to be there.

Q. Did they act like they didn't want to be around Mr. Pepe?

A. No. I saw them ran over to hug Mr. Pepe.

On cross-examination, Patricia Donahue established that Mao only worked at Pepe's house for six months in 2005, and not during the first half of 2006 when most of the alleged abuse took place. She also asked questions based on the handwritten letter Pepe sent back home in which he described his daily routine:

Q. When you were at Mr. Pepe's house, did Mr. Pepe ever tell you that the girls would give him a massage at 12:00 and then you would come at 1:00?

A. Can you please repeat the question?

Q. Did Mr. Pepe ever tell you that he had [Kanya, Sita, and Rotha] give him a massage right before you came over?

A. No.

Un Son, the priest from St. Joseph Catholic Church Phnom Penh, testified that Pepe had approached him and volunteered to help with whatever work the church needed done. The priest said it was he, not Pepe, who suggested they collaborate in distributing school supplies to children. The priest also testified, "I took him to the church in Svay Pak."

On cross-examination by Donahue, Father Un Son acknowledged that Svay Pak was a well-known destination for people who wanted to have sex with children. He also testified:

Q. Now, Father . . . you never went to Mr. Pepe's house, did you?

A. No.

Q. You have never been there?

A. That's correct.

Q. You don't know who else lived in the house, do you?

A. Yes. I don't know. That's correct.

Q. He never told you that he had children living at his house, did he?

A. No.

A similar pattern of examination and cross-examination occurred when Ung Huot, the former Cambodian prime minister, took the witness stand. On direct examination he testified about Pepe's work distributing school supplies to needy children. But on cross-examination, prosecutor John Lulejian delivered a rapid-fire set of questions:

Q. You have never been at defendant's house have you?

A. No.

Q. Never been inside the defendant's bedroom?

A. No.

Q. Never seen who lives in defendant's house?

A. I never been to his house.

Q. In fact, you don't really know that much about the defendant, do you?

A. No.

Defense attorney Charles Brown called Sander De Montero, the husband of Nary's sister Borat, to the witness stand. De Montero testified that Pepe worked as a professor and wanted to help impoverished children:

Q. At some point, Mr. De Montero, did you discuss with Mr. Pepe the idea of educational outreach to the poor communities of Cambodia?

A. Yes. We did discuss about how to make a plan in order to further our outreach to the children in the suburb.

Q. Whose idea was that originally?

A. It's Mr. Michael Pepe's idea.

On cross-examination, Lulejian tried to paint De Montero as a fixer—someone paid by Pepe to derail the prosecution. De Montero admitted that after Pepe's arrest he received expense money via Nary and talked with Pepe by phone more than two dozen times:

Q. During your telephone calls with the defendant, the two of you talked about working to reunite the victims with their families and take them out of the shelters?

A. Yes.

Khieu San, a member of Cambodia's National Assembly, testified on direct examination by Carlton Gunn that Pepe distributed school supplies to more than ten thousand students. On cross-examination, Lulejian focused on what happened within the walls of Pepe's villa:

Q. When you were at the defendant's home, did you see children there?

A. Sometimes I do.

Q. How old were the children?

A. To me maybe look like 13.

The defense also called Michael Maloney, a clinical psychologist who taught at UCLA and had been a key defense witness in the McMartin case.[7] Dr. Maloney testified he had concerns about the interview techniques investigators used when speaking with the victims—the implication being that adults in the room may have put words into the victims' mouths.

"And I read a number of these interviews," said Dr. Maloney. "I actually counted . . . every single utterance of everybody in the room. And in one it was like 12,600 words from interpreters and interviewers and 1,088 from the child." On cross-examination, Donahue zeroed in on this subject:

Q. Dr. Maloney, you are not saying that if an interview question is leading, that means the information provided by the child necessarily is untrue; right?

A. That's correct.

Q. In fact, one of the best ways to ensure that information provided by a child is not false is to look and see if there is information that corroborates what the child has said; right?

A. Correct.

Regarding corroborating information, Maloney acknowledged he wasn't aware of the incriminating photos recovered from Pepe's computer. "Purposely unaware," he said. "I just wanted to focus on the interviews."

On the twelfth day of the trial, the defense rested. Michael Pepe, exercising his constitutional right to remain silent, didn't take the witness stand.

Before the lawyers delivered closing arguments, Judge Fischer read aloud the jury instructions. She told the jurors that the government needed to establish three elements to prove Pepe committed a crime under the PROTECT Act: (1) he was a US citizen, (2) he "traveled in foreign commerce," and (3) he engaged in "illicit sexual conduct."

Judge Fischer explained that travel in foreign commerce "means traveling from one country to another country." She said "illicit sexual conduct" could be any one of certain prohibited acts involving minors, such as having commercial sex with someone under eighteen years old.

With these legal standards as the backdrop, prosecutor Patricia Donahue stepped to the podium and addressed the jury. "We submit to you that all of this evidence that you have seen over the past couple of weeks proves beyond a reasonable doubt that the defendant is guilty of all seven counts charged in the indictment.

"He bought the teachers at their school. He had the second in command in the school coming and tutoring them. He bought the parents. . . . He has got the former Prime Minister of Cambodia coming in here and testifying on his behalf. He locked these girls' world down. There was no place for these girls to go other than to stay at his house and submit."

But defense attorney Charles Brown argued that the government's evidence didn't withstand scrutiny. "It's not just the fact that the interviews themselves were suggestive," he said. "The other evidence really raises doubt about what the girls said occurred while they were at Mr. Pepe's house. The demeanor of the girls in photos . . . their statements that have been attributed to them raise serious concern about what they say happened."

Brown characterized the American criminal justice system as "one big quality control process." He told the jurors, "You are the gatekeepers of that process" and urged them to protect the justice system's integrity.

"It's even more so in a case like this where they're bringing in foreign witnesses, foreign evidence, foreign procedures, questionable evidence, questionable witnesses, questionable interviews.

"We ask that you hold the government to its high burden of proof in this case. We ask that you hold the government to its standards. Our standards. Not Cambodian standards. U.S. standards.

"The government has not met its burden of proof in this case. And we ask that you return a verdict of not guilty."

Late in the day, the twelve jurors retired to deliberate. The following morning—day thirteen of the trial—the jurors returned to their room and deliberations continued.

At 10:30 a.m. the jurors sent word to Judge Fischer that they'd reached a unanimous verdict. The prosecution and defense teams assembled in the courtroom; marshals led Pepe in to hear the verdict read. The seven victims, who'd been returned to their lodgings, weren't close enough to the courthouse to attend.

The jurors filed in and took their seats. Juror #11, who worked at a nonprofit think tank and had a master's degree in journalism, identified himself as the foreperson. He handed the verdict form to the bailiff and Judge Fischer read it aloud:

Michael J. Pepe, guilty as charged on all seven counts.[8]

Tom Tallone, a mechanical engineer, served as Juror #3. When interviewed for this book on July 30, 2020, he said that inside the jury room, once the jurors finished with preliminaries and got down to business, "it only took about twelve minutes" before they voted to convict Pepe.

"The guy is a serious dirtbag," he said. "I had no reservations."

***

Judge Fischer scheduled a sentencing hearing for September 2008, marking the beginning of what's often a complicated process. Sentencing in federal court can stretch over many months as the judge reviews a presentencing report, weighs briefs submitted by the prosecution and defense, reads letters from victims and concerned citizens, and holds hearings in which the lawyers argue, victims speak, and the defendant is given the right to be heard.

In the case of *USA v. Pepe*, while the sentencing process moved forward at a snail's pace, the government celebrated what it viewed as a major victory. "Predators such as Mr. Pepe should realize that their unspeakable acts will not go unpunished," trumpeted US attorney Thomas O'Brien in a press release.[9]

The following year, Attorney General Eric Holder held a ceremony in Washington, DC, to honor outstanding Department of Justice employees. The honorees included prosecutor Patricia Donahue, her second chair John Lulejian, and a third lawyer on the case, Elizabeth Yang. Also receiving awards were Foreign Service National Vansak Suos and ICE special agents Gary Phillips, Eddy Wang, and Paul Carbone.

Said the attorney general, "Each of these dedicated servants has carried out the important mission of the Department of Justice and has done so with excellence and distinction."[10] The unwitting irony in his statement would soon become apparent.

CHAPTER THIRTEEN

Pulling Back the Veil on the Murder Case

WHILE MICHAEL PEPE CONTINUED TO AWAIT SENTENCING, THE CASE
took a mind-boggling turn. Prosecutor John Lulejian informed DOJ
ethics personnel that he suspected the lead ICE agent on the case, Gary
Phillips, of carrying on a secret affair with Ann Spiratos, the Vietnamese
interpreter at trial.

The DOJ immediately launched an investigation. It turned out that
Phillips and Spiratos first met when the government team traveled
to Cambodia for Sang's deposition. Two months later, when Phillips
returned to the United States with the victims, he met the interpreter
again.

Spiratos said in a sworn statement that she and Phillips "worked
together for long hours most days" and on one occasion had lunch alone.
Another time, they spent a day "sightseeing in local beach neighborhoods" and "had dinner together that evening." Spiratos said that they
first had sex on Phillips's birthday in June 2008.

Phillips's sworn statement offered a somewhat different account. He
said that after the victims flew to California, he encountered Spiratos at
the mock trial staged by Donahue and Lulejian. "As we became friends
over the next few weeks, we had a spontaneous physical relationship."

Phillips said that the relationship turned sexual "sometime after the
start of trial or near the end of the trial." He also said that they had a
romantic encounter when taking the victims to Disneyland.

Pepe's attorney Charles Brown responded by filing a motion for a
new trial. Brown argued that the sexual relationship between Phillips

and Spiratos caused the interpreter to slant the testimony in favor of the government. Brown also claimed that Spiratos instilled bias in Moryvann Paigne, the Khmer interpreter.

In what appears to have been an exercise of professional courtesy, Brown applied for permission to file the new trial motion under seal, meaning it wouldn't be made public. Judge Fischer, apparently furious about the alleged misconduct, refused to grant the request, stating, "This case received media attention—at least some of which was initiated by the government. The prosecution consumed a significant amount of public funds. The public has a right to know the grounds for the motion."

A headline in the *LA Times* blared, "Verdict in Key Child-Sex Trial at Risk."[1] Special Agent Phillips, when asked during the DOJ's investigation to explain behavior that imperiled the case along with his career, claimed Lulejian encouraged him to have an intimate relationship with Spiratos. He said that when she came aboard the case, Lulejian told him, "Wait until you see who I hired, she is Vietnamese and she is very hot."

Phillips also said that when the government team traveled to Cambodia to take Sang's deposition, Lulejian told Phillips to "take care" of Spiratos and not leave her alone in a foreign country. Lulejian denied these allegations.

Phillips became the subject of an internal ICE investigation and ended up retiring—an ignominious ending to what had been a stellar career.[2] Spiratos lamented that her court reporting practice took a dive after she followed her heart instead of her head.

"I feel like I'm a scapegoat," she told the *LA Times*. "It takes two, right? Not just me."[3]

Meanwhile, from behind bars at MDC in downtown Los Angeles, Michael Pepe worked to undermine the outcome of the case. He groused to Sander De Montero, "The judge is a bitch."

Firing off instructions via phone calls and letters, Pepe conceived a multiprong strategy—or in the eyes of the US government, an elaborate conspiracy. The facts came to light after Australian Federal Police executed a search warrant at De Montero's home in Victoria, Australia, and seized a trove of correspondence. Additional evidence came from tape-recorded phone calls Pepe made to De Montero from MDC.

The correspondence and recordings showed that Pepe instructed De Montero to contact Sang in Prey Sar prison and obtain a declaration in which she recanted her trial testimony. Pepe said that getting the declaration "would be easy, [and] just take a little money," and that Sang needed to realize "who is going to save her ass and who butters her bread."

The erstwhile professor discussed strategies to ensure the girls would be unavailable to testify if Judge Fischer granted a new trial. He told De Montero to "help move them out to the provinces." He also mentioned establishing a "scholarship fund."

Pepe alluded to the cash required for these efforts, which he called "grease." He said when De Montero needed more money, Pepe's sister Elaine Pepe-Williams would forward it along via MoneyGram. There was also mention of wire transfers to De Montero from Pepe's account at the CBC Federal Credit Union.

"Put whatever resources we can into getting this all done," Pepe told De Montero. "It is important!"

But Pepe cautioned De Montero to be careful in dealing with defense attorneys Carlton Gunn and Charles Brown. "These guys, even though they are my attorneys, have different ethical standards," said Pepe.

Pepe ended up succeeding with one of his schemes. In a handwritten document dated July 6, 2010, signed by Sang and marked on each page with a fingerprint, she stated in Khmer translated to English, "I never sold any child to anyone named MICHAEL PEPE. I helped him once when he was ill and from that time on he became my friend." This was virtually the same language used in a sample declaration that Pepe had drafted and sent to De Montero.

After Pepe's attorneys submitted this declaration to Judge Fischer as a basis for seeking a new trial, prosecutor Patricia Donahue fired back. Her papers detailed the elaborate and well-funded conspiracy by Pepe and De Montero to bribe Sang into providing a false declaration.

Faced with evidence that Pepe engaged in witness tampering, the defense counsel withdrew the motion for a new trial based on Sang's recantation. But the motion to void the verdict based on the sexual relationship between Phillips and Spiratos remained pending, awaiting a decision by Judge Fischer.

Because Pepe's victims were minors at the time they testified, by law their testimony had been videotaped, to help assure there was no undue influence by any of the adults in the courtroom. These videotapes allowed other translators to review how Spiratos and Paigne translated what the girls said. This painstaking review, followed by briefing from counsel and a hearing before Judge Fischer, stretched over many months.

According to the defense's translator, there were instances where the translation at trial didn't match with the witness's testimony and was done in a manner that favored the prosecution. In their motion for a new trial, Pepe's counsel cited this exchange from Patricia Donahue's examination of Chavy:

Donahue: "When you say, 'I wouldn't sleep with him,' what do you mean?"

Interpreter: "When you said that you wouldn't sleep with him, what do you mean you wouldn't sleep with him?"

Witness: "I didn't sleep because I was afraid of him."

Interpreter: "I meant that I wouldn't let him insert his penis into my vagina."

But most of the alleged mistranslation was more subtle, such as in this example offered by the defense's translator:

Donahue: "How did you get to Michael's house?"

Interpreter: "Who took you to Michael's house?"

Witness: "Aunty Sang."

Interpreter: "Sang."

When Judge Fischer issued a ruling on the new trial motion, she noted that the allegations only involved the Vietnamese interpreter Ann Spiratos, not the Khmer interpreter Moryvann Paigne. The judge blasted the "egregious misconduct by the case agent and Vietnamese interpreter" but denied Pepe's motion for a new trial, saying any errors likely reflected "the inherent imprecision of translation" and didn't have a material effect.

At this juncture, more than five years had passed since the jury convicted Pepe under the PROTECT Act. At last, the stage was set for the erstwhile professor to be sentenced.

The sentencing process began back in 2008, soon after the jury returned a guilty verdict. To accommodate the victims, Judge Fischer set a hearing where they could make statements to the court.

The seven little girls from Cambodia gathered in Judge Fischer's courtroom along with Don Brewster and other guardians. As Pepe and his lawyers sat and watched, along with prosecutors, observers, and a reporter from the *LA Times*, one by one the victims stepped up to speak. Their statements were short and to the point.[4]

"I want to say hello to everyone who is here," said Kanya. "And thank you for allowing me here to speak. Thank you for helping me find justice and believe in me. Thank you for the government."

When Thang came forward, she also expressed gratitude: "I would like to thank the Court to allow me to be here. I want to grow up to be a doctor. That's all."

Rotha told Judge Fischer, "I want to say I do not want this to happen again to other children. When it happened to us, it made us very painful. I am happy today because I see justice. I just want to say thank you that you helped me find justice here."

Don Brewster addressed the defendant directly: "Mr. Pepe, I'd like you to know that I've been praying for you," he said. "Praying you would admit what you have done, that you would take responsibility for torturing and raping little girls, that you would step forward with the courage to do that, and that you wouldn't be asking the Court for leniency."

Pepe, dressed in a prison jumpsuit, remained silent, as he had throughout the trial. Nothing in his demeanor gave any clue about what he might be thinking.

Because of the lengthy process surrounding the motion for a new trial, the final stage of sentencing didn't occur until 2014. At that point it seemed clear the court wouldn't grant Pepe leniency. The US ambassador to Cambodia had sent a letter to Judge Fischer:

"Mr. Pepe's actions were reprehensible and have tarnished the image of the American people. . . . It is my hope that a strong sentence will not only provide the victims with some comfort that justice was done, but encourage other victims also to fight for their rights."

At the conclusion of the final sentencing hearing, Judge Fischer sentenced Pepe to the maximum of thirty years on each of the seven counts. The judge ordered him to serve the sentences consecutively—a total of 210 years.

"Monstrous does not begin to describe the crime and the harm done to the victims," said the grim-faced federal judge. She also said that Pepe showed "absolutely no remorse."[5]

After Pepe was hauled away to begin serving his 210-year sentence, most observers thought the case was over. Although defense counsel promptly filed a notice of appeal, Pepe's heinous behavior, evidenced by heart-wrenching testimony from the girls and documented in explicit photos, left no room for arguing the jury got it wrong.

When Michael Westerman heard that Michael Pepe had in effect been sentenced to life in prison, he felt a measure of satisfaction that justice had been served. "Nothing's ever going to bring back my mom," said Michael. "But at least he isn't going scot-free."

At that point, Michael was the sole surviving immediate family member of Barry and Louise. Even though more than twenty years had passed since the couple disappeared, he often found himself missing his mother.

"My relationship with her was taken away," he said. "I still think of times when I wish she was there to share."

As for how he felt about Pepe, Westerman had this to say: "I want him to feel some of the pain that we felt. He thinks he's smarter than everyone and he's going to get out. I hope it never happens."

Perhaps in the case of Barry and Louise Berman, as retired Inyo County Deputy Leon Boyer lamented, Pepe "skated and skated and skated." But when it came to his rape and torture of seven girls in Cambodia, the disgraced professor wouldn't get away with it, or would he?

***

When Michael Pepe was sentenced in 2014, I read about the case in the *LA Times* but beyond that didn't take note. Although some law enforcement officials knew that the professor who preyed on girls in Cambodia was also the former Marine suspected in the murders of Barry and Louise Berman, the connection hadn't yet been made public.

Coincidentally, at about the same time Pepe was sentenced, I began to wonder what became of the Berman case. I knew their remains had turned up several years after they vanished, but I didn't recall the details about the apparent murders. Yet the incident still affected me; it tinged my view of Saline Valley, a place I cherished, and made me wary when traveling there.

While in college decades earlier I'd heard talk about Saline Valley and its clothing-optional hot springs.[6] I first ventured there in 1977, together with four buddies, in a faded-purple Rambler station wagon. As we soaked in a pool, drinking beer and smoking weed, I stared at the Inyos, a wall of mountains that seemed impenetrable yet alluring.

I returned the following spring, and on a backpacking trip with three other guys, started climbing from Saline Valley up the east side of the Inyo range. But we were desert mountaineering novices, and the adventure was ill-planned.

Partway up the mountain, while two of the guys remained at camp, I set out with James Morrison, nicknamed "Mo," for what was supposed to be a morning hike in search of water—we were almost out. Wearing shorts and T-shirts and carrying but one quart of water between the two of us, we kept climbing higher, lured by the sight of a snowy summit that looked to be "right there."

Many hours later, as the sun descended and the air turned cold, Mo and I started up the final ridge. As we pushed toward the peak, what had begun as a day-hike became something more perilous but also more profound.

Looking back, it's easy to catalog the factors: rarified air, dehydration, lack of food, physical exhaustion, impressionability of youth, and the fact we got high along the way. But none of that means what we experienced wasn't "real."

The ridge leading to the top was formed of chalk-white dolomite, steep and crumbling, and streaked with orange lichen. Along this ridge grew ancient bristlecone pines—a hanging garden, achingly beautiful, like a Japanese painting brought to life.

Many of the trees were so old they appeared barren, with gold- and gray-colored wood that had been baked and polished by the passage of time. Yet there would often be a strip of living bark winding up the trunk to sustain branches that still produced pine cones.

Mo and I felt blessed to be among these ancient trees, but after many hours of hiking up the mountain we were suffering ill effects. When I inhaled, my body felt hollow, and despite the exertion of climbing a steep mountain, my skin turned clammy. A feeling of anxiety pressed against my temples like a vise.

The bristlecone pines seemed to take notice. Like sentient beings, they reached out with sturdy limbs to lend a helping hand. As Mo and I grabbed the limbs and pulled ourselves upward, we realized we weren't alone. We were among the elders of planet earth, and they spoke to us mutely, and offered encouragement.

The weathered branches told of sun and wind, of passing clouds and falling snow. The gnarled roots told of centuries-long struggles as rocks fell and earth slid and the roots grappled to retain a foothold.

The trees urged us to keep going, to keep trying, because this is what living things do. Why were we here? Because we were alive. Life itself was the raison d'être—it required no other rationale.

The sun was setting by the time the trees thinned, the ridge rolled away, and Mo and I found ourselves on top. We gazed westward across Owens Valley to the Sierra Nevada—a wall of granite and ice stretching north to south as far as the eye could see. We lingered until the sun dropped below the Sierra summits before turning east again in the direction of Saline Valley.

We only made it down a thousand vertical feet before darkness forced us to bivouac. We spent the night huddled around a fire, melting snow in a battered two-gallon tin canteen that Mo had found along the way—a relic from olden mining days.

A waning quarter moon rose at midnight, illuminating the magical landscape. In the wee hours, a great horned owl alighted atop a dead tree and stared down at us with luminescent eyes.

Mo and I didn't make it back to camp until the following night. Meanwhile, our two buddies, Steve Bailey and Colin Gavin, drove out of Saline Valley into Lone Pine and reported us missing. A helicopter dispatched by the Inyo County's SAR team, with Steve riding shotgun,[7] finally spotted me and Mo as we waited in the shade in Saline Valley at the base of the Inyos sipping water from the two-gallon canteen.

This incident marked a turning point in my life. Mo and I cofounded an outdoor group called Desert Survivors.[8] As we worked to protect desert wilderness by signing up members for our group, launching letter-writing campaigns, meeting with elected officials, and making impassioned speeches at public hearings, I ended up applying to law school. All the while my love affair with Saline Valley and its surrounds led me to return time and again in search of adventure, inspiration, and solace.[9]

But after two hippie-type campers disappeared from the hot springs in January 1986, and their remains later turned up in a shallow grave, the valley didn't seem quite so idyllic. That's why I decided, nearly three decades after Barry and Louise vanished, to investigate the case.

I started by calling Morgan Irby, a longtime desert exploration partner. A unique individual with a combination of eccentricity and intellect, he embodied sheer animal strength and had a physique like Mr. Clean, with massive biceps and a shaved head. He'd devoted decades of his life to being a firefighter—refusing promotions so he could be first off the truck when it rolled up to the scene. Irby spoke several languages and often sprinkled his dialogue with quotes from Shakespeare, the Bible, Arthur Miller, Bob Dylan, and the like.

As Irby and I spoke, he reminded me of a trip we took in April 1987 to the Saline Valley region, about fifteen months after the Bermans disappeared, and before their remains had been found. Starting northwest of Saline Valley at a remote location accessible by four-wheel-drive, we set out on foot, each of us carrying more than eight gallons of water in our ninety-pound backpacks. From there we headed southeast along the crest of the Saline Range, a maze-like moonscape of intertwined ridges and high plateaus.

Spurred by fear of running out of water, we hiked from dawn to dusk. Along the way we talked about the missing couple from Santa Barbara. I half expected to find their remains, but we saw no sign of creatures other than insects, lizards, and an occasional bird.

A notable exception came on the afternoon of our second day. After we'd spent hours crossing terrain that was silent and still, the furious whir of a rattlesnake sent a jolt of electricity down my spine. I froze, looked around and saw it: a sidewinder, brown and tan, tightly coiled and bristling with energy.

I stepped back but Irby moved closer. He doffed his pack and crouched down, teasing the boundary of the snake's striking distance.

Most people, if they'd been struck by a rattlesnake before, endured skin-splitting swelling and searing pain, spent a week in intensive care, and returned to the ICU after a sudden relapse, would stay the hell away. But instead of being once bitten twice shy, Irby kneeled next to the rattlesnake and addressed it as "my demon brother."

Late in the afternoon of the third day, down to less than two quarts of water each, Irby and I descended the southern flank of the Saline Range and landed along the Corridor. We continued down to Upper Warm Springs—the undeveloped hot springs about two miles above Palm Spring. As we rested in the shade, I wondered whether the missing couple from Santa Barbara had passed this way, and what sort of demon they might have encountered.

Now it was springtime 2014, and Irby was relating to me what he remembered about the Berman murders and making suggestions about who to contact. From there I began tracking down witnesses, reaching out to law enforcement, submitting public record requests, and reading everything I could find about the case.

After months of digging, and by building on the work of Deputy Leon Boyer and other law enforcement officials, I formed a theory about what may have happened in Saline Valley when Barry and Louise disappeared. Unraveling the different threads, and then tying them together, I began drafting an article laying out the evidence.

Saline Valley's otherworldly terrain, profound silence, and geographic isolation gave "regulars" and other visitors a sense they'd escaped the bounds of conventional society. In this unique setting, a sort of desert Eden, people who ventured into the valley could revel in an aura of unfettered freedom.

Visitors who camped at the hot springs found themselves among like-minded folks, situated at a magical oasis surrounded by inhospitable desert. This imparted a sense of shared experience—like passengers aboard a ship at sea.

The hot tubs enhanced this feeling of connectedness. When visitors shed their clothes and stepped into the water, often sipping drinks and passing joints, social barriers dissolved, and strangers became friends. How could you feel wary while relaxing in a bath?

When Barry and Louise drove into Palm Spring campground on January 5, 1986, they parked their pickup and changed into bathing suits. As they soaked in Wizard Pool under a blanket of stars, they chatted with Michael Pepe, Brian Casey, and Greg Snyder. The five of them shared tidbits of personal information and talked about the wonders of Saline Valley.

In this setting it would have been natural for Louise to engage in animated conversation, respond with a laugh, and do all this in a genuine, open-hearted manner. As her former best friend Eleanor Snow said, "Louise was friendly with everyone."

Pepe, who was young and solidly built, with a full head of hair and mellow voice, possessed his own sort of charm—we know this because by then he'd been married twice and had a girlfriend who felt comfortable going camping with him. Marston Mottweiler said Pepe had a soft manner—not what you'd expect from a Marine. And he was a person of accomplishment: Marine Corps officer, college graduate, and MBA student.

Among military men such as Pepe, the hot springs had a reputation as a place abounding with naked hippie girls. Pilots made daring flyovers just to catch a glimpse of bare breasts and curved hips.

Pepe's personal history—especially his later years in Cambodia— proved he viewed females as objects for desires that at best were kinky and unconventional, and at worst, violent and perverse. From his warped perspective, friendly conversation with an engaging female might have been viewed as an invitation for sex.

According to retired deputy Leon Boyer, "Louise was kind of a flirt, she made Barry jealous sometimes. Maybe Pepe misinterpreted?"

As Pepe, Barry, Louise, and the two motorcycle riders chatted in Wizard Pool, the Bermans mentioned wanting to visit the Hogan. Pepe had experience with touring Saline Valley; during the interrogation by sheriff's investigators, he mentioned exploring the Corridor, Upper Warm Springs, and various petroglyph sites.

The next morning, the Bermans left camp and began walking up the Corridor. Because they left their cameras behind, it's doubtful they intended to take a long hike. Also, a few days earlier, before leaving town, Louise told Pauline Colbert that she felt footsore and didn't plan to do much hiking.

The gravesite where the Bermans's remains turned up lies about seven miles in distance and one thousand feet in elevation above the hot springs. A daylong hike to and from that location would be a daunting challenge for most people, and well beyond the range of Louise. For this reason, it's reasonable to surmise the Bermans must have ascended the Corridor, at least part way, by motor vehicle.

This leads to the question: What vehicles were seen along the Corridor on January 6? Brian Casey observed Pepe unloading camping gear from the back of his Datsun truck, and then Pepe drove away from Palm Spring, headed in the same direction as Barry and Louise. His pickup was the only passenger vehicle known to have traveled the Corridor that day—and it had a cab big enough to accommodate three people.

Brian Casey, Greg Snyder, and Mark Muscio also headed up the Corridor by vehicle, but they rode Yamaha dirt bikes designed to carry only a single rider. During my investigation I examined one of the dirt bikes, which Casey kept stored under a tarp outside his house in the Sierra foothills. The dirt bike had a small, narrow seat, and didn't have any passenger foot pegs.[10]

According to Casey, back at Palm Spring, late in the day, when talk around camp turned to the couple from Santa Barbara, Pepe told the other campers he "may have" seen the pair hiking up the Corridor.

He also acknowledged this possibility in his interview with sheriff's investigators.

Pepe was sexually aggressive, and sheriff's investigators theorized he made a sexual proposition to the Bermans. We don't know if this occurred, but we do know that within minutes of meeting Katy Aberdeen, a total stranger, Pepe floated the idea of engaging in a threesome.

The Bermans were devotees of Radha Soami, a conservative faith with a strict set of rules. Although Barry appeared quiet and unassuming, he was a man of deeply-held principles—while still a child he pushed back against the lifestyle and mores of his wealthy, powerful father. As Dr. Koplin said, Barry had his "own internal compass."

Anne Sullivan said Barry might've been a virgin when he met Louise, which means he also lacked experience being with a romantic partner in an awkward, three-way situation. Put another way: Barry wasn't accustomed to watching someone hit on his wife, because back home, people respected the boundaries of their relationship.

Although Barry came across as a hippie-type, the hardworking blacksmith was lean and muscular. His friend George Ziegler said he had "the build of a weightlifter."

Pepe was a US Marine and former high school football lineman who simmered from the pressures of a stressful job, a troubled marriage, and three kids. Beneath his mild-mannered exterior lurked a Jekyll and Hyde personality. "He could explode," said his sister Maureen O'Hara.

We also know that Pepe didn't like being challenged. When he was a boy, walking home after target shooting with Bill Haigler, thugs in a car tried to grab his .22. He refused to let go—even as he got dragged down the street. When the girls in Cambodia screamed or squirmed, he hit them—hard.

Marine Corps training wasn't about proportionate response or turning the other cheek. Pepe had been schooled in hand-to-hand combat, and he told Mottweiler and Gray he always carried a handgun when traveling alone in the desert.

The methodical concealing of Barry and Louise's bodies called to mind Marine Corps officers' school at Quantico, where candidates learned how to "act in the fog of war." Think about it: If you'd just killed two people, wouldn't your first instinct be to run away?

But someone trained to be coolheaded would have wanted to hide the bodies. The desert dry wash where their remains turned up offered a workable solution: far from camp, off the beaten path, yet accessible by a two-wheel-drive pickup.[11]

The grave itself was in a side channel of the wash—a narrow trough with steep walls. This meant the bodies could be buried without digging a hole, and afterward covered with rocks and dirt so the grave would blend in with the surrounding terrain.

The Bermans' remains included fragments of underwear, but the Nikes, previously discovered near Lower Warm Springs, were gone. Nor was there any sign of backpacks, heavy clothing, or other items that are slow to decay. Louise's jewelry and Barry's silver belt buckle also went missing. All of this indicates a remarkable level of planning.

The burial process must have been physically and emotionally challenging. First came the awful task of removing clothing and dragging the bodies into the makeshift grave. After that came the real work: hauling rocks and shoveling sand and dirt. Not everyone could handle such a task—it required strength and stamina, along with a shovel such as the one Pepe carried in the bed of his pickup.

The handcuff key found amid the Bermans's remains called to mind Pepe's behavior inside his Phnom Penh villa. When the little girls struggled or resisted, he bound their hands and legs with lengths of rope.

Around midday on January 6, the three motorcycle riders, who were taking their time and exploring washes and spurs, came riding up the Corridor. Based on site visits and an examination of Muscio's photos, it appeared they stopped for lunch about half-a-mile north of the gravesite.

At the gravesite, deep inside a wash, someone working to bury the Bermans could have peeked over the top of a cutbank and seen the riders in the distance. We don't know if Pepe did this, but we do know that later in the day, back at camp, he said he saw the riders go by.

We also know from Katy Aberdeen that when Pepe returned to camp, he was "all dirty" and "super nervous." He bummed a pack of cigarettes in exchange for a can of peaches. We also know from Veronica

McClintock, who was a secretary at the Marine Corps logistics base in Barstow, that when Pepe went back to work after the trip, he acted jumpy and kept taking a lot of smoke breaks.

In the November 1986 interview, when Inyo County sheriff's investigators asked Pepe what he did on January 6, Mottweiler recalled that the Marine captain's answers were "resistive—not forthcoming." Pepe changed his story repeatedly, claimed he didn't remember, and seemed to be trying to deflect attention onto other people and incidents.

Pepe's account of returning to camp and finding "some of my gas was missing and the truck appeared to be out of position" sounded like an attempt to disassociate himself from wherever the truck was earlier in the day. It's also noteworthy that not long after the trip he painted and sold the pickup.

When Pepe's father Joseph was asked to comment on the case, he said, "I think my son's been implicated in something he didn't do. He happened to be the closest guy around."

But law enforcement officials believed they had the right man, and my investigation revealed extensive circumstantial evidence to support this belief. With decades gone by since Barry and Louise turned up dead in Saline Valley, and no arrest made in the case, it seemed high time to pull back the veil on the murder case and let the public know the facts.

CHAPTER FOURTEEN

"Suspect in Unsolved Murders Set to be Freed"

THE ARTICLE I PENNED, ENTITLED "DOUBLE MURDER IN THE MOJAVE," ran as a five-thousand-word cover story in *LA Weekly* in March 2015.[1] The story broke the news that former Marine Corps captain Michael J. Pepe was the prime suspect in the unsolved murders of Barry and Louise. The story also linked the Berman case to the same perpetrator who, while working as a professor in Cambodia, raped and abused underage girls.

At the time my article ran, Pepe was being housed at the maximum security United States Penitentiary (USP) in Tucson, Arizona, situated in the open desert about seventeen miles southeast of downtown. Behind the tilt-up concrete walls, under sallow neon lights, Pepe was serving time with about 1,300 other convicted felons.[2]

He'd been transported to USP Tucson after being sentenced by Judge Fischer. Following a standard Bureau of Prisons screening interview, he'd been assigned to the general population. Although in some prisons his status as child molester—"chomo" in jailhouse jargon—would have made him a marked man, at USP Tucson he was one of many convicted sexual predators.

High-profile deviants such as Brian David Mitchell, who kidnapped fourteen-year-old Elizabeth Smart and held her captive for eight months, got sent to USP Tucson.[3] So did Larry Nassar, the former USA Gymnastics team doctor who sexually assaulted at least 265 young athletes.[4]

The Bureau of Prisons concentrated sex offenders in a single location to provide safety in numbers, and to enable them to participate in treatment programs without fear of reprisal. But that didn't necessarily mean that other inmates would have known about Pepe's horrific offenses.

After my article ran, *LA Weekly* received a letter from Quincy Walters, an inmate at USP Tucson. Walters claimed Pepe had been bragging about murdering people. Jill Stewart, a hard-bitten newspaper veteran who at that time served as managing editor, sent me an email on May 11, 2015: "Probably BS but maybe not."

Background research revealed that Walters, thirty-one, was a repeat offender sentenced to eighteen years for robbing a bank in Texas. After being sent to USP Tucson, Walters eventually ended up with Pepe as his cellmate. This put them in close contact for long hours every day, so presumably they shared information about their personal histories and talked about how they came to be incarcerated.

Among prisoners there's an unwritten code of conduct—and one of the designated offenses is being a "rat." When Walters reached out to *LA Weekly* saying Pepe bragged about killing people, this raised a threshold question: Why would Walters want to rat out his cellmate?

In federal prison, inmates with a record of good behavior are allowed to send and receive emails via a subscription service called CorrLinks.[5] Following his outreach to *LA Weekly*, Quincy Walters traded emails with Louise's son Michael Westerman, and he also exchanged letters and emails with me.

According to Walters, after Pepe arrived at USP Tucson, other inmates preyed on the overweight, middle-aged new arrival by "pressing" him for food and commissary items. Because Pepe was Walters's "cellie" and seemed like an "alright guy," Walters and his friends "took him in under our protection."

Walters said Pepe claimed to be in prison for wire fraud and money laundering—respectable crimes in jailhouse culture. But after reading the *LA Weekly* article, Walters realized that Pepe brutalized preteen girls. Even at USP Tucson, these crimes could make the offender a prison pariah.

Walters said he had two choices when he learned Pepe was a "chomo": "Stab and beat the shit out of Pepe" or "do the same thing he did to me, betray his trust." Walters said he chose the latter.

"I don't know if you've ever met Pepe personally, but he's a arrogant and cocky mutha fucka, who thinks he's smarter than the world," Walters wrote. "Cause he's actually proud of those killings, he also thinks he was doing something cool by having sex with all those kids and just paying the families pretty much pocket change (as he calls it)."

Walters sent a long email to Michael Westerman on August 28, 2015, setting forth what Walters claimed were "Pepe's words" about the events in Saline Valley back in January 1986. Walters's email began by saying Pepe met the Bermans at the hot springs.

"Pepe told them he was familiar with the area, and that he had been exploring and found some new hot springs, and how he finds different little artifacts and things like that. . . . Pepe promised to show them some of the un-explored areas, where he found the natural hot springs and artifacts."

According to the email, Pepe gave directions to Barry and said he'd meet them later. After Pepe caught up, the Bermans climbed into his truck. Pepe asked if they wanted to have a little fun, and suggested they smoke some hashish, but Barry turned the offer down.

"[T]hat's when Pepe said the lady can speak for herself. And Pepe, says that's when the husband starts acting like a asshole, and tells him to let them out the truck."

Walters's email said Pepe pulled over and the Bermans got out. Pepe got out too and the situation escalated.

"[Pepe] ask him, 'why is he acting like a dick, all he's trying to do is have a little fun.' The husband doesn't respond, he just walks away, and Pepe catches up to him, but when he catches up, he grabs your mother hand and ask her, why is she with this jerk, the husband then pushes Pepe, and Pepe rushes him and grabs him around his throat, the husband then punches Pepe in the nose."

Pepe allegedly told Walters that Barry pulled a pickax, although where this tool came from wasn't explained. Then the altercation turned deadly.

"Pepe shot him in the stomach with a snub nose .357, when he shot him, your mother tried to run, but Pepe caught her and handcuffed her arm thru the window to the steering wheel."

Walters' email said that Pepe finished off Barry by stabbing him in the neck with a KA-BAR fighting knife. Pepe allegedly killed Louise by strangling her with a "tent coil." Then he buried the bodies.

"I know the paper said something about a belt buckle and wedding ring. But Pepe also took a chained watch from the husband and some gold bangles from your mother. And the handcuff key was his, he lost it when he was digging the grave."

A few months later, Walters's friend Daniel Blount, an inmate at USP Tucson convicted of trafficking and abusing adult prostitutes, sent an email alleging that he'd heard Pepe tell the same story.[6] But were these accounts by Blount and Walters credible?

Prisons are known to be rife with snitches who are out for revenge, seeking an advantage, or trolling for attention. When interviewed for this book on September 13, 2019, Blount was candid about his hope that cooperating with authorities would win him an early release.[7]

"I'm not going to lie to you," said Blount. "I'd like to get a time cut."

Another factor to consider was whether Pepe would talk openly about killing people—especially in front of men half his age who had long criminal histories. Also, alliances in prison often form along racial lines; Walters and Blount are Black while Pepe is White.[8]

But it's also conceivable that Pepe bragged about killing the Bermans in hopes of elevating his jailhouse status or building relationships with prisoners who could protect him. Respect and friendship are two of the most precious commodities in prison, which can mean the difference between hard time and an easier ride, and even between life and death.[9]

Turning to the specifics of Walters's email, the notion that Barry took offense over an offer of hashish seemed unlikely. Among people in Barry's circle, who grew up in the 1960s, marijuana and hashish weren't regarded as offensive, even though drugs were prohibited under Radha Soami's precepts. After all, Barry carried hash in his backpack the first time he visited the dera. But what if Pepe suggested that Louise and Barry do more than just get high with him?

The allegation that Pepe strangled Louise with a coil of tent rope sounded plausible. But when the Inyo County coroner examined the Bermans's remains, he found a woman's hyoid bone. There was no mention in the coroner's report of any damage to it.

The hyoid, a U-shaped bone in the center of the throat, fractures in about 30 percent of strangulation cases. However, breakage is less likely in cases of "ligature strangulation" such as with a rope.[10]

Walters's mention of "natural hot springs" was interesting, because the *LA Weekly* article didn't mention Upper Warm Springs, which was the undeveloped set of hot springs about two miles up the Corridor from Palm Spring. Either Walters made a good guess, or he obtained that information somewhere else.

Walters's reference to "gold bangles" was also intriguing, because the *LA Weekly* article didn't refer to Louise's necklaces. She usually wore two gold-mounted pendants: one a small purple quartz crystal, the other a freshwater pearl. These items of jewelry didn't turn up when sheriff's investigators excavated the grave.

In the end, whether to believe the accounts of Walters and Blount would depend in large measure on their perceived credibility. In connection with this book, I interviewed them, separately, over the phone. To me, both men came across as convincing, but I didn't meet them in person.

They were, however, interviewed by a veteran sheriff's investigator from Inyo County face-to-face, and he reached the same conclusion. This came about because after I started investigating, then-sheriff Bill Lutze in Inyo County decided to have his office review the files again. He assigned the case to Dan Williams, a former college baseball player and longtime criminal investigator who'd grown up in Independence.

"Bill was 100 percent supportive," Williams said when interviewed for this book on November 4, 2017. "He was working here as a lieutenant when it happened. He always wanted resolution."

As Williams read through the case files, he noticed a glaring omission. "There was no homicide investigation," he explained. "There was a missing person report, but after the bodies were found, Cheryl Craycraft got involved and our office never followed up."

Williams set out to rectify the situation. Just as Craycraft did years earlier, he made the rounds to interview witnesses, including Brian Casey, Katy Dunsmuir, Pepe's former wives, and Pepe's longtime best friend Bill Haigler.

Although Williams declined to share details about his findings, he hinted that he'd uncovered fresh information from people close to Pepe. He also confirmed that he'd received valuable assistance from "other agencies" (presumably NCIS) but declined to elaborate.

Williams did confirm that he interviewed Quincy Walters and Daniel Blount at USP Tucson. The veteran investigator sized up the two inmates as "serious people" who had "believable reasons for talking."

After a two-year investigation, Williams completed a homicide report that the sheriff's office forwarded to Inyo County district attorney Thomas Hardy. Shortly afterward Williams retired, but he stayed in close contact with county officials, expecting his report would lead to murder charges being filed against Pepe. He also reached out to Louise's son Michael Westerman.

"Dan Williams let me know what was going on," said Michael. "He was sure it was Pepe. He pointed out all the inconsistencies in the recorded statement."

But on the eve of what would have been Louise Berman's eighty-fourth birthday, DA Hardy sent an email to me and Michael Westerman:

"After my review, I have determined that at this point in time there is not sufficient evidence to file a criminal complaint against Michael Pepe for the deaths of Barry and Louise Berman. While I, along with the investigators involved in the case, believe he is a very likely suspect, the available, admissible evidence could not prove him guilty beyond a reasonable doubt."

Former Inyo County officials, who asked not to be named, said the DA's decision came as no surprise. "Hardy's that way," said one of the former officials. "He doesn't file unless it's a slam dunk."

Because more than thirty years had passed since the Bermans were murdered, and the sheriff's office had invested a huge amount of money and time investigating the case, I felt that there should be full disclosure. I authored an opinion piece that ran in the local paper the *Inyo Register* under the headline, "Berman murders: Press charges or open files." The article argued that "family members, and the public, deserve to know the facts."[11]

But Sheriff Lutze said his office "would not be inclined to release the report . . . as it is still an open homicide case." After Lutze retired, his successors took the same position.

At this juncture, Williams's report detailing the evidence that his homicide investigation uncovered is locked away at the sheriff's office in Inyo County. It's anyone's guess whether the report will ever see the light of day.

***

As Williams completed his report about the Berman murders, another drama played out: in the federal sex crimes case of *USA v. Pepe*. After Judge Fischer sentenced Pepe to 210 years for brutalizing seven underage girls in Cambodia, attorneys for the former professor filed an appeal on his behalf to the 9th Circuit Court of Appeals.[12]

Every convicted criminal is entitled to pursue an appeal, so this wasn't a surprise. The pertinent question was whether Pepe had a realistic chance of overturning the jury's verdict.

Most observers didn't think Pepe had a prayer. Besides the overwhelming evidence of guilt and heinous nature of the crimes, the primary arguments his appellate counsel raised had been considered and rejected in a prior 9th Circuit case, *USA v. Clark*, which arose from strikingly similar facts.[13]

Michael Lewis Clark, a military veteran, maintained a bank account and mailing address in the United States and took occasional trips home, but made Cambodia his primary residence. When Clark got caught in a guesthouse engaged in sex acts with underage boys in Phnom Penh, the Cambodian National Police arrested him, and he was brought to the United States to face federal charges.

After Clark entered a plea bargain, the judge sentenced him to eight years in prison, remarking that the defendant "purchased these children for less money than you pay for a latte here in Seattle."[14] But as part of the agreement Clark preserved his right of appeal, enabling his counsel to argue that the PROTECT Act exceeded Congress's constitutional authority to regulate conduct overseas.

The constitutional "hook" for the PROTECT Act was language in Article I of the US Constitution granting Congress the power "to regulate commerce with foreign nations."[15] Did this language, known as the "foreign commerce clause," give Congress the authority to prohibit an American from paying children in foreign countries to have sex? The 9th Circuit said yes, so long as the government proved the defendant "traveled in foreign commerce."

In Clark, the defendant's most recent travel from the United States to Cambodia occurred less than two months before he got caught with the underage boys. The 9th Circuit concluded that this was sufficient travel to satisfy the statute but said in a footnote, "Whether a longer gap between the travel and the commercial sex act could trigger constitutional or other concerns is an issue we leave for another day."[16]

This footnote created a possible loophole that Pepe's appellate counsel, Deputy Federal Public Defender James Locklin, sought to exploit. Locklin, pale and bespectacled, had the cerebral look of someone who spends long hours in a law library, and he was known as a brilliant and tenacious advocate.

After both sides filed extensive briefs, Pepe's appeal was scheduled for a hearing in February 2017 at the 9th Circuit's courthouse in Pasadena, California.[17] Locklin sat at the table reserved for the appellant's counsel. At the opposite table sat prosecutor Patricia Donahue and a co-counsel, Nancy Spiegel.

Three black-robed judges entered and took their seats on the elevated bench. At stage left sat Jacqueline Hong-Ngoc Nguyen, a Barack Obama appointee with an extraordinary personal history. Born in Vietnam, Nguyen moved to the United States as a ten-year-old after Saigon fell in 1975. For a while, she and her family lived in a tent at Camp Pendleton—the same Marine Corps base where Pepe had been sent to boot camp.

On stage right sat a senior judge, Andrew J. Kleinfeld, at that time age seventy-two. He'd traveled from his chambers in Fairbanks, Alaska, to attend the argument in Pasadena. Judge Kleinfeld, who'd been elevated to the 9th Circuit by George H. W. Bush, had a reputation as a salty conservative with a libertarian streak.

In the middle sat the chief judge of the 9th Circuit, Sidney Runyan Thomas. Chief Judge Thomas, originally from Montana, had been nominated to the court by Bill Clinton. Balding and with a gray beard, Judge Thomas seemed like a Barry Berman type: He didn't say much, but when he did speak, people listened.

When the court called the matter of *USA v. Pepe*, Locklin stepped to the podium. His primary argument: Pepe lived as an expat in Cambodia and wasn't "traveling in foreign commerce" when he raped and abused the seven girls.

In legalese, Locklin said that there wasn't sufficient "nexus" between Pepe's travel and the illicit conduct to satisfy the US Constitution. He also invoked the "rule of lenity," meaning if a criminal statute can be interpreted more than one way, then the interpretation most lenient—in other words, most favorable to the defendant—should be adopted by the court.

After Nancy Spiegel began arguing the travel issue on behalf of the government, Judge Kleinfeld interjected. Remarking that the statutory reference to travel "must mean something," he launched into a hypothetical scenario about a widow collecting life insurance and moving to Belize.

"She's there for ten or twenty years . . . and she has a little affair with a beach boy," posited Kleinfeld. He asked Spiegel if the move to Belize many years earlier counted as "travel" under the PROTECT Act.

Judge Kleinfeld's implausible scenario seemed to catch Spiegel off guard, and she replied in general terms that the statute had no time limit. Kleinfeld pressed his point: "What about my widow and a beach boy. Is she a felon under the statute?"

"Well, it just depends," said Spiegel.

Patricia Donahue, sitting at counsel table, looked concerned as Spiegel continued to argue. Judge Kleinfeld, perhaps sensing weakness in the government's position, kept pressing.

"I want to know if the widow, who's been living in Belize for the ten or twenty years since her husband died . . . gets it on with the beach boy . . . is she a felon under the statute?"[18]

Spiegel replied, "There is no temporal element in this statute."

Judge Nguyen jumped in, asking why the government needed to take such an extreme position. After hearing this from a judge who might have been regarded as sympathetic toward the prosecution, and with more tough questions being fired from the bench, Spiegel reversed course.

"There is a point where it's too attenuated," she conceded.

Judge Thomas spoke up, his measured voice carrying extra force because of his role as chief judge. "Where is that point?" he asked.

Siegel, looking flustered, replied, "It needs to depend on the reasonableness of all the facts in the case."

To observers sitting in the courtroom, this exchange seemed to undermine the government's case because Siegel appeared unsure about the very statute she was supposed to be explaining and defending.

After the oral argument ended, the court took the matter under submission: Rulings on appeal aren't issued from the bench. The government team gathered in the hallway and talked anxiously. Locklin appeared confident as he strode toward the parking lot accompanied by his wife, who'd come to watch her husband in action.

At the 9th Circuit Court of Appeals, the average time between oral argument and decision was forty-five days. But in *USA v. Pepe*, months dragged by without any announcement. When the one-year anniversary of oral argument came and went, still there was no decision.

Finally, in July 2018, the 9th Circuit ruled. The thirty-one-page opinion, authored by Judge Nguyen and joined in by Judge Kleinfeld, vacated Pepe's conviction on the grounds that Judge Fischer gave the jury improper instructions for determining whether Pepe "traveled in foreign commerce."[19]

The two-judge majority held, in essence, that the government needed to prove Pepe was still a traveler when he raped and tortured the underage girls. Because the evidence at trial suggested Pepe was an expat living permanently in Phnom Penh, the government hadn't met its burden of proof. The appellate court vacated his conviction and remanded the case to Judge Fischer.

Chief Judge Thomas dissented, arguing that the Clark case was controlling law and the travel required under the statute occurred when Pepe flew to Cambodia.

Hoping other judges on the 9th Circuit might view the case the same way as Judge Thomas, the government petitioned for a rehearing by an eleven-judge panel instead of only three judges. This gambit, the legal equivalent of a Hail Mary pass, came up short—the petition was denied.[20]

News of the 9th Circuit's decision shocked most observers. Years of legal work and millions of taxpayer dollars had been spent in bringing a serial child rapist to justice. Despite the overwhelming evidence of Pepe's guilt and a unanimous verdict by a jury of his peers, his convictions had been tossed aside.[21] The *Inyo Register* ran a story of mine under the headline, "Suspect in unsolved murders set to be freed."[22]

The government's sole recourse for salvaging Pepe's conviction was to file a petition with the US Supreme Court. I wrote an opinion piece that ran on the front pages of *L.A. Daily Journal* and *San Francisco Daily Journal*—periodicals that are widely read in California's legal community—arguing that the Supreme Court should reverse the 9th Circuit because "travels in foreign commerce" simply meant the defendant traveled to a foreign country, not that the defendant still needed to be a traveler when the illicit sex occurred.[23]

But when the government asked the 9th Circuit for an extension of time so the US solicitor general could decide whether to seek Supreme Court review, the appellate court refused.[24]

The 9th Circuit's evisceration of the sex crimes case against Michael Pepe left many people feeling outraged. "I think it's appalling," said juror Tom Tallone. "It says something about our legal system and how people can get away with things."

"This is unbelievable," said Michael Westerman, after learning that Pepe prevailed on a technical argument about statutory construction. "I hope the feds don't give up after all this effort."

CHAPTER FIFTEEN

Driven to Dominate and Inflict Pain

INSTEAD OF GIVING UP AND SETTING PEPE FREE, THE GOVERNMENT doubled down. One of the ICE officials involved in the case, who asked not to be named because they aren't authorized by the Justice Department to comment publicly, said, "This is a fight to the death."

Within the US Attorney's office, the case was reassigned to Stephanie Christensen, a rising star who'd attended UCLA law school and previously worked for one of Los Angeles's premier law firms.[1] Christensen made a bold move: She abandoned the original charges and filed a new grand jury indictment charging Michael Pepe with two counts of "travel with intent to engage in illicit sexual conduct" and two counts of "aggravated sexual abuse of a child."[2]

Charging Pepe under these statutes meant the government didn't need to prove he was still a traveler when the sexual assaults occurred. But the strategy was risky, because the government now faced a formidable burden: proving Pepe had criminal intent when he departed the United States and flew to Cambodia.

Under counts one and two, the statute required proof that Pepe traveled "for the purpose of engaging in illicit sexual conduct." Counts three and four required proof hc "knowingly crossed a state line with the intent to engage in a sexual act." How would the government convince a jury that Pepe possessed the requisite state of mind?

On the defense side, Charles Brown remained on the case, backed by Howard Shneider, a gregarious public defender who played well in front of juries, and Isabel Bussarakum, a Yale Law School graduate. As often happens in complex criminal cases, after the government filed the new indictment, the defense went on the attack by filing a host of pretrial motions.

In one motion, Pepe's counsel asked Judge Fischer to declare the two statutes unconstitutional and throw the case out. In another motion, the defense argued that Pepe's photos of the girls had been illegally seized and searched and should be excluded from use at trial.[3]

The government matched these moves by bringing in two more top-flight lawyers: Damaris Diaz, a Harvard graduate, and Lynda Lao, who'd spent twelve years working for the FTC in Washington, DC. The reconfigured prosecution team spent long hours researching and writing opposition papers.

Meanwhile, with his convictions vacated, Pepe was once again innocent until proven guilty in the eyes of the law. No longer a felon, he was transferred from USP Tucson into the custody of the US Marshal's office in L.A. While this was still a form of detention, pretrial custody afforded him more privileges and cushier living conditions.

Judge Fischer scheduled the new trial for October 2019, but the defense's flurry of motions consumed many months. Eventually, the judge held a hearing and denied the defense motions. At that point, she continued the trial date until March 2020, admonishing counsel that she wouldn't tolerate further delays.

Then the COVID-19 pandemic struck, upending life around the world and creating massive problems for the US justice system. How could juries be empaneled, witnesses called, and trials held, when doing so would endanger people's lives? Days before Pepe's trial was scheduled to commence, the Central District of California issued an order suspending jury trials until further notice.

Facing no other choice, Judge Fischer continued Pepe's trial to September 2020. As that date approached, and with the pandemic still raging, defense counsel and the government stipulated to another continuance, and the judge agreed. The trial in the case was pushed back nearly a year, to August 2021.

***

Wednesday, August 4, 2021, brought temperate weather to Los Angeles, with clear skies and a temperature in the low seventies—spring-like conditions rather than the usual summertime heat. As a transport van carried Michael Pepe to the courthouse, he could see scenes of everyday life: pedestrians strolling along sidewalks, coffee shops serving morning brew, cars and trucks navigating traffic, workers walking into office buildings.

All that stood between Pepe and the delicious freedom he hadn't tasted since the Cambodian police arrested him back in 2006 was the jury of twelve people that had been empaneled in Judge Fischer's courtroom the day before.

As with the first trial, jury selection had been a chess game. First, the prospective jurors filled out questionnaires that asked about matters such as whether they'd been sexually abused or had any connections to law enforcement.

Next, inside the courtroom, Judge Fischer and counsel for both sides asked follow-up questions. During this process, at least half-a-dozen prospective jurors disclosed information about sexual abuse. Interestingly, in the first trial only one person had done so. Perhaps the #MeToo movement had heightened awareness of the issue and made people more willing to talk about it.

The most powerful account came from a preschool teacher named Maria, talking about one of her students. "A child was a victim of sexual abuse by someone in his family," she explained. "And I saw the damage that that child had and it's very emotional for me. It's very emotional. He was just a five-year-old and it was very sad for me."

Judge Fischer asked Maria if she could set aside her feelings and decide the case based on the facts and the law. Maria shook her head. "I will find it troubling, very troubling, to find somebody who done that innocent," she said.

Judge Fischer dismissed Maria for cause. Other prospective jurors, sitting in the courtroom as she spoke, or watching by video feed, heard Maria's heartfelt words. This could be viewed as a favorable development for the government.

But in the defense's favor, some prospective jurors expressed skepticism about applying US law to conduct in a foreign country. A man named David was outspoken about the subject.

"I'm one who believes that if a crime is committed in another country, that country should be solely responsible for trying that person for that crime," said David. He explained that in his view, bringing charges against someone for conduct abroad was "an overreach of US policy." As with Maria, Judge Fischer dismissed David for cause, but other jurors heard what he said.

Another juror, a man named Frederick who formerly served in the US Navy stood out but not in a good way. He had courtroom observers rolling their eyes. Instead of answering the judge's questions, he rattled on and on.

"Well, I know what goes on in other countries," said Frederick, talking about his travels in Asia. "I even shopped for some stuff to bring my wife from there. You know, it's like cheaper or something. Took a tour of like the river with the shops along there in Bangkok. Just there for one day."

Outside the hearing of the jury, Judge Fischer remarked to counsel, "I can't imagine him being on a jury but I don't know if that's grounds for cause." She asked if the government had anything to say about the issue, "other than he'll never shut up back in the jury room."

Judge Fischer ended up dismissing Frederick for cause, along with several others. She also excused a handful of people because of personal issues like a scheduled surgery or work-related conflict.

After Judge Fischer ruled on the challenges for cause, the lawyers for both sides had an opportunity to use their allotted peremptory challenges to remove prospective jurors they viewed as unfavorable. The defense struck ten people and the government struck six.

By the time the culling process ended, nearly forty people had cycled through Judge Fischer's courtroom to seat a panel of twelve—and this didn't include the alternates.

The next morning, after the transport van carrying Pepe arrived at the courthouse, US marshals shuttled him via wheelchair into courtroom 7D. His health had deteriorated in the thirteen years since the first trial: he suffered from diabetes, morbid obesity, asthma, arthritis, and heart disease. The sixty-seven-year-old defendant took a seat at the defense table, wearing headphones, black-rimmed glasses, and a face mask, and watched as the trial got underway.[4]

Because of COVID-19 restrictions, the jurors sat socially distanced in the spectators' section. Observers, media, and interested parties were relegated to courtroom 9B two floors above, where the proceedings could be viewed by video feed.

When time came for the government's opening statement, Damaris Diaz, a personable woman with five years' experience as a federal prosecutor, stepped to the podium. She told the jury that the government would focus on two trips taken by Pepe while he was living in Cambodia: the first in May 2005 to attend his son Jason's high school graduation in New Mexico, and the second in August–September 2005 to attend his daughter Andrea's wedding, also in New Mexico.

Because Pepe's state of mind would be the key issue in the case, Diaz explained the government's theory in simple terms. She told the jury that when Pepe returned from the United States to his villa in Phnom Penh, his underlying motivation was sexual.

"During this trial, you will learn that in Cambodia you could buy children for sex," said Diaz. "In Cambodia, poor parents sold their daughters to foreigners for sex, and the evidence will show that defendant bought children for sex. It will show that Michael Pepe traveled to Cambodia so that he could rape and sexually abuse little girls."

Speaking on behalf of Michael Pepe, federal defender Isabel Bussarakum, who like Diaz was an ambitious young lawyer with an Ivy League pedigree, unveiled the defense's theme.

"The real issue is: Did Mr. Pepe commit a crime here in the United States when he got on the plane headed to Cambodia in May and September of 2005? The evidence will show that Mr. Pepe did not have the state of mind necessary to be guilty of the charges when he boarded those two flights."

Bussarakum told the jury the evidence would show that by 2005, her client had built a life in Phnom Penh replete with a job, house, wife, and car. "Mr. Pepe is not guilty of these charges because the evidence will show that when he boarded those two flights his purpose was simply to go home, to go home to Cambodia where he had been living since 2003."

The tagline—*going home*—gave the defense a rallying cry it lacked in the first trial. Sometimes all a defense lawyer can do is nitpick the prosecution's evidence, grasping for shreds of doubt. But a defense with a clear theme is much more powerful.

Observers watching the live feed in courtroom 9B fell silent during Bussarakum's opening statement—and some who favored the prosecution became anxious. The argument announced by Bussarakum opened a plausible pathway for Pepe to win acquittal.

***

The following day, the first victim to testify—we've assigned her the pseudonym Rotha—entered the courtroom. She wore a sweater and skirt, her black hair falling to her shoulders, her face protected by a clear shield rather than a mask. The sight of her stunned observers who'd been following the case since the outset and remembered her as a little girl.

The girl Pepe called "Smiley" was nine years old when she was brought to his villa in Toul Kork. When she testified at the first trial, she was one day shy of her twelfth birthday. She was now a graceful twenty-five-year-old who'd been adopted by an American family, educated, and granted US citizenship.

Speaking in lightly accented English, in a voice that was soft but clear, Rotha told the jury how her birth family lived in a shanty built on stilts along the edge of the Mekong River Delta. After the house burned down, the family lived for a while in a tent. Rotha couldn't afford to go to school, and in a place so disadvantaged it was common for underage girls to be sold into the sex trade.

Rotha testified that Michael Pepe's gated compound, situated in an upscale part of town, was an improvement over the squalor of the slums. She described the interior of the villa as having a stairway to the second floor, a balcony where she and the other girls played, "our room" with a shared king bed and stuffed animals, and Pepe's bedchamber down the hall.

"It was nicer than my home," she told the jury. "We had food to eat. We were able to go to school. I like those things."

Rotha identified Pepe by a photograph that was offered into evidence. She told about being taught to perform oral sex on him, and how she serviced him every day. He had a pea-sized bump on his inner thigh. Afterward, he'd tip her one dollar. Sometimes he snapped naked photos. Once they watched a pornographic version of *Snow White*.

"There was no emotion," she said. "I do my job." She explained to the jury that a dollar could buy breakfast for herself and her two little brothers. Besides, said Rotha, she had no choice.

"Where could I run?"

Michael Pepe, sitting at the defense table in a white shirt and black jacket, and flanked by his lawyers, stared helplessly at the "Smiley" who now, with grace and gravitas, had turned into one of his most powerful accusers.

***

The next victim to testify we've called Kanya—she was brought to Pepe's villa by Sang, who she called his "best friend and assistant." Kanya described Pepe as tall and overweight, with light eyes and dark hair. She said he smoked and drank a lot of coffee and tea. She described his demeanor as serious.

"He got angry sometimes," said Kanya. "He could be mean."

Kanya testified that she was twelve years old, prepubescent and a virgin, when Sang brought her to Pepe's villa. Sang instructed her to go into his bedroom and "do whatever he asked me to do."

But Kanya said she struggled as Pepe raped her, even though she'd been given a drink laced with a drug that made her drowsy. Pepe responded by tying her feet and arms to the side of the bed and hitting her in the face until she passed out.

"I woke up with a pool of blood," she told the jury. "I was in pain for a long time, about a week."

Sang warned Kanya that if she didn't behave, she'd get sent to a brothel where she'd be forced to have sex with many men. Sang also said that Kanya should "lay low and stay in the room" when other people visited the villa.

Now, some sixteen years later, having matured into a dignified young woman, Kanya seemed calm and centered as she faced the man who violated her.

"I want him to stay where he is right now in jail," she told the jury.

***

A series of other young women who'd been victimized by Michael Pepe when they were children took the witness stand over the course of three trial days and testified about what happened.

Suong told the jury, "I think it was the third time that he raped me and my thing was torn apart. And at that time I had to go to the hospital and we had to have it stitched up."

Duyen testified that Pepe tied her up and "hit me on my face." Afterward, he raped her. When asked how she felt when this happened, Duyen responded, "A lot of pain."

Thang, who was the little girl spotted by an anti-trafficking investigator in 2006, told the jury why she was thrown out of Pepe's house: When Pepe forced her to give him oral sex, she bit his penis, and when he raped her, she wouldn't stop screaming.

Thang told the jury that at one point she found her way to the balcony and yelled to the neighbors. "I was standing there calling out and ask for help, but the neighbor did not understand me."

***

The testimony about Pepe merging sexual behavior with acts of violence corresponds with what medical professionals have learned about sexual sadism. One team of researchers defined sexual sadism as "behavior and fantasy which is characterized by a wish to control another person through domination, humiliation, or inflicting pain for the purpose of producing sexual arousal."[5]

Reflecting on what happened in January 1986 in Saline Valley, if Pepe killed Barry and Louise, as many people believed, then the question followed whether the alleged murders arose in part from a sadistic sex drive, "an excessive need to control and dominate others," and not merely from an altercation that spiraled out of control.[6]

Deputy Boyer, who had an instinct for truth, felt strongly that Pepe had a sexual motivation. "He'd come alone, hung around, ogled at girls," said the plainspoken lawman. Consistent with this, Katy Aberdeen said that after Pepe returned to Palm Spring campground on January 6, 1986, all dirty and acting nervous, he had sex on his mind.

"He started talking about threesomes," she said. "He told us he'd been in a threesome."

According to Pepe's cellmate Quincy Walters, Pepe bragged about the killings, saying he shot Barry with a handgun, handcuffed Louise to his pickup, finished Barry off with a KA-BAR knife, then strangled Louise with a coil of tent rope.

If Pepe killed the Bermans as Walters alleged, absent a confession there's no way of knowing if he was driven by a desire to dominate and inflict pain, or if he was simply finishing off a fight. But we do know a key fact about Pepe's relationship with his third wife Tatiana, the twenty-something Russian woman.

"Tatiana said Michael was sexually deviant," said Pepe's sister O'Hara. "He hurt her."

Once Pepe's marriage to Tatiana crumbled and he landed in Cambodia, he had the time, background, and financial means to remake his life. He became a professor and began teaching at a university. He moved into a walled villa with a gate guard. He cozied up to Cambodian elites.

What did Pepe want when he built a life of privilege and influence? In her opening statement, Demaris Diaz framed the question this way: "So how do you know what Michael Pepe intended to do in Cambodia? Just look at what he did."

Pepe selected victims who were young, weak, and powerless, and housed them at his villa. Behind the doors of his bedroom, he tied them up and raped them—bloodying the sheets and leaving the girls to suffer. And if they dared to resist, he was ruthless.

In an article about sex crimes, a former NYPD homicide division commander wrote, "Human behavior, though unpredictable, is oftentimes repetitive."[7] Is it possible that the violence Pepe inflicted on the little girls in Cambodia was a repeat of the past—in essence a rerun of what happened to Louise and Barry in Saline Valley?

Chapter Sixteen

Pepe Began Sputtering Questions

Faced with a series of young women who told the jury about being tortured and raped by Pepe, Charles Brown and the defense team made a strategic decision not to attack the testimony directly. In the first trial, Pepe's attorney Carlton Gunn tried that approach and it failed to resonate—or even to spark a serious discussion. Recall what juror Tom Tallone said: It only took the jurors "about twelve minutes" to convict him.

Since then, the situation for the defense had only gotten worse. Besides the fact that the victims were now grown women who delivered forceful testimony in well-spoken English, the #MeToo movement had altered societal perspective on the dynamics of sexual abuse. No longer would it be an effective technique to show a child rape victim a photo taken by Pepe while she was playing, and remark, "It looks like you're having fun there."

This time around, the defense team declined to ask any questions of Kanya. As for Rotha, they gently cross-examined her about dates when the events took place, suggesting because she was so young at the time, there might be some doubt. This could help defuse the theory that Pepe was intending to have illicit sex when he flew back to Cambodia in May and September 2005. Indeed, for the most part the victims' testimony involved assaults by Pepe in 2006—months after he took the two trips that were the focus of the government's case. The same was true about the digital photos recovered from his devices: the metadata revealed that most of the pictures were taken after May and September 2005.

Because of this, uncertainty began to form about the government's case. Was the fact that the lion's share of the evidence concerned actions taken by Pepe in 2006 sufficient to raise reasonable doubt about whether Pepe had criminal intent in 2005, when he boarded the return flights at LAX?

After the government rested its case, the defense called its first witness, Richard Williams, the retired law enforcement officer who was married to Pepe's favorite sister Elaine.

As Deputy Federal Defender Isabel Bussarakum began direct examination of Williams, the purpose of her questions soon became clear: to show the jury that when Pepe traveled back to Cambodia in 2005, he was simply *going home.*

Williams testified that when he and his wife Elaine visited Pepe in 2004, they found the part-time professor enjoying a "definitely upper-class" lifestyle. Pepe's Toul Kork villa was, Williams said, "ten times better, if not more," than the places he'd lived in the United States.

Williams recited the relevant facts: Pepe owned a Jeep SUV; he taught at Pannasastra University; he attended a local Catholic church; he volunteered at the veterans' association; he carried a Cambodian driver's license; and he had an account at a Phnom Penh bank.

Williams testified that when Pepe visited the United States in 2005 for his son's graduation and daughter's wedding, the retired Marine Corps captain routinely called Nary, who was in Cambodia, and talked with her for long periods of time.

Pepe's intent, Williams told the jury, was to fly home to his wife and his house in Cambodia and live there for the rest of his life:

Q. Did Mr. Pepe ever communicate to you any plans to move back to the United States?

A. No.

Q. And based on your observations, was Cambodia Mr. Pepe's home?

A. Yes.

Ms. Bussarakum: No further questions, Your Honor.

When Pepe's sister Elaine took the witness stand, she echoed her husband's words about her brother's life in Cambodia. She testified that Michael lived with Nary, taught at the university, and did charitable work distributing school supplies to children. Pepe's lawyer Howard Shneider asked:

Q. Based on your trip in 2004, and based on all of your communications with your brother, did he intend to stay in Cambodia long term?

A: He intended to be living there permanently.

The defense's next witness, former Cambodian prime minister Ung Huot, testified by video conference from Melbourne, Australia, where he lived part of the time. He told the jury about collaborating with Pepe to launch an "executive training program" in Cambodia. This paved the way for Shneider to ask:

Q. How long do you think it would have taken to get the program up and running?

A. I think it could be about a few months, maybe a year.

Q. Okay. What about, though, to see the program fully developed. How long would that take?

A. Many years. Five, ten years, who knows.

The defense also called two of Pepe's children as witnesses. First came Jason Pepe, thirty-four, a solar salesman living in New Mexico. Jason testified about his high school graduation in 2005, when his dad flew in from Cambodia. Howard Shneider asked:

Q. While your dad was at Rio Rancho for your graduation, at some point did he ask you to live with him in Cambodia?

A. He did, yes. He invited me to live out there. He said I was eighteen now, and I could live, you know, where I wanted to and explore the world. . . . I thought about it a little bit, but ultimately I decided it probably wasn't for me. . . .

Q. Did he come back—I think he mentioned for your sister Andrea's wedding as well?

A. That's right, yes . . .

Q. After your dad came out to New Mexico for your sister's wedding, did he go back to his home in Cambodia?

A. Yeah. That is my understanding, he went back then as well.

The final defense witness was Pepe's daughter Andrea Morales, forty, who also worked in the solar business in New Mexico. Morales told the jury that after her dad retired from the Marine Corps, his standard of living declined.

"He seemed to move where he could find a job," she said. "He always lived in one-bedroom apartments, studio apartments, not always in the nicest places."

According to Morales, in Cambodia her dad enjoyed a much better lifestyle. He landed a teaching job. He went on trips to explore the countryside. He met and married Nary. "He was happy, he was excited. He was in love."

Isabel Bussarakum asked Morales about her father's trip to Albuquerque to attend her wedding:

Q. After attending your wedding, did your dad return home?

A. He did . . .

Q. In 2005, did your dad tell you he had plans to stay in Cambodia long term?

A. I mean that was—that's what we felt was going to happen. There wasn't a conversation, it's just that sort of what his life was.

Q. Based on your conversations and interactions with your dad, was Cambodia his home?

A. Yes.

Following this exchange about Michael Pepe *going home*, the defense rested.

The next morning, Judge Fischer instructed the jury about the law they should apply when deciding the case. The judge spent a long time reading the jury instructions aloud—they were written in legalese that wasn't easy to understand. But the judge also said that the instructions would be available in the jury room for their reference.

The prosecution and defense teams knew that the jurors, once alone in their room, might read the instructions and talk about what they meant. This often happened in jury trials once the jury retired to deliberate. As the discussion got underway in the awkward early moments, the jurors would begin combing through evidence and instructions, trying to find answers.

Because of this well-known dynamic, both sides realized that the precise language of the jury instructions could be critical to the outcome. Prior to trial, the prosecution and defense had sparred about what the jury should and shouldn't be told. Everyone knew that even a single word or phrase might end up swaying the outcome.

Three of the instructions were of key importance. One was a standard instruction about the government's burden to prove its case beyond a reasonable doubt: "Proof beyond a reasonable doubt is proof that leaves you firmly convinced the defendant is guilty."

The phrase *firmly convinced* was important for Pepe's defense. Given that intent was a pivotal element of the charges against him, and given that it wasn't possible to read Pepe's mind, would the government's evidence leave the jury *firmly convinced* he had criminal intent when he traveled from the United States to Cambodia in May and September 2005?

But the government had one advantage: it wasn't required to prove that sex with underage girls was Pepe's sole reason for traveling back to Cambodia. Instead, the jury instructions recognized that a person might have various reasons for traveling.

For the First and Second Counts of the indictment, jury instruction 23 set the standard. It said that the government needed to prove that a "dominant, significant, or motivating purpose" of Pepe's travel was to engage in illicit sexual conduct.

For the Third and Fourth Counts of the indictment, the government's burden was slightly different: proving beyond a reasonable doubt that Pepe "crossed a state line with the intent to engage in a sexual act with a person who was under the age of 12 years." However, the government didn't need to prove that Pepe had a specific victim in mind.

***

Language from these instructions played a central role in the closing arguments. For the government, Stephanie Christensen stepped to the podium, and in a crisp voice, she addressed the panel of women and men.

"How do you know what someone intended to do? You look at what they did."

Illustrating her argument with a PowerPoint presentation, Christensen showed photos of the underage girls Pepe allegedly abused, and said, "This was his dominant, significant, or motivating purpose for his travel in 2005. In Cambodia, you could buy children for sex."

Christensen moved through images of Pepe's travel itineraries, his villa in Toul Kork, and the children who lived there. Weaving words and images into a seamless flow, Christensen kept hammering home her argument about intent.

"This is jury instruction 23. I encourage you to read it when you get back there because you might have been surprised given defense counsel's opening statement claiming that if defendant was flying home, as she called it, somehow, he's not guilty of a crime.

"Not so. Don't be fooled. A person can have multiple purposes for travel. They can have multiple motives for travel, and each may prompt in varying degrees the act of making the journey.

"What we have to prove as the government is that beyond a reasonable doubt that illicit sexual conduct was a dominant, significant, or motivating purpose of his travel to Cambodia in 2005. And it was. Sexually abusing those little girls was defendant's everyday life. It was his dominant, significant, or motivating purpose."

By the end of Christensen's argument—confidently delivered and compelling in its reasoning—the defense faced an uphill battle. In less than an hour, the talented assistant US attorney had buttressed the government's case point by point and directly attacked the defense's theme that Pepe was simply *going home.*

When Deputy Federal Public Defender Howard Shneider stepped to the podium to argue on behalf of Michael Pepe, he began by acknowledging the abuse suffered by the victims.

"We're not here to say otherwise," he said. "There's a reason we did not cross-examine any of the women who came to tell their stories about the sex acts in Cambodia."

The personable defender told the jury that he understood the range of emotions they must have felt during the trial: "Sympathy, empathy, compassion for the women who told their stories. Maybe sadness, anger."

But he urged the jury to "follow the court's instructions and put your emotions to the side." Shneider told the jury they were duty-bound to decide the case based on a strict application of the law to the facts.

"The government is required to prove to you what was going on inside Mr. Pepe's mind when he was on those flights in Los Angeles on the tarmac in May and September of 2005. Mr. Pepe's purpose was to *go home,* to go back to his life in Cambodia . . . in Cambodia where he had lived since March of 2003. Cambodia, where he had a job. Cambodia, where he had a wife. Cambodia, where he had all of his belongings.

"Cambodia was his home and that was his purpose for getting on those flights."

***

The bailiff led the jury down the hall to a vacant courtroom, where they could spread out the exhibits on conference tables and sit in a socially distanced circle during the discussion. Meanwhile, the bailiff stood post just outside the door, ensuring that no one could interfere in the deliberations.

The jury's first order of business was selecting a foreperson. After a few people said they weren't interested, someone looked at Juror #2 and asked, "How about you?"

Cody Hoffman, then twenty-nine, agreed to assume the role, but when interviewed for this book on August 13, 2021, said that he felt the pressure of being put in such a weighty position. Hoffman decided to use the same sort of methodical approach he applied in his environmental science work for the California state park system. He took out the verdict form, and based on the questions presented by the judge, began working with his colleagues to arrive at the answers.

Unlike in the first trial, the jury's deliberation wasn't a short process. They devoted a long afternoon to the issue of Pepe's state of mind.

"The crux was intent," Hoffman said afterward. "We spent a lot of time really going through the prosecution and defense's evidence. We wanted to make sure we had no doubts."

Late in the day, Hoffman called for an informal vote. "We were all on the same page. I said, let's sleep on it."

Early the following morning, the jury resumed deliberations. "Some people wanted to look at the evidence," said Hoffman. "I thought about the film *12 Angry Men*."[1]

At last, everyone agreed it was time to take a vote. Hoffman led the jury through the five-page verdict form, and as the jury voted, he checked the applicable boxes. At 10:05 a.m., he handed the bailiff a preprinted form, indicating that the jury had reached a unanimous verdict.

Judge Fischer summoned the lawyers, and federal marshals went to fetch Michael Pepe. Because I'd written a letter to Judge Fischer asking to be present for the verdict, she allowed me to don a face mask and take a seat in the courtroom, which faced the defendant.

The bailiff led the jury back down the hall to courtroom 7D. Hoffman, who worked part time as a conditioning coach, said later, "My heart rate was higher."

After Judge Fischer asked, "Who is our foreperson," Hoffman identified himself. The judge instructed him to give the verdict form to the bailiff. "It was now out of my hands," said Hoffman later.

Judge Fischer reviewed the form and then read the verdict aloud, count by count: "We, the jury in the above-entitled cause, unanimously find the defendant Michael Joseph Pepe guilty as charged."

Sitting at the defense table, Pepe blinked rapidly and his face reddened. He watched as the judge polled the seven women and five men, asking each of them, "Are those your verdicts?"

After every juror said yes, Judge Fischer excused them. "Members of the jury, you've now completed your service as jurors on the case; and on behalf of the United States District Court and all of us here, I want to thank you for giving your time and efforts to the administration of justice in this community."

Once the jurors departed, Judge Fischer scheduled a sentencing hearing. When she left the courtroom, two marshals emerged from a side door with Pepe's wheelchair. As the disappointed defendant stood up, he said to his attorneys, "I'm not really surprised."[2]

***

On Valentine's Day 2022, exactly sixteen years after Michael Pepe purchased a little girl to bring to his villa as a celebratory treat, federal marshals transported him from a secure nursing home facility to First Street Courthouse, then wheeled him into Judge Fischer's courtroom. It was mostly empty. Unlike at trial, there weren't any family members or friends there to support him.

None of the victims attended—their work was finished. Despite having been subjugated and abused, despite the efforts by Pepe and Sander De Montero to silence them, and despite being forced to face their abuser and his attorneys not once but twice in open court, they'd somehow found the courage to persevere.

Now they were off living their lives. According to Don Brewster, some of the young women have decided to focus their careers on helping other survivors of sexual abuse.

Pepe sat at the defense table flanked by his lawyers. His hair was gray, as were his mustache and goatee. His standard-issue clothing was also gray: a simple pullover, cheap trousers, and plastic slip-on shoes. His hands were in cuffs, shackled to a chain around his waist.

A presentencing report had been prepared for Judge Fischer, and both sides had submitted briefs. The defense argued for a sentence of twenty-five years, saying Pepe's "age and feeble health mitigate against the imposition of a sentence of death in prison."

The prosecution countered that Pepe's health problems didn't stop him from "taking Viagra and drugging, beating, and raping children on a near daily basis in Cambodia." The government's position was that Pepe should be sentenced to 210 years—the same as before.

After a few minutes of dispassionate oral arguments by counsel, Judge Fischer pronounced the sentence. She read a statement rejecting the defense's contention that a life sentence would be unduly harsh.

"Mr. Pepe confined numerous preteen girls in his home under conditions that weren't merely unduly harsh; they were torture. Compared to the horrors he inflicted on these children, his life in prison does not come close to being unduly harsh."

Judge Fischer imposed a maximum of thirty years on each of the first two counts. On The Third and Fourth Counts, the maximum allowable was life in prison, but Stephanie Christensen cautioned the judge against giving Pepe a life sentence, saying this could open the door to a legal challenge that the sentencing was vindictive.

Judge Fischer heeded the government's advice and settled on a sentence of 210 years on each of the Third and Fourth Counts, and she ruled that all four terms would run concurrently. This meant the 210-year total matched exactly with the outcome of the first trial.[3]

After Judge Fischer adjourned the hearing and left the courtroom, a discussion ensued between Pepe's counsel and one of the marshals, who explained that imposition of sentence meant Pepe would be transferred from pretrial custody of the US Marshal's office to long-term custody of the Bureau of Prisons—perhaps that very day.

Upon hearing this news, Pepe seemed agitated, asking if he'd be placed in a Level 4 care facility, which is reserved for the most severe medical cases and offers more comfortable living conditions.[4] The marshal shrugged, saying this decision would be left to BOP.

Pepe began sputtering questions about what would happen to him now. The marshals responded by sitting him down in his wheelchair and rolling him out the side door.

When retired deputy Leon Boyer learned about the outcome of Pepe's sentencing, his response was simple and enthusiastic: "That's great news!" Michael Westerman, the sole surviving immediate family member of Barry and Louise Berman, likewise breathed a sigh of relief.

"It has been a long road," he said. "Finally, it's done."

Conclusion

Near the beginning of this project, I drove into Saline Valley to hunt for Barry and Louise's gravesite. After making a right turn where Bat Rock used to be, I crossed the valley floor and parked my old Toyota 4Runner at Palm Spring campground, intending to sleep there for the night and drive up the Corridor first thing in the morning.

It was late spring, well past the high season, and with temperatures approaching ninety degrees. I was the only one in camp. I stripped off my dusty clothes, settled into Wizard Pool, and popped a cold beer. It was a moment of tranquility in one of my all-time favorite places.

But when the sun dipped toward the horizon, the wind kicked up and sand began to blow. As the sandstorm intensified, the sky turned blood red. Soon the Inyo Mountains vanished from view.

When night fell the wind shrieked and moaned. Palm fronds rattled overhead like loose storm shutters. Then bats appeared, dozens of them, darting and diving over Wizard Pool, and brushing past my wet scalp.

As blowing sand stung my face, I wondered if this is what happens when you investigate an unsolved double homicide. Had I stirred up demons?

But by dawn the sky was clear, and the wind had eased to a whisper. I threw open the doors of the 4Runner, and in the back where I'd slept, I propped against a pillow and began writing notes.

I might've lounged there all morning, pecking at my laptop, except a pair of songbirds came dancing into view, and I thought about Barry and Louise. It was time to get on with it.

Many years have passed since that trip into Saline Valley, and now I've written what I found. Maybe someday new information will emerge, or maybe not. Perhaps the Inyo County Sheriff's Office will release Dan Williams's homicide report, but I'm not holding my breath. Although I haven't given up hope that Michael Pepe will eventually grant me an interview, his sister Andrea says that will never happen.

So is this really the end of the Berman case, even though not all the questions have been answered?[1]

Because Michael Westerman says he feels a sense of closure, I suppose that's good enough for me. As for Barry and Louise, I'd like to believe their spirits live on like the pair of songbirds—dancing, singing, and reminding us to get on with it.

NOTES

CHAPTER ONE

1. Tom Ganner's "The Saline Valley Chronicles" was a key source of information about the culture and geology of Saline Valley. "Major Tom" was also involved in some of the events reported on in this book. See "The Saline Valley Chronicles," Time & Space Nature Adventures, accessed May 5, 2018, https://timenspace.net/saline-valley-chronicles/.

2. The author's website includes copies of official reports from the Inyo County Sheriff's Office, including items not previously made public. However, the sheriff's office withheld some key documents. See www.dougkariauthor.com.

3. See W. A. Chalfant. *The Story of Inyo* (self-pub.,1980).

4. "[I]n its infancy, Inyo County experienced its share of violence. Territorial and mining claims were often disputed, and in some cases, the disputes ended tragically. There are many reports of shootings in the mining towns, robberies on the open, desolate highways, and drunken brawls in the townships. Many crimes went unreported because, as mentioned in some historical accounts, local citizens did not want to inconvenience the sheriff because of the great distance he had to travel. The sheriff and his deputies (and there were very few deputies) had to be brave, tough and resourceful. One colorful story speaks of how several men were discovered 'stealing ropes with horses attached' in an Inyo County township and were later found hanging from telegraph poles. It was assumed the men committed suicide" (Inyo County, n.d., "A Brief History of the Inyo County Sheriff's Office," https://www.inyocounty.us/services/sheriff).

5. To place the time frame in historical context, 1986 was one year into Ronald Reagan's second term as president. Reagan's image as a bastion of old-fashioned American values had resonated in rural Inyo County, and on Election Day 1984 he'd garnered 5,863 votes, representing more than 70 percent of the total ballots cast. There was also a local connection, because many county residents still remembered seeing Reagan, back in 1974 when he was California's governor, riding on horseback in the Mule Days parade.

6. Chicago shut out the LA Rams 24–0, and New England beat Miami 31–14.

7. Quotation marks indicate that the words were said to or overheard by me, made in a recorded statement, written in a letter or email, or quoted in a newspaper article.

8. Ganner (see note 1), points out that a valley typically has a stream or river running through it, but Saline Valley is a basin, making it more a "bolson" in a geological sense. Per https://www.britannica.com/science/bolson, a "bolson" (from Spanish *bolsón,* "large

purse"), is "a semiarid, flat-floored desert valley or depression, usually centered on a playa or salt pan and entirely surrounded by hills or mountains."

9. Millions of years ago, much of Inyo County was submerged. See Christopher Norment, *Relicts of a Beautiful Sea: Survival, Extinction, and Conservation in a Desert World* (Durham: University of North Carolina Press, 2014), describing how, in a handful of isolated habitats, ancient aquatic species such as salamanders and pupfish still manage to survive.

10. Over the years, Bat Rock was painted and repainted in various color schemes, often with a bat depicted in angular black and the underlying rock in green or white. The National Park Service buried Bat Rock after gaining jurisdiction over Saline Valley in 1994.

11. The history of the hot springs scene is subject to differences of recollection and opinion. Besides Ganner (see note 1), a key source of historical information about Saline Valley was Timothy A. Dahlia, *Saline Valley History* (self-pub, 2019).

12. Near Saline Lake was a site where members of the Ko'ongkatün Band of Timbisha Shoshone once lived in an agricultural village, holding onto a parcel of their homeland for decades after the end of the "Indian War," as settlers called it, and establishment of Inyo County, in 1866. But in 1952, the last of the Timbisha in Saline Valley were driven out by a fight over water rights. The fight began after Ambrose "Monty" Monteith acquired a mining claim at the mouth of Hunter Canyon, overlooking the Timbisha village. Monteith, a former enlisted man who called himself "Colonel," was a swindler who'd done time in San Quentin prison. Monteith dammed a stream that the Timbisha used to irrigate their farmland, his plan being to create a scenic pond and build vacation cabins. To guard the place that Monteith dubbed "Camp Vega," he recruited a young man named Johnny Chavez off the mean streets of east LA. Monteith's water grab spurred a pair of Shoshone teenagers to confront Chavez. According to the boys, Chavez ran them off at knifepoint. The next day the youngsters returned with a rifle and shot Chavez. After he retreated to a cabin, the boys lit the building afire. Chavez perished and the Timbisha boys were arrested on murder charges. See "Indian Boys Admit Slaying Caretaker," Ventura Star-Free Press, February 19, 1952.

13. See Harlan D. Unrau, "A History of the Lands Added to Death Valley National Monument by the California Desert Protection Act of 1994," September 1977, Death Valley National Park Special History Study.

14. According to Ganner (see note 1), the tub was installed by the Civilian Conservation Corps in the 1930s at the same time a dirt road was bulldozed into Saline Valley.

15. "The Inyo Mountains forming the western boundary of Saline Valley have the steepest relief of any mountain range in the United States," Ganner, "The Saline Valley Chronicles."

16. In the early years, visitors sometimes soaked in the natural hot springs. But after the water was piped in for use in bathing, drinking, cooking, and washing dishes, the "source pools" became off limits. Ganner writes in "The Saline Valley Chronicles": "There was only one rule that I can remember. Do not soak in the source."

17. According to Ganner in "The Saline Valley Chronicles, "Sunshine was a hippie from San Francisco who, around 1968, crafted the peace sign using a rake."

18. See Martin Forstenzer, "A Fine Soak That Treats Body and Soul: Hippies discovered the Saline Valley hot springs in the 1960s. Today's eclectic users say the experience is worth the trip on 50 miles of bad road," *LA Times* (quoting then-sergeant Dan Lucas from the Inyo County Sheriff's Office), November 24, 1992, https://www.latimes.com/archives/la-xpm-1992-11-24-mn-1136-story.html.

19. The tradition among hot springs regulars was to use nicknames or "handles," reportedly because some might be running from the law.

20. According to Ganner in "The Saline Valley Chronicles," a local resident named Dan Roman gave the radio to Chili Bob. Roman owned a convenience store along Highway 395 in Olancha.

21. Some sources refer to the campground as "Palm Springs" (plural) rather than "Palm Spring" (singular).

22. Lucas's marching orders were delivered by Lieutenant Bill Lutze, who was later elected sheriff of Inyo County. While Lutze was sheriff, he directed his office to cooperate with the author's investigation.

23. Dorsey ended up being voted out of office in 1990. Several years later he was convicted on multiple counts arising from embezzlement of more than $100,000 in "special funds" that had been earmarked for the fight against narcotics. See Bennett Kessler, "Sentence of Ex-Sheriff Fuels Anger," *LA Times*, April 9, 1996, https://www.latimes.com/archives/la-xpm-1996-04-09-mn-56457-story.html.

24. For a copy of Sergeant Lucas's report on the Berman case, see www.dougkariauthor.com.

25. Lucas's report listed the five SAR team members as Pat Elliott, Bob West, Bob Wilson, Guy Godfrey, and BLM ranger Bruce Albert.

26. A washboard dirt road results from passing vehicles bouncing up and down. Over time, the bouncing shapes the dirt into a washboard pattern, which makes for rough and rattly driving.

27. At that time, there were two spur roads leading from Saline Valley Road to the hot springs. The spur road that most visitors used was Bat Rock Road, also called North Warm Springs Road. Farther south, a rough and often muddy spur road known as Artesian Road or South Warm Springs Road skirted past tamarisk trees near Saline Lake. Nowadays, Artesian Road is closed to vehicles.

28. The Corridor crosses over Steel Pass, elevation 5,111 feet, and descends the gorge that nowadays is called Dedeckera Canyon. The rocky canyon derived its name from *Dedeckera eurekensis*, a rare flowering plant first identified by the late Mary DeDecker of Independence, a self-taught botanist who became the leading authority on native plants of the California desert. Mary once told the author a story about hiking alone in the Eureka Dunes when an eagle flew overhead, carrying a kill in its talons. A small bird was pestering the eagle, so the eagle dropped its kill, which landed at Mary's feet. It was a great horned owl. "That must've been an interesting few minutes when the eagle took the owl," said Mary. See "Steel Pass," DeathValley.com, accessed September 12, 2021, https://www.deathvalley.com/index.php/exploring-death-valley/backcountry-4x4/326-steel-pass.

29. Desert dry washes are stream beds formed by intermittent rainfall. Cutbanks, also called river cliffs, form along the outside edge of the stream beds.

Chapter Two

1. Lucas's report says that SAR team member Pat Elliott had a camper-type key that was used to unlock the pickup's camper shell.

2. One camera was 35mm, while the other was an Instamatic point-and-shoot camera that used 126 film cartridges—a popular camera during the latter half of the twentieth century. See https://ohio5.contentdm.oclc.org/digital/collection/artifacts/id/575/ (information about Instamatic cameras).

3. See Mike Renta, "Operation Reports," China Lake Mountain Rescue Group (operations report for the Berman search and rescue effort), May 1986, https://www.clmrg.org/taluspile/tp%20065.pdf.

4. A sheriff's investigative report identified the pharmacy as "Wilson's," which is presumed to mean Dwayne's Friendly Pharmacy, owned by Dr. Dwayne Wilson. See https://www.facebook.com/dwaynespharmacy/.

5. See Renta, "Operation Reports" (identifying the group's participants in the search by last name: Renta, Green, Jones, Mitchell, Gleason, Geyer, Ingle, McDowell, Silverman, Hill, Roberts, Roseman, Rockwell, Burge, and Ringrose).

6. By this time, using a spare set of keys discovered inside the cab, the pickup had been moved to the search and rescue base camp, which was located above Lower Warm Springs.

7. See "Bodies of long-missing Reagan neighbors found at Saline Valley," *Inyo Register*, November 16, 1988) (quoting a story from years earlier).

8. The cabin was built by a longtime prospector named Roy "Red" Braden, and veteran Saliners referred to it as "Braden's Cabin" rather than "Wolfman's Cabin."

9. Says Tom Ganner, "Wolfman was a rather nefarious personality who was never a welcome visitor to camp." See "The Saline Valley Chronicles," Time & Space Nature Adventures, accessed February 28, 2018, https://timenspace.net/saline-valley-chronicles/.

10. A copy of the report is available at www.dougkariauthor.com.

11. See Richard A. Brook, "Inferences Regarding Aboriginal Hunting Behavior in the Saline Valley, Inyo County, California," *Journal of California and Great Basin Anthropology*, 2, no. 1 (1980) (stating that the structure was likely built sometime after 1931).

12. Ruth stayed home in Beverly Hills. "Mrs. Berman wasn't the kind you would imagine going out camping—ever," said Dinnes.

13. I made numerous attempts to reach Nixon for comment but never received a response.

14. In April 1987, seven members of China Lake Mountain Rescue Group followed up on a tip from two dowsers who claimed to have pinpointed the location of the Bermans' bodies in Saline Valley. Nothing came of this effort. See Mike Renta, "Operations Reports," China Lake Mountain Rescue Group, June 1987, https://www.clmrg.org/taluspile/tp%20071.pdf.

Chapter Three

1. Satguru in Sanskrit means a "true guru"—an enlightened spiritual guide as opposed to a mere teacher.

2. The quote is from a Beverly Hills High School alumni page, and the author also interviewed Ziegler. See https://www.bhhs1968.com/class_profile.cfm?member_id =383751.

3. On January 3, 1986, Reagan met with Mexican president Miguel de la Madrid in Mexicali. See Reagan Foundation (January 3, 1986). "White House Diaries," Ronald Reagan Presidential Foundation & Institute, accessed May 10, 2023, https://www .reaganfoundation.org/ronald-reagan/white-house-diaries/diary-entry-01031986/.

4. Love was a longtime friend of Arthur Korb, who in turn was one of Barry's close friends.

5. See "Woman lost as storm sweeps car down creek," *Santa Barbara News-Press*, January 24, 1983.

6. When interviewed for this book, Joseph Ehret, who formerly managed the ranch for Jules, said El Capitan was mainly a horse ranch but also included agricultural land where Jules planted nine hundred acres of avocados.

7. Unless otherwise noted, quotes from Jules Berman are from his oral history. See "Interview of Jules Berman," 1996, Entrepreneurs of the West, UCLA Oral History Program, Center for Oral History Research, Charles E. Young Research Library, https:// oralhistory.library.ucla.edu/catalog/21198-zz0008zqjm.

8. During the twentieth century, Schenley was one of the largest liquor companies in the United States. The company's headquarters, staffed by more than eight hundred employees, occupied five floors of the Empire State building, making Schenley the largest tenant employer in residence. See ScotchWhiskey.com (Schenley Industries), https:// scotchwhisky.com/whiskypedia/5996/schenley-industries/.

9. See Leonard Sloane, "Jules Berman Returns to Liquor Business," *New York Times*, December 29, 1981.

10. Jules originally co-owned the Kahlua brand, but his partner disagreed with Jules's strategy of reinvesting profits into marketing, so Jules bought his partner out. Given the subsequent success of Kahlua, Jules's former partner likely regretted the decision. "I bet that guy pooped in his pants for years to come," remarked Jules's former secretary Valerie Dinnes when interviewed for this book on September 6, 2021.

11. See Myrna Oliver, "J. Berman; 'Mr. Kahlua' Was Developer, Donor," *LA Times*, July 22, 1998, https://www.latimes.com/archives/la-xpm-1998-jul-22-mn-6063-story.html.

12. Jules bought the hunting preserve, located on Goose Lake, along with Robert W. Prescott, founder of the air cargo service Flying Tigers, which was later merged into Federal Express. See Wikipedia (Robert William Prescott), https://en.wikipedia.org/wiki /Robert_William_Prescott.

13. See "Television Highlights," *San Bernardino Sun*, August 5, 1964.

14. See "Ranch Bought for $4 Million," *San Bernardino Sun*, February 3, 1965.

15. When Ruth was a girl, Switzerland was home to scores of finishing schools where wealthy families sent their daughters to learn English riding, French, and European manners—skills considered essential for upper-class girls. See Alice Gregory, "Lessons

from the Last Swiss Finishing School," *The New Yorker*, October 1, 2018. Les Fougeres, a well-known boarding school operated by Mssr. and Mme, Chaubert-Félix, was located in Lausaane on the shores of Lake Geneva. See NotreHistoire (photo of Les Fougères), https://notrehistoire.ch/entries/KgQYAml2Ywv.

16. Many boys of Barry's era learned the basics of electronics by building a Heathkit. See Lou Frenzel, "Heathkit: An Employee's Look Back," November 30, 2020, https://www.electronicdesign.com/blogs/contributed-blogs/archive/communiqu/article/21148923/electronic-design-heathkit-an-employees-look-back.

17. "The ultimate example of modern youth rebellion, however, would have to be the counterculture of the 1960s. And to a certain degree, this is simply the classic story of young people lashing out against the values and goals of their parents—only, in this case, the behaviors of these hippies were, to put it lightly, a bit more extreme." See Paul Swendson, "The Ultimate Generation Gap of the 1960s." Soapboxie, October 19, 2022, https://soapboxie.com/social-issues/The-Ultimate-Generation-Gap-of-the-1960s.

18. See Rob A. Campbell, "L.A. STORIES: Uncovering a History as Wild as the Canyon Itself," *LA Times*, November 8, 1995, https://www.latimes.com/archives/la-xpm-1995-11-08-ls-691-story.html.

19. Dr. Judy Sund, a professor specializing in art of the Americas who interviewed Jules Berman, wrote that "the deliberate and unacknowledged vulgarization of another culture's funerary goods—to commercial ends—might be categorized as appropriation of a particularly imperialist and exploitative sort." See Judy Sund, "The Preke Speaks: Kahlua's Co-option of West Mexican Burial Effigies," *Visual Resources*, vol. 16.

20. See "State Commissioners turn down Clay license," *Redlands Daily Facts*, July 13, 1967.

21. A British magazine called *The Spectator* said in 1971: "Not for nothing is the youth culture characterized by sex, drugs and rock 'n' roll." See Alan Cross, "Where Did the Phrase 'Sex, Drugs and Rock'n'Roll' Actually Come From?" *Journal of Musical Things*, April 6, 2016, https://www.ajournalofmusicalthings.com/phrase-sex-drugs-rocknroll-actually-come/.

22. School records show that Barry attended Cal Poly from September 1969 to June 1970. In between graduation from high school and starting college, Barry and a friend took a long road trip around the western United States and into Canada.

23. Mary later received a master's degree in psychology and a master's degree in acupuncture and Chinese herbal medicine. She began her career by studying polarity therapy—a term coined by Randolph Stone, an osteopath who founded the practice. See Life Energy Institute, "About Polarity Therapy" accessed June 9, 2020, https://psychcentral.com/health/polarity-therapy.

24. See Sandip Roy, "50 years in, India is celebrating the Beatles' infamous trip to the country," TheWorld, March 5, 2018, https://theworld.org/stories/2018-03-05/50-years-india-celebrating-beatles-infamous-trip-country.

25. The Beatles arrived in India with much hoopla, bringing along a celebrity entourage that included Mike Love of the Beach Boys and the actress Mia Farrow. Within weeks, all four band members departed in disillusionment, amid allegations the guru made a sexual overture to Farrow. See Molly Langmuir, "Mia Farrow Takes an Unflinching Look

at Her Past in the Wake of the #MeToo Movement," *Elle*, October 10, 2018, https://www
.elle.com/culture/movies-tv/a23653929/mia-farrow-women-in-hollywood-me-too/.

26. Katherine Wason, a Radha Soami devotee, wrote: "Quietly and modestly He sat
there, as would any ordinary man, yet the deliverance of hundreds of thousands of souls
rested on His shoulders. Only three feet away from me sat the Living Lord," Katherine
Wason, *The Living Master* (RSSB: 1966), 160.

27. See Jack O. Baldwin, "Rare Horses Come to U.S.," *Long Beach Independent*, May
5, 1970.

28. Jules filed suit, claiming thousands of signatures should be invalidated because the
UCSB students weren't permanent county residents. After a painstaking review, a judge
upheld eight thousand signatures, enough to qualify the referendum for the November
1970 ballot. The battle took another turn when Santa Barbara County District Attorney
David Minier, a headline-grabbing crusader, filed felony charges against the two housewives, alleging they'd altered some of the signatures. But a judge threw out the charges,
the referendum went before voters, and the zoning change necessary for Jules's planned
development went down to defeat by a vote of 46,861 to 33,322. See Margaret Connell,
"Selma Rubin Saves El Capitan Canyon!! (37 Years Ago)," Santa Barbara Independent,
November 1, 2007, https://www.independent.com/2007/11/01/selma-rubin-saves-el
-capitan-canyon-37-years-ago/.

29. See Tony Mostrom, "1960s Canyon Culture Has Been Preserved in Amber in a
Little Foothills Spot," *LA Weekly*, April 9, 2016, https://www.laweekly.com/1960s-canyon
-culture-has-been-preserved-in-amber-in-a-little-foothills-spot/.

30. For more about this wild phase in Leary's life, see Nina Burleigh, "A Return Trip to
Timothy Leary's Psychedelic, Day-Glo Mexico," NY Times, May 10, 2022, https://www
.nytimes.com/2022/05/06/travel/mexico-timothy-leary-psychedelics.html.

31. See "Jimi Hendrix Sets Guitar On Fire at Monterey Pop Festival (1967)." YouTube.
https://www.youtube.com/watch?v=1ZiFUN8cIuo.

32. Radhi Soami allows adherents to practice other faiths while following the Path, so
Barry wasn't heretical in becoming an ordained minister in the Universal Life Church.
Founded by Kirby J. Hensley in Modesto, California, the church became known for its
mail-order ordination, which allowed everyday people to perform legal weddings in
California and several other states. See Wikipedia (Universal Life Church), https://en
.wikipedia.org/wiki/Universal_Life_Church.

33. Paan, also known as betel pepper leaf, is a stimulant chewed by millions of people in
India. See SpruceEats, "What Is Paan? A Guide to Paan and Its Use in Indian Cuisine,"
September 7, 2022, https://www.thespruceeats.com/definition-of-paan-1957541.

CHAPTER FOUR

1. The student body at Belmont, an urban high school, included students of diverse
backgrounds and ethnicities. Activist and folk singer Odetta Holmes and actress Reiko
Sato were two notable Belmont alumni from the postwar era.

2. The clerk's office was located in the former Clark County courthouse, a 1914 Classic
Revival building designed by Frederic DeLonchamps, a mining engineer with little formal training who became one of Nevada's leading architects. The building was demolished

in the 1950s. See "1914 Las Vegas Post Card—Clark County Court House- DeLongc-hamps," January 17, 2018, http://captainhistory.com/wordpress1/2018/01/17/337/.

3. Around the time of the divorce, just before rollout of the Salk vaccine, Woodward caught polio. He was hospitalized in an iron lung, and although he recovered, the disease left him with a paralyzed arm. He passed away in 2014 at age eighty-one.

4. Gatto was found slumped over a desk with a gunshot wound to his abdomen. The police offered a $50,000 reward and launched a massive search for suspects, but to date the case hasn't been solved. Meanwhile, news reports have focused on internecine feuding in the family, alleging that in the months preceding his death, Gatto considered removing his daughter Nicole from his will.

5. See Ari Bloomekatz, "Artists, students call Joseph Gatto 'great educator of the arts,'" *LA Times*, November 15, 2013, https://www.latimes.com/local/lanow/la-me -ln-artists-remember-joseph-gatto-20131114-story.html#:~:text=Artists%20and%20art %20students%20from,and%20promoter%20of%20the%20arts.

6. The marriage was so fleeting that Louise's eldest son Michael didn't know about it until the author showed him a copy of the marriage license many years later.

7. The Santa Clara River was forever linked to Inyo County by a terrible and tragic event. In the early 1900s, legendary engineer William Mulholland spearheaded a massive project in which the City of Los Angeles acquired land along the Owens River and built a 230-mile aqueduct to carry the water south. As demand for water increased, Mulholland decided the system needed more storage near its terminus. He spearheaded the design and construction of a huge reservoir situated in a canyon called San Francisquito. But as St. Francis Dam filled with water, it began springing leaks. Around midday on Wednes-day, March 26, 1928, Mulholland walked across the top of the dam and pronounced it safe. A supremely confident man who'd spent his life accomplishing the impossible, Mul-holland had never experienced a worst-case defeat. Shortly before midnight on March 27, only hours after Mulholland gave a thumbs-up, St. Francis Dam collapsed. A wall of water surged downcanyon into the Santa Clara River basin, all the way to the ocean, and at least 430 people lost their lives. See Doyce B. Nunis Jr., ed., *The St. Francis Dam Disaster Revisited* (Long Beach, CA: Historical Society of Southern California, 1995)

8. Box Canyon had a calamitous history. In 1949, a passenger plane approaching Bur-bank Airport clipped a rocky hilltop above the canyon, killing thirty-five people. Near the accident scene, a stone monastery housed a religious cult. After the plane crash, cult members clad in flowing robes helped pull survivors from the wreckage. The cult leader, who called himself "Krishna Venta," was a former mental hospital patient named Frank Pencovic. Although Pencovic required his disciples to remain celibate, he routinely availed himself of conjugal relations with his female followers—including women married to other men. In 1958, two cuckolded husbands bought dynamite, stuffed it into a musette bag, and went to the monastery. The subsequent explosion killed ten people—including the two bombers, Pencovic, and several disciples and children. Surviving cult members still lived in Box Canyon when Louise moved there in 1962 and settled into married life with Wes Westerman. See Matthew Duersten, "The Bizarre Story Behind the Suicide of a SoCal Cult," *LA Times*, December 10, 2018, https://laist.com/news/la-history/bizarre -story-behind-the-suicide-bombing-of-a-socal-cult.

9. The author interviewed Westerman by phone on May 19, 2014, and again on April 11 and April 16, 2017. In June 2017, he agreed to meet in person at his house in Elk Creek, California. But while driving down to Elk Creek from Washington State, Westerman fell asleep at the wheel. His pickup truck rolled, he sustained grave injuries, and after a months-long struggle, he passed away at age eighty-five.

10. "Revered by the Indians, the Pagosa (a Ute word meaning 'healing' or 'boiling water') hot springs were frequented by many of the tribes." See "History of Archuleta County," Archuleta County, Colorado, accessed June 11, 2020, https://www.archuletacounty.org /101/History-of-Archuleta-County.

11. Jim struggled with alcoholism for much of his life and passed away in 2012.

12. After Barry and Louise vacated the cottage at El Capitan and moved into their house atop Refugio Road, Nold and Laura moved into the cottage. About a year before Nold and Laura split up, a section of the oceanfront cliff fell away, and Laura's dog vanished. A few years after Barry and Louise went missing, a resident at the property died when a train struck his car as he crossed the tracks outside the gate.

CHAPTER FIVE

1. The Tehachapi and Santa Ynez mountains are part of the Transverse Ranges, which due to "tectonic rotation" run east to west, rather than north to south like most mountain ranges in the West. See Thomas Bailey and Richard Jahns, accessed April 30, 2023, "Geology of the Transverse Range Province, Southern California," https://authors.library .caltech.edu/101236/1/Jahns_1954p83.pdf.

2. "Not the law, but the land sets the limit. Desert is the name it wears upon the maps, but the Indian's is the better word. Desert is a loose term to indicate land that supports no man; whether the land can be bitted and broken to that purpose is not proven." Mary Austin, *The Land of Little Rain* (New York: Houghton and Mifflin). See https://www .gutenberg.org/files/365/365-h/365-h.htm for a complete copy of her celebrated book.

3. Friends of the Bermans said they were private rather than prudish and may have been reserved about shedding their clothes in an unfamiliar setting.

4. The author located Dale and Katy on May 30, 2014, when they were living together in a remote desert town. As Katy spoke warily from the doorway, Dale stood behind her, naked and still wiry at almost eighty years old, smiling broadly and chiming in with occasional comments. But Dale was having health problems, so Katy cut the interview short, saying they needed to focus on "positive healing energy" rather than "dredging up the past." Dale passed away in 2015.

CHAPTER SIX

1. See Sheila Kennedy, "Puzzle of Missing Family Remains Unsolved," *Santa Barbara News-Press*, July 19, 1987.

2. See Ann Japenga, "A Couple Disappear in Bermuda Triangle of Death Valley," *LA Times*, December 21, 1986, https://www.latimes.com/archives/la-xpm-1986-12-21-vw -3821-story.html.

3. "On November 18, 1978, Peoples Temple founder Jim Jones [led] hundreds of his followers in a mass murder-suicide at their agricultural commune in a remote part of the South American nation of Guyana. Many of Jones' followers willingly ingested a poison-laced punch while others were forced to do so at gunpoint. The final death toll at Jonestown that day was 909; a third of those who perished were children." See "Mass suicide at Jonestown," History.com, accessed January 15, 2023, https://www.history.com/this-day-in-history/mass-suicide-at-jonestown.

4. The 2018 Netflix documentary series "Wild Wild Country" brought the invasion back to life for millions of viewers worldwide. See Troy Patterson, "'Wild Wild Country' Is a Tabloid Epic of the American Frontier," *The New Yorker*, April 11, 2018, https://www.newyorker.com/culture/on-television/wild-wild-country-is-a-tabloid-epic-of-the-american-frontier.

5. See Sam Kemp, "Barker Ranch: The abandoned gold mine that became Charles Manson's hideout," *Far Out Magazine*, June 19, 2022, https://faroutmagazine.co.uk/barker-ranch-charles-mansons-hideout/.

6. Timothy Dahlia, Saline Valley History, Inyo County California, 1800s to 2000s (self-pub. 2019), includes a photo on page 163 of Manson at Lower Warm Springs.

7. At the invitation of Arthur Korb, in 2014 the author attended a satsang at the Science of the Soul Center in Petaluma, California, hosted by Charan Singh's nephew and successor Gurinder Singh. Several of Barry's friends attended this event.

8. "From 1980 to 2008, nearly 1 out of 5 murder victims were killed by an intimate partner. . . . In fact, available research shows that women are more likely to be killed by an intimate partner (husband, boyfriend, same-sex partner, or ex) than by anyone else." See VAWnet, "The Scope of the Problem: Intimate Partner Homicide Statistics," accessed January 15, 2023, https://vawnet.org/sc/scope-problem-intimate-partner-homicide-statistics.

9. Muscio permitted the author to examine and copy his original photos.

10. When interviewed for this book, Brian Casey described "Humboldt lady" as a hippie-type who offered the other campers marijuana brownies.

11. The reporting party wasn't identified in the sheriff's report.

12. According to the sheriff's report, Nixon drove to the scene on February 18, 1986, with Deputy J. P. Jones.

13. A copy of Boyer's composite drawing can be seen www.dougkariauthor.com.

14. As cofounder of the outdoor group Desert Survivors, the author was deeply involved in the desert protection movement. See Frank Wheat, *California Desert Miracle: The Fight for Desert Parks and Wilderness* (Chula Vista, CA: Sunbelt Publications, 1999).

15. The petition was posted by Saline Preservation Association (SPA), an organization "created to respond to concerns brought about by the proposed California Desert Protection Act." Although SPA favors protection of Saline Valley, the organization is leery of government interference and supports "traditional human presence that emphasizes responsible individual freedom of choice." See Saline Preservation Association, https://salinepreservation.org/.

16. Between 2014 and 2018, the author sent Pepe multiple requests for comment. Although people who knew him confirmed he received the requests, he never responded.

In 2022, the author sent another request via his lawyer Charles Brown, which was declined.

Chapter Seven

1. Assisted by Bridget Yin, the author interviewed Joseph Pepe on January 20, 2015, six years before his death at age ninety. Dorothy Pepe passed away in 2004.
2. Brian died in 2001 of pancreatic cancer.
3. Haigler made the statement outside his home in Nevada on December 28, 2015.
4. Camp Pendleton, one of the largest Marine Corps bases in the United States, was formerly a horse and cattle ranch called Rancho Santa Margarita y Las Flores. The base covers more than 180 square miles of coastal terrain in northern San Diego County, and traces to a grant held by Pio Pico, the last Mexican governor of Alta California. See USMC, accessed June 18, 2020, "MCB Camp Pendleton," https://www.pendleton .marines.mil/Main-Menu/History-and-Museums/.
5. See USMC, "Quantico: Crossroads of the Marine Corps," Accessed June 19, 2020, https://www.usmcu.edu/Portals/218/Quantico-%20Crossroads%20Of%20The %20Marine%20Corps.pdf.
6. See USMC, "MCAS Iwakuni, Japan," accessed May 10, 2023, https://www .mcasiwakuni.marines.mil/.
7. See Katharine Moon, "Military Prostitution and the U.S. Military in Asia." *The Asia-Pacific Journal* 7, no. 6 (2009), https://apjjf.org/-Katharine-H.S.-Moon/3019/article .html.
8. Carpenter, who served in law enforcement for thirty-seven years, passed away in 2020.
9. See "Carol Anilda, Michael Pepe Exchange Vows," *Oxnard Press-Courier*, October 2, 1975.
10. See CA Superior Court-San Diego, Case #D101882 (March 3, 1976). Carol Ann Pepe v. Michael Joseph Pepe. Pepe's sister Andrea recalled that the marriage lasted about two years.
11. "Officership Foundations B1X0856 Student Handout," USMC The Basic School.
12. Pepe underwent ground supply training at Camp Lejeune, a 246-square-mile base along the coast of North Carolina. See https://www.lejeune.marines.mil/.
13. See Quote Investigator, An Army Marches On Its Stomach," October 15, 2017, https://quoteinvestigator.com/2017/10/15/army/.
14. In an effort to improve management within the armed forces, the Defense Officer Personnel Management Act of 1980 required the military to remove officers who weren't selected for promotion. See Bernard D. Rostker, Harry J. Thie, James Lacy, Jennifer H. Kawata, and Susanna W. Purnell, "The Defense Officer Personnel Management Act of 1980: A Retrospective Assessment." RAND Corporation, accessed May 11, 2023, https: //www.rand.org/pubs/reports/R4246.html.
15. The aide de camp for a brigadier general would wear an aiguillette with two loops, while aides to higher-ranking personnel would wear up to four loops. See USMC, "Marine Corps Uniform Regulations," May 1, 2018, https://www.marines.mil/portals/1/ Publications/MCO%201020.34H%20v2.pdf?ver=2018-06-26-094038-137.

16. Felicia didn't respond to multiple requests for comment, and her last name has been omitted to protect her privacy.

17. Under military law, adultery was illegal if it harmed "good order and discipline" and could bring "discredit upon the armed forces." But during the pre #MeToo era the tendency was to look the other way. See Ian Fisher, "Army's Adultery Rule Is Don't Get Caught." *New York Times*, May 17, 1997, https://www.nytimes.com/1997/05/17/us/army-s-adultery-rule-is-don-t-get-caught.html.

CHAPTER EIGHT

1. NIS went through various name and abbreviation changes before becoming NCIS. For simplicity, the agency is mostly referred to in this book as "NIS." See H. Paul Mullis, "A Brief History of the Naval Criminal Investigative Service," accessed August 12, 2023, https://ncisahistory.org/wp-content/uploads/2017/07/A-Brief-History-of-the-Naval-Criminal-Investigative-Service-Editor-H.-Paul-Mullis-1997.pdf.

2. In this book, the interview transcript is the source of most of the quotes from Pepe. The author obtained a copy of the transcript in 2014 after Inyo County sheriff Bill Lutze invited the submission of a request under the California Public Records Act. Lutze said that his office would consent to producing the transcript in hopes the author's investigation would turn up leads.

3. A few months before the interview, the F-18 had seen combat for the first time—in a bombing attack on Libya that purportedly killed Muammar Gaddafi's adopted daughter. See Andrew Glass, "U.S. planes bomb Libya, April 15, 1986." Politico, April 15, 2019, https://www.politico.com/story/2019/04/15/reagan-bomb-libya-april-15-1986-1272788.

4. Racetrack Playa is a lakebed that is dry most of the time. After years of theorizing and debate, scientists in 2013–2014 established that a rare combination of light winds and thin ice causes the rocks to move, which leaves the telltale tracks. See NPS, "The Racetrack," last updated September 29, 2021, https://www.nps.gov/deva/planyourvisit/the-racetrack.htm.

5. See TopGear, "History lesson: The Datsun name," July 16, 2013, https://www.topgear.com/car-news/classic/history-lesson-datsun-name.

6. See Brian Fitch, "The Truth About Lying: What Investigators Need to Know," FBI Law Enforcement Bulletin, June 10, 2014, https://leb.fbi.gov/articles/featured-articles/the-truth-about-lying-what-investigators-need-to-know.

7. This was a fifteen-minute topographic map, the most detailed map of the Saline Valley Warm Springs area available at that time.

CHAPTER NINE

1. California's Dealer's Record of Sale (DROS) protocol includes a background check form, reporting system, and gun registration system.

2. In his interview with sheriff's investigators, Pepe said he expected to be leaving his job soon, so the transfer may have already been in the works.

3. One report said Michael Keating, aka "Caveman Mike," was later spotted at a bar, but the legend of his disappearance persists, and there have been other strange incidents at the hot springs. In December 2020, the body of Donald Vanneman III turned up in one of the source pools. Speculation was he disregarded the prohibition on bathing in the source pools and became overheated. See Ashley Harrell, "San Francisco man's unusual death in Death Valley thermal pool alarms hot springs community," SF Gate, updated January 23, 2021, https://www.sfgate.com/california-parks/article/san-francisco-death-valley-saline-warm-springs-15886069.php. In May 2021, Robert "Bob" Wildoner, another visitor, went missing from the campground, leaving his keys and cell phone behind. Investigation by the author with assistance from Stuart Jeffries turned up one of Wildoner's sandals, leading to a theory that he may have fallen and injured himself and sought refuge in a nearby cave. See Doug Kari, "New clue emerges in veteran's Death Valley disappearance," *Las Vegas Review-Journal*, March 27, 2023, https://www.reviewjournal.com/local/local-nevada/new-clue-emerges-in-veterans-death-valley-disappearance-2751732/.

4. See Ann Japenga, "A Couple Disappear in Bermuda Triangle of Death Valley," *LA Times*, December 21, 1986, https://www.latimes.com/archives/la-xpm-1986-12-21-vw-3821-story.html.

5. Deputy Boyer's sketches can be seen at www.dougkariauthor.com.

6. See Sheila Kennedy, "Puzzle of Missing Family Remains Unsolved," *Santa Barbara News-Press*, July 19, 1987.

7. Kennedy, "Puzzle."

8. Ibid.

9. The author obtained a photo of the hiker, which was sent to various desert mountaineers from that era, but the author was unable to identify him. The case files provided by the Inyo County Sheriff's Office didn't include his name.

10. See Tom Ganner, "A Collection of Recollections of Days Gone By," Time and Space Nature Adventures. Https://timenspace.net/saline-valley-chronicles/. In 2016, when the author interviewed Ganner he proved to have a lyrical way with words, saying at one point: "The desert is a paradox. It's barren and arid and can kill you. It has creatures that can bite and sting. It's a collection of ugly things that transcend into beauty. And the silence is so profound that it has a presence."

11. Robert Pollard aka "Chili Bob" died in 1998 at age fifty-two.

12. See PBS, "Learning from Skeletons," History Detectives Special Investigations. Https://www.pbs.org/opb/historydetectives/technique/learning-from-skeletons/index.html.

13. See John Kendall, "Remains of Long-Missing Couple Found in Desert," *LA Times*, November 16, 1998, https://www.latimes.com/archives/la-xpm-1988-11-16-mn-305-story.html.

14. The coroner's report and autopsy report can be seen at www.dougkariauthor.com.

CHAPTER TEN

1. See Myrna Oliver, "J. Berman; 'Mr. Kahlua' Was Developer, Donor," *LA Times*, July 22, 1998, https://www.latimes.com/archives/la-xpm-1998-jul-22-mn-6063-story.html.

2. See "Neighbors From Hell: Furious Locals Accuse Brad Pitt and Angelina Jolie of Destroying Fragile Californian Coastline," Radar, April, 26, 2013, https://radaronline.com/exclusives/2013/04/brad-pitt-and-angelina-jolie-accused-of-destroying-worlds-most-fragile-coastline/.

3. "Martin" (February 12, 2006). ExSatsangi Support Group (former Yahoo Public Group with 532 members).

4. See Phillip Athey, "Marine commandant considers major changes to improve force retention," Marine Times, October 3, 2019, https://www.marinecorpstimes.com/news/2019/10/03/marine-commandant-considers-major-changes-to-improve-force-retention/.

5. Tatiana didn't respond to requests for an interview, and to protect her privacy her last name has been omitted.

6. Excerpts from court transcripts related to Pepe can be seen at www.dougkariauthor.com.

7. For a feverish view of Cambodia's underbelly at the turn of the twenty-first century see Amit Gilboa, *Off the Rails in Phnom Penh: Into the Dark Heart of Guns, Girls, and Ganja* (Bangkok: Asia Books).

8. One commentator wrote, "I can't think of anything on earth that could prepare you for Cambodia. The extreme poverty, the corruption, the appalling history, the crime, the lack of personal safety must all be taken into account," Phil Ross, "Cambodia-The Wild West of Asia," Stickmanbangkok, April 15, 2004, https://www.stickmanbangkok.com/readers-submissions/2004/04/cambodia-the-wild-west-of-asia/.

9. Also identified as "Sang Chi Chhouern" or "Chheang Thi-San." A witness at a later court proceeding explained that "Sang" was her nickname and "Basang" was equivalent to saying, "Ms. Sang."

10. See Ramses Amer, "The Ethnic Vietnamese in Cambodia: A Minority at Risk?" *Contemporary Southeast Asia*, September 1994.

11. See James Welsh, "Officials Defend Testimonies in US on Behalf of Pedophile," *Cambodia Daily*, June 26, 2008, https://english.cambodiadaily.com/news/officials-defend-testimonies-in-us-on-behalf-of-pedophile-58244/.

12. A team of undercover investigative journalists secretly recorded a foreigner who was attempting to rationalize child prostitution in Cambodia. "With 13 and 14-year-olds, by the time she gets to Svay Pak she's probably had sex a hundred times. . . . You didn't turn her, you didn't make her do that. You're taking advantage of the situation and the opportunity and it's not your fault." See "It's like a sweet shop: if this girl's not right, get another," *The Telegraph*, September 15, 2002, https://www.telegraph.co.uk/news/worldnews/asia/cambodia/1407280/Its-like-a-sweet-shop-if-this-girls-not-right-get-another.html.

13. In a letter Pepe sent home to his family, later recovered by law enforcement, he stated, "I had gotten the idea that it was OK, even expected. . . . [A friend] bragged more than once that he had 23 children living at his house."

14. Sometimes called Toul Kouk or Khan Toul Kouk.

15. FUNCINPEC derives its name from a French acronym for Front uni national pour un Cambodge indépendant, neutre, pacifique, et coopératif, which in English translates

as "National United Front for an Independent, Neutral, Peaceful, and Cooperative Cambodia." When Pepe arrived in Cambodia the party still had influence, but since then its power has waned. See Wikipedia (FUNCINPEC), https://en.wikipedia.org/wiki/FUNCINPEC.

16. Foreign Service National employees are citizens of the countries where the US State Department maintains diplomatic posts and consulates.

Chapter Eleven

1. Norodom Sihamoni became the king of Cambodia in 2004, shortly after the abdication of his father, Norodom Sihanouk. It's not clear which king's picture hung in Pepe's villa. See Seth Mydans, "Abdication by Cambodia's King Throws His Nation Into Confusion," *New York Times*, October 8, 2004, https://www.nytimes.com/2004/10/08/world/asia/abdication-by-cambodias-king-throws-his-nation-into-confusion.html.

2. See "Ethnic Vietnamese in Cambodia Left in Limbo Without Citizenship," Radio Free Asia, May 19, 2014, https://www.rfa.org/english/news/cambodia/vietnamese-03192014205359.html.

3. McCallum, who like Pepe worked as a teacher, was arrested by Cambodian police in 2008. See Phorn Bopha, "UK Man Charged for Creating Child Pornography," Cambodia Daily, December 3, 2008, https://english.cambodiadaily.com/news/uk-man-charged-for-creating-child-pornography-59294/.

4. This version of events came from the author's interview of Vansak Sous. When IJM was asked to comment, a spokesperson for the organization declined to provide any details, saying they don't reveal their investigative methods. For a somewhat different version of how IJM's investigation uncovered Pepe's abuse, see Katherine Wood, "Sex-Trafficking in Cambodia Assessing the Role of NGOs in Rebuilding Cambodia," Spring 2014, https://digitalcommons.liberty.edu/cgi/viewcontent.cgi?article=1439&context=honors.

5. ICE boasts of being "a leader in the global fight against human trafficking, proactively identifying, disrupting and dismantling cross-border human trafficking organizations and minimizing the risk they pose to national security and public safety." See ICE, "Role of ICE," accessed June 23, 2020, https://www.ice.gov/features/human-trafficking#:~:text=training%20and%20awareness.-,Role%20of%20ICE,national%20security%20and%20public%20safety.

6. For a profile of Vansak, see David Henshaw, "The US agents tracking down sex tourists in Cambodia," BBC, January 20, 2011, https://www.bbc.com/news/world-us-canada-12298870.

7. Other evidence seized inside Pepe's villa included baby oil, a "bestiality CD," pornographic movies, tampons, and a game called "Body Parts."

8. Pepe deleted the images but didn't overwrite the data.

9. See Thai Tha, "Cambodia's Prey Sar Prison Like Being 'in Hell' Former Inmate Says," Radio Free Asia, March 3, 2017, https://www.rfa.org/english/news/cambodia/prison-03032017132739.html#:~:text=Confinement%20in%20Cambodia's%20notorious%20Prey,%2C%2025%2C%20said%20on%20Feb.

10. See "14 Years: The Horrors of Prey Sar," *Khmer Times*, June 16, 2016, https://www.khmertimeskh.com/24870/14-years-the-horrors-of-prey-sar/.

11. See "A day in the life of Prey Sar Prison, Cambodia," *InsideTime*, April 1, 2013, https://insidetime.org/a-day-in-the-life-of-prey-sar-prison-cambodia/.

12. See "US Citizen arrested for having sex with young girls in Cambodia," KI-Media, June 2, 2006, http://ki-media.blogspot.com/2006/06/us-citizen-arrested-for-having-sex.html.

13. See James Welsh, "Officials Defend Testimonies in US on Behalf of Pedophile," *Cambodia Daily*, June 26, 2008, https://english.cambodiadaily.com/news/officials-defend-testimonies-in-us-on-behalf-of-pedophile-58244/.

14. Pepe was concerned that his connections might not be enough. He wrote in a letter sent home to his family, "Unfortunately, most of my 'power guys' were removed in a coup a few months ago."

15. PROTECT is an acronym for Prosecutorial Remedies and Other Tools to End the Exploitation of Children Today. See PROTECT Act (2003). Pub. L. No. 108–21, 117 Stat. 650.

CHAPTER TWELVE

1. See Greg Krikorian, "Ex-Marine to face U.S. charges in Cambodian child-rape case," *LA Times*, February 10, 2007, https://www.latimes.com/archives/la-xpm-2007-feb-10-me-marine10-story.html.

2. For an unvarnished description of MDC see Zoukis Consulting Group, "MDC Los Angeles—Metropolitan Detention Center Los Angeles," accessed May 10, 2023, https://federalcriminaldefenseattorney.com/federal-bureau-prisons/mdc-los-angeles/.

3. See USDC C.D. CA, Case #2:06-mj-01717-DUTY. USA v. Michael Joseph Pepe.

4. Sander De Montero, sometimes spelled as "Sander de Montero," was a Melbourne resident who was formerly involved with the Cambodian government.

5. At the time it was the longest criminal trial in US history, and at a cost of $15 million, the most expensive. The case ended with no convictions. One defendant, Ray Buckley, spent five years in prison. See Douglas Linder, "The McMartin Preschool Abuse Trial: An Account," Accessed April 30, 2023, https://famous-trials.com/mcmartin/902-home.

6. Once assigned to Judge Fischer, the case became USDC C.D. CA, Case #CR-07–168 DSF. USA v. Michael Joseph Pepe.

7. See Famous-Trials.com, "Testimony by Dr. Michael Maloney," accessed May 10, 2023, https://www.famous-trials.com/mcmartin/917-maloneytestimony.

8. Douglas Gillison, "California Jury Convicts US Man in '06 Sex Case," June 3, 2008, *Cambodia Daily*, https://english.cambodiadaily.com/news/california-jury-convicts-us-man-in-06-sex-case-81738/.

9. See DOJ, "Ex-Marine Guilty of Using Drugs and Force to Have Sex With Young Girls in Cambodia," May 29, 2008, https://www.justice.gov/archive/usao/cac/Pressroom/pr2008/074.html.

10. See DOJ, "Attorney General Holder Recognizes Department Employees and Others for Their Service at Annual Awards Ceremony," October 21, 2009, https://www.justice.gov/opa/pr/attorney-general-holder-recognizes-department-employees-and-others-their-service-annual.

CHAPTER THIRTEEN

1. See Scott Glover, "Verdict in key child-sex trial at risk," *LA Times*, November 20, 2010, https://www.latimes.com/archives/la-xpm-2010-nov-20-la-me-child-sex-prosecution-20101120-story.html.

2. At this time, Phillips was an ICE section chief, and his role in the Pepe case had brought him a measure of renown. See Sara Giboney, Sara, "Undercover agent: Child sex abuse must be talked about," World Herald News Service, April 9, 2009. Https://nonpareilonline.com/archive/undercover-agent-child-sex-abuse-must-be-talked-about/article_fb02678f-a622-57cb-b50b-4afda57e1fab.html

3. See Glover, "Verdict," n.173.

4. Scott Glover, who later became an investigative reporter for CNN, covered the hearing as a staff writer for the *LA Times*. He wrote this about one of the victims: "She eyed the defendant, who had done unspeakable things to her and six other girls. He was seated just a few feet away with a smirk on his face." See Scott Glover, "Abused girls testify in U.S.," *LA Times*, September 26, 2008, https://www.latimes.com/archives/la-xpm-2008-sep-26-me-kids26-story.html.

5. Victoria Kim, "Ex-Marine convicted of sex acts with young girls in Cambodia gets life," *LA Times*, February 28, 2014, https://www.latimes.com/local/lanow/la-xpm-2014-feb-28-la-me-ln-cambodia-child-sex-sentence-20140228-story.html.

6. Thanks to the author's sister Karen Jarrell, who explored Saline Valley before he did.

7. The helicopter time cost $700. Steve, perhaps inspired by participating in the search, eventually became a paramedic—including eleven years aboard a helicopter performing hair-raising rescues in Yosemite and the Sierra Nevada.

8. See Desert Survivors, https://www.desert-survivors.org/.

9. All three of the author's children were baptized under a waterfall near the base of McElvoy Canyon, one of the precipitous Inyo canyons that opens into Saline Valley.

10. See MotorcycleSpecs, "Yamaha IT 175," Https://www.motorcyclespecs.co.za/model/yamaha/yamaha_it175d.htm; MotorcycleSpecs, "Yamaha IT 200," Https://www.motorcyclespecs.co.za/model/yamaha/yamaha_it200%2084.htm.

11. To test whether Pepe's two-wheel-drive Datsun pickup could have handled the terrain, the author kept his 4Runner in two-wheel-drive when driving up the Corridor to explore the grave site.

CHAPTER FOURTEEN

1. See Doug Kari, "Double Murder in the Mojave: a 1986 double murder cold case in the Mojave Desert is finally unraveling," *LA Weekly*, March 10, 2015, https://www.laweekly.com/a-1986-double-murder-cold-case-in-the-mojave-desert-is-finally-unraveling/.

2. For an inmate's view of USP Tucson see Danny Fabricant, "The Federal Prison System and the Tucson Penitentiary," February 14, 2013, https://fastandfuriousandfabricant.wordpress.com/2013/02/14/the-federal-prison-system-and-the-tucson-penitentiary/.

3. See Melinda Rogers, "Elizabeth Smart kidnapper booked at federal prison in Arizona," Salt Lake Tribune, September 15, 2011, https://archive.sltrib.com/article.php?id=52500560&itype=CMSID.

NOTES

4. See Kim Kozlowski, "Larry Nassar now housed in Arizona prison," Detroit News, February 11, 2018, https://www.detroitnews.com/story/news/local/michigan/2018/02/09/larry-nassar-milan/110251634/.

5. See Zoukis Consulting Group, "Corrlinks.com Inmate Email/TRULINCS Federal Prison Email," updated June 9, 2023, https://federalcriminaldefenseattorney.com/prison-life/corrlinks-inmate-email-trulincs/.

6. For an account of Blount's criminal history, see Laurie Mason Schroeder and Peter Hall, "'Violent' sex trafficker gets 24-plus years in federal prison," February 6, 2015, *Morning Call*, https://www.mcall.com/2015/02/06/violent-sex-trafficker-gets-24-plus-years-in-federal-prison/.

7. See George T. Wilkerson, "It's Surprisingly Tough to Avoid Snitching in Prison," The Marshall Project, July 19, 2018, https://www.themarshallproject.org/2018/07/19/it-s-surprisingly-tough-to-avoid-snitching-in-prison.

8. See "Prison is a Real-Life Example of the World White Supremacists Want," The Marshall Project, August 24, 2017, https://www.themarshallproject.org/2017/08/24/prison-is-a-real-life-example-of-the-world-white-supremacists-want.

9. See G. F. Cornelius, "Understanding Prison Culture Is the Key to Inmate Management," *Corrections Today*, December 1992, https://ojp.gov/ncjrs/virtual-library/abstracts/understanding-prison-culture-key-inmate-management, accessed May 6, 2023.

10. See Dean Hawley, "Death by Strangulation." *Journal of Forensic Sciences*, http://www.markwynn.com/wp-content/uploads/death-by-strangulation.pdf.

11. Doug Kari, "Berman murders: Press charges or open files," *Inyo Register*, May 3, 2018.

12. See U.S. Court of Appeals 9th Cir., Case #14–50095. USA v. Michael Joseph Pepe.

13. See USA v. Clark, 435 F.3d 1100 (9th Cir. 2006).

14. See "Man sentenced for sex with Cambodian boys," *The Spokesman-Review*, June 26, 2004, https://www.spokesman.com/stories/2004/jun/26/man-sentenced-for-sex-with-cambodian-boys/.

15. Article I, Section 8, Clause 3 of the US Constitution empowers Congress "to regulate commerce with foreign nations, and among the several states, and with the Indian tribes."

16. Article I, Section 8, Clause 3 of the US Constitution.

17. See USA v. Pepe (February 8, 2017). (The hearing video can be viewed by entering Case #14–50095), https://www.ca9.uscourts.gov/media/.

18. The author sent a letter to Judge Kleinfeld's chambers posing a list of questions such as: "What is a 'beach boy'? By 'beach boy' did you mean an underage boy on a foreign beach who is sexually exploited by an American?" As expected, the judge didn't repond.

19. USA v. Pepe, 895 F.3d 679 (9th Cir. 2018).

20. The procedure, called a petition for a hearing en banc, allows an opportunity for all judges within the appellate circuit to weigh in. But because this requires an enormous investment of judicial resources, en banc petitions are rarely granted. See Marc Poster, "Taking It To the Banc," accessed April 30, 2023, https://www.gmsr.com/wp-content/uploads/2016/06/Taking-it-to-the-Banc.pdf.

21. The decision also fit with the 9th Circuit's reputation as a liberal outlier compared to other appellate circuits, prone to rulings that are often overturned by the Supreme Court. See Dylan Matthews, "How the 9th Circuit became conservatives' least favorite court," Vox, January 10, 2018, https://www.vox.com/policy-and-politics/2018/1/10/16873718/ninth-circuit-court-appeals-liberal-conservative-trump-tweet.

22. The author didn't write the headline and it wasn't accurate, but it expressed the fears of many people who'd been following the case. See Doug Kari, "Suspect in unsolved murders set to be freed," *Inyo Register*, July 17, 2018. The headline of an article the author wrote for *LA Weekly* was more measured. See Doug Kari, "Appellate Court Reverses Sex Crimes Conviction of Double-Murder Suspect," *LA Weekly*, July 23, 2018, https://www.laweekly.com/appellate-court-reverses-sex-crimes-conviction-of-double-murder-suspect/.

23. See Doug Kari, "High court should hear child rape case," *SF Daily Journal* and *LA Daily Journal*, November 1, 2018.

24. Most likely the Supreme Court would not have agreed to take the case. The procedure, called a petition for writ of certiorari, asks the Supreme Court to grant a hearing, but the court has discretion over which petitions to grant—and the odds were less than 1 in 50. See U.S. Courts, "About the Supreme Court," accessed May 10, 2023, https://www.uscourts.gov/about-federal-courts/educational-resources/about-educational-outreach/activity-resources/about#:~:text=The%20Supreme%20Court%20agrees%20to,asked%20to%20review%20each%20year.

CHAPTER FIFTEEN

1. The law firm is Munger, Tolles & Olson LLP, founded in 1962 by Charles Munger, who later went to Berkshire Hathaway as Warren Buffet's right-hand man.

2. Pepe was charged under 18 USC § 2423(b) and 18 USC § 2241(c).

3. Motions seeking to exclude evidence under the Fourth Amendment of the US Constitution, which bars "unreasonable searches and seizures," are a common feature of criminal cases. See Cornell Law School, "Motion to suppress," accessed May 10, 2023, https://www.law.cornell.edu/wex/motion_to_suppress#:~:text=The%20concept%20of%20a%20motion,from%20unlawful%20searches%20and%20seizures.

4. See Doug Kari, "Retrial begins for ex-Marine accused of sex crimes in Cambodia," Long Beach Post, August 6, 2021, https://lbpost.com/news/michael-pepe-cambodia-retrail-marines#:~:text=Charles%20Brown%2C%20one%20of%20Michael,where%20he%20sexually%20abused%20girls.

5. See Wade C. Meyers, Lawrence Reccoppa, Karen Burton, and Ross Ross, "Malignant Sex and Aggression: An Overview of Serial Sexual Homicide," *Bulletin of the American Academy of Psychiatry and the Law* (1993), https://jaapl.org/content/jaapl/21/4/435.full.pdf.

6. See J. Levin and J. A. Fox, *Mass Murder: America's Growing Menace*, New York: Plenum Press.

7. See Vernon J. Geberth, "The Classification of Sex-Related Homicides," Practical Homicide Investigation, 1996, http://practicalhomicide.com/articles/sexrelatedhomicides.htm.

CHAPTER SIXTEEN

1. The movie *12 Angry Men*, a 1957 film starring Henry Fonda as juror #8, portrayed one man's struggle change the minds of the other eleven jurors. See IMDB, "12 Angry Men (1957)," accessed February 21, 2022, https://www.imdb.com/title/tt0050083/.

2. See Doug Kari, "Jury finds former U.S. Marine guilty of molesting girls in Cambodia," *Long Beach Post*, August 12, 2021, https://lbpost.com/news/jury-finds-former-u-s-marine-guilty-of-molesting-girls-in-cambodia/#:~:text=The%20federal%20court%20jury%20found,illicit%20sexual%20conduct%20with%20minors.

3. See Doug Kari, "Former professor sentenced to 210 years in Cambodia sex crimes case," Long Beach Post, February 14, 2022, https://lbpost.com/news/crime/michael-pepe-cambodia-sex-crimes-sentence#:~:text=A%20judge%20in%20Los%20Angeles,sentence%20would%20be%20unduly%20harsh.

4. Fewer than 1 percent of federal prison inmates qualify for Level 4 care. As of November 2023, Pepe is again housed at USP Tucson, which doesn't offer Level 4 care.

CONCLUSION

1. On August 28, 2023, the Ninth Circuit issued a unanimous opinion affirming Pepe's conviction. See U.S. Court of Appeals 9th Cir., Case #22–50024. USA v. Michael Joseph Pepe. See also https://www.youtube.com/watch?v=hAdRj8uDYbI_(video of the argument).

BIBLIOGRAPHY

BOOKS

Abbey, Edward. *Desert Solitaire: A Season in the Wilderness*. New York: Ballantine Books, 1971.

Austin, Mary. *The Land of Little Rain*. New York: Houghton Mifflin, 1903.

Beverly Hills High School, *Watchtower*. Beverly Hills, CA: Beverly Hills High School, 1968.

Chalfant, W. A. *The Story of Inyo*. Chicago: Hammond Press, 1922.

Columbus, Frank, ed. *Advances in Psychology Research*, Vol. 7. Hauppage, NY: Nova Science Publishers, 2001.

Dahlia, Timothy. *Saline Valley History*. Privately Published, 2019.

DeDecker, Mary. *Mines of the Eastern Sierra*. La Siesta Press, 1966.

———. *White Smith's Fabulous Salt Tram*. Yucca Valley, CA: Sagebrush Press, 1975.

George, Uwe. *In the Deserts of this Earth*. New York: Harcourt Brace Jovanovich, 1977.

Gilboa, Amit. *Off the Rails in Phnom Penh: Into the Dark Heart of Guns, Girls, and Ganja*. Bangkok, Thailand: Asia Books, 2000.

Hall, Clarence, Jr., ed. *Natural History of the White-Inyo Range*. Berkeley: University of California Press, 1991.

Hueneme High School. *Voyage*. Oxnard, CA: Hueneme High School, 1971.

Juergensmeyer, Mark. *Radhasoami Reality: The Logic of a Modern Faith*. Princeton, NJ: Princeton University Press, 1995.

Levin, J. and J. A. Fox. *Mass Murder: America's Growing Menace*. New York: Plenum Press, 1985.

Likes, Robert C. and Glenn R. Day. *From This Mountain – Cerro Gordo*. Bishop, CA: Chalfant Press, 1975.

Mann, Bill. *Guide to The Remote and Mysterious Saline Valley, Volume 4*. Visalia, CA: Shortfuse Publishing Company, 2002.

Murphy, Bob. *Desert Shadows: A True Story of the Manson Family in Death Valley*. Yucca Valley, CA: Sagebrush Press, 1993.

Nadeau, Remi. *City Makers*. Garden City, New York: Doubleday & Co., 1948.

———. *Silver Seekers*. Santa Barbara, CA: Crest Publishers, 1999.

Norment, Christopher. *Relicts of a Beautiful Sea: Survival, Extinction, and Conservation in a Desert World*. Durham: University of North Carolina Press, 2014.

Nunis, Doyce B., Jr., ed. *The St. Francis Dam Disaster Revisited*. Long Beach, CA: Historical Society of Southern California, 1995.

Schumacher, Genny. *Deepest Valley*. San Francisco: Sierra Club, 1962.

Southern Inyo AARP. *Saga of Inyo*. Covina, CA: Taylor Publishing Company, 1977.

Steward, Julian H. *Ethnography of the Owens Valley Paiute*. Berkeley: University of California Press, 1993.

Sturtevant, William C., ed. *Handbook of North American Indians*, Vol. II, Great Basin. Washington, DC: Smithsonian, 1986.

Van Horn, Lawrence F. *Native America Consultations and Ethnographic Assessment, the Paiutes and Shoshones of Owens Valley, California*. Washington, DC: National Park Service, 1995.

Wason, Katherine. *The Living Master*. Punjab Province, India: Radha Soami Satsang Beas, 1996.

Wheat, Frank. *California Desert Miracle: The Fight for Desert Parks and Wilderness*. Chula Vista, CA: Sunbelt Publications, 1999.

JOURNALS

Amer, Ramses. "The Ethnic Vietnamese in Cambodia: A Minority at Risk?" *Contemporary Southeast Asia* 16, no. 2 (September 1994): 210–38.

Bailey, Thomas, and Richard Jahns. (n.d.). "Geology of the Transverse Range Province, Southern California." *Geology of Southern California. California Division of Mines and Geology Bulletin* 1, no. 170 (1954): 83–106, https://ia800703.us.archive.org/12/items/boxsouthgeology00calirich/boxsouthgeology00calirich.pdf.

Brennan, Tim, and Svein Magnussen. "Research on Non-verbal Signs of Lies and Deceit: A Blind Alley." *Frontiers in Psychology* 11 (December 14, 2020), https://www.frontiersin.org/articles/10.3389/fpsyg.2020.613410/full.

Brook, Richard A. "Inferences Regarding Aboriginal Hunting Behavior in the Saline Valley, Inyo County, California." *Journal of California and Great Basin Anthropology* 2, no. 1 (1980): 60–79.

Burgess, Ann W., Carol R. Hartman, and Arlene McCormack. "Sexual Homicide: A Motivational Model." *Journal of Interpersonal Violence* 1, no. 3 (September 1986): 251–72.

Cornelius, G. F. "Understanding Prison Culture Is the Key to Inmate Management." *Corrections Today* 54, no. 8 (December 1992): 138–73.

Darjee, Rajan. "Sexual Sadism and Psychopathy in Sexual Homicide Offenders: An Exploration of Their Associates in a Clinical Sample." *International Journal of Offender Therapy and Comparative Criminology* 63, no. 9 (March 2019): 1738–65.

Fowler, Catherine S. "Applied Ethnobiology and Advocacy: A Case Study from the Timbisha Shoshone Tribe of Death Valley, California." *Society of Enthnobiology* 39, no. 1 (May 2023): 1.

Meyers, Wade C., Lawrence Reccoppa, Karen Burton, and Ross McElroy. "Malignant Sex and Aggression: An Overview of Serial Sexual Homicide." *Bulletin of the American Academy of Psychiatry and the Law* 21, no. 4 (1993): 435–51, https://jaapl.org/content/jaapl/21/4/435.full.pdf.

Moon, Katharine. 2009. "Military Prostitution and the U.S. Military in Asia." *The Asia-Pacific Journal* 7, no. 6 (January 12, 2009), https://apjjf.org/-Katharine-H.S.-Moon/3019/article.html.

Rand, Erin J. "PROTECTing the figure of innocence: child pornography legislation and the queerness of childhood." *Quarterly Journal of Speech* 105, no. 3 (June 2018): 251–72.

Roof, Steven, and Charlie Callagan. "The Climate of Death Valley, California." *American Meteorological Society* (December 2003): 1725–40, file:///C:/Users/Doug/Downloads/1520-0477-bams-84-12-1725.pdf.

Sund, Judy. "Beyond the Grave: The Twentieth Century Afterlife of West Mexican Burial Effigies." *The Art Bulletin* 82, no. 4 (December 2000): 734–67.

———. "The Preke Speaks: Kahlua's Co-option of West Mexican Burial Effigies." *Visual Resources* XV (2000): 169–84.

NEWSPAPERS AND MAGAZINES

Colton Courier. 1952. "Teenagers Confess Burning Man Alive." February 18, 1952.

Daily Breeze. 1986. "Desert parks bill lauded." February 9, 1986.

Deccan Herald. 2022. "Clash between Nihang Sikhs and Radha Soami sect followers in Punjab, 11 injured," September 4, 2022, https://www.deccanherald.com/national/north-and-central/clash-between-nihang-sikhs-and-radha-soami-sect-followers-in-punjab-11-injured-1142167.html.

Desert Sun. 1973. "Ancient Mexican Art Shown." March 9, 1973.

Desert Sun. 1986. "Desert bill on rough road." June 14, 1986.

Inside Time. 2013. "A day in the life of Prey Sar Prison, Cambodia," April 1, 2013, https://insidetime.org/a-day-in-the-life-of-prey-sar-prison-cambodia/.

Khmer Times. 2016. "14 Years: The Horrors of Prey Sar," June 16, 2016, https://www.khmertimeskh.com/24870/14-years-the-horrors-of-prey-sar/.

Lompoc Record. 1970. "County voters decided to prevent development of El Capitan Ranch." November 4, 1970.

Los Angeles Daily News. 1990. "Sweet Secret Kahlua Finds Marketing Is Key Ingredient to Success." March 10, 1990.

Los Angeles Times. 1925. "Saline Valley Road Bid Asked." March 23, 1925.

Los Angeles Times. 1932. "Gold Vein Opened Up By Deluge." June 20, 1932.

Los Angeles Times. 1935. "Mine Promoter Faces Charges." October 2, 1935.

Los Angeles Times. 1946. "Supplies Flown to Marooned Sierra Miner." December 7, 1946.

Los Angeles Times. 1962. "Year-Round Resort." January 7, 1962.

Long Beach Independent. 1964. "Hartford's Estate Sold for $2 Million." November 9, 1964.

Long Beach Independent. 1966. "Huntington Harbour Sales." September 25, 1966.

Oxnard Press-Courier. 1973. "Elaine J. Pepe Becomes Bride." April 18, 1973.

Oxnard Press-Courier. 1975. "Carol Anilda, Michael Pepe Exchange Vows." October 2, 1975.

Pasadena Independent. 1962. "Man Found Alive After 3-Day Ordeal in Desert." August 4, 1962.

Redlands Daily Facts. 1967. "State Commissioners turn down Clay license." July 13, 1967.

Santa Barbara News-Press. 1983. "Woman lost as storm sweeps car down creek." January 24, 1983.

San Bernardino Sun. 1964. "Television Highlights." August 5, 1964.

San Bernardino Sun. 1965. "Ranch Bought for $4 Million." February 3, 1965.

San Bernardino Sun. 1965. "Brown Names Commissioner." September 23, 1965.

San Francisco Examiner. "Housing for the Very Rich Only." June 18, 1965.

San Pedro News-Pilot. 1968. "Mexican art pieces on exhibit." April 13, 1968.

The Spokesman-Review. 2004. "Man sentenced for sex with Cambodian boys." June 26, 2004.

The Telegraph. 2002. "It's like a sweet shop: if this girl's not right, get another," September 15, 2002, https://www.telegraph.co.uk/news/worldnews/asia/cambodia/1407280/Its-like-a-sweet-shop-if-this-girls-not-right-get-another.html.

Ventura Star-Free Press. 1952. "Indian Boys Admit Slaying Caretaker." February 19, 1952.

Ventura Star-Free Press. 1965. "Fuzzy Pup Joins Cupid in Tale of Lost Wallet." August 30, 1965.

Athey, Phillip. 2019. "Marine commandant considers major changes to improve force retention." *Marine Times*, October 3, 2019, https://www.marinecorpstimes.com /news/2019/10/03/marine-commandant-considers-major-changes-to-improve -force-retention/.

Baldwin, Jack O. 1970. "Rare Horses Come to U.S." *Long Beach Independent*, May 5, 1970.

Bhattacharya, Abheek. 2012. "The Cambodian Wild West." *Wall Street Journal*, May 10, 2012, https://www.wsj.com/articles/SB10001424052702304203604577395600458028114.

Bloomekatz, Ari. 2013. "Artists, students call Joseph Gatto 'great educator of the arts.'" *Los Angeles Times*, November 15, 2013, https://www.latimes.com/local/lanow /la-me-ln-artists-remember-joseph-gatto-20131114-story.html#:~:text=Artists %20and%20art%20students%20from,and%20promoter%20of%20the%20arts.

Bopha, Phorn, and Katies Nelson. 2008. "UK Man Charged for Creating Child Pornography." *Cambodia Daily*, December 3, 2008, https://english.cambodiadaily.com/ news/uk-man-charged-for-creating-child-pornography-59294/.

Brantingham, Barney. 2012. "The DA Who Loved Headlines." *Santa Barbara Independent*, February 23, 2012.

Brean, Henry. 2018. "Officials end 'hands off' policy for offbeat Death Valley hot springs." *Las Vegas Review-Journal*, May 8, 2018, https://www.reviewjournal.com/news/officials-end-hands-off-policy-for-offbeat-death-valley-hot-springs/.

Brean, Henry. 2019. "Nudity OK at Death Valley hot springs, but burros, palms must go." Las Vegas Review-Journal, May 10, 2019, https://www.reviewjournal.com/ news/politics-and-government/nudity-ok-at-death-valley-hot-springs-but-burros -palms-must-go-1660979/.

Burleigh, Nina. 2022. "A Return Trip to Timothy Leary's Psychedelic, Day-Glo Mexico." *New York Times*, May 10, 2022, https://www.nytimes.com/2022/05/06/travel/mexico-timothy-leary-psychedelics.html.

Campbell, Rob A. 1995. "L.A. STORIES: Uncovering a History as Wild as the Canyon Itself." *Los Angeles Times*, November 8, 1995, https://www.latimes.com/archives/la -xpm-1995-11-08-ls-691-story.html.

Chaba, Anju Agnihotri. 2020. "Explained: Who are the Rhada Soami Satsang Beas, the 'dera' at the heart of allegations against the Singh brothers." *Indian Express*, July 6, 2020, https://indianexpress.com/article/explained/explained-who-are-radha-soami -satsang-beas-dera-malvinder-shivinder-singh-religare-6068897/.

Chawkins, Steve, and Fred Alvarez. 2002. "Priest Charged in Sex Abuse of Boys in Oxnard, CA." *Los Angeles Times*, March 28, 2003.

Chiu, David. 2020. "Jonestown: 13 Things You Should Know About Cult Massacre." *Rolling Stone*, May 29, 2020, https://www.rollingstone.com/feature/jonestown-13 -things-you-should-know-about-cult-massacre-121974/.

Connell, Margaret. 2007. "Selma Rubin Saves El Capitan Canyon!! (37 Years Ago)." *Santa Barbara Independent*, November 1, 2007, https://www.independent.com /2007/11/01/selma-rubin-saves-el-capitan-canyon-37-years-ago/.

Denman, Lori. 2020, "Strategic Desecration of a Local Sacred Native America Site." *Citizens Journal*, February 12, 2020, https://www.citizensjournal.us/strategic-des -ecration-of-the-sacred/.

Duersten, Matthew. 2018. "The Bizarre Story Behind the Suicide of a SoCal Cult." *Los Angeles Times*, December 10, 2018, https://laist.com/news/la-history/bizarre-story -behind-the-suicide-bombing-of-a-socal-cult.

Fieldman, Charlie. 2017. "Sexual sadism: 'It's a question of degree, not of nature.'" *Montreal Gazette*, April 12, 2017, https://montrealgazette.com/news/local-news/ studying-sexual-sadism-its-a-question-of-degree-not-of-nature.

Fisher, Ian. 1997. "Army's Adultery Rule Is Don't Get Caught." *New York Times*, May 17, 1997, https://www.nytimes.com/1997/05/17/us/army-s-adultery-rule-is-don -t-get-caught.html.

Forstenzer, Martin. 1992. "A Fine Soak That Treats Body and Soul: Hippies discovered the Saline Valley hot springs in the '60s. Today's eclectic users say the experience is worth the trip on 50 miles of bad road." *Los Angeles Times*, November 24, 1992, https://www.latimes.com/archives/la-xpm-1992-11-24-mn-1136-story.html.

Gee, Marcus. 2007. "For today's pedophiles, it's all too easy." *Globe and Mail*, November 10, 2007, https://www.theglobeandmail.com/news/world/for-todays-pedophiles -its-all-too-easy/article22625144/.

Gervais, Mike. 2015. "Investigators renew look at '86 double murder." *Inyo Register*, March 14, 2015.

Giboney, Sara. 2009. "Undercover agent: Child sex abuse must be talked about." *World Herald News Service*, April 9, 2009.

Gillison, Douglas. 2008. "California Jury Convicts US Man in '06 Sex Case." *Cambodia Daily*, June 3, 2008, https://english.cambodiadaily.com/news/california-jury-con -victs-us-man-in-06-sex-case-81738/.

Glover, Scott. 2010. "Verdict in key child-sex trial at risk." *Los Angeles Times*, November 20, 2010, https://www.latimes.com/archives/la-xpm-2010-nov-20-la-me-child-sex -prosecution-20101120-story.html.

————. 2008. "Abused girls testify in U.S." *Los Angeles Times*, September 26, 2008, https://www.latimes.com/archives/la-xpm-2008-sep-26-me-kids26-story.html.

Graham, Chuck. 2021. "Movie Magic in the Alabama Hills - Eastern Sierra Backdrop Featured in Numerous Films." *Santa Barbara Independent*, November 29, 2021, https://www.independent.com/2021/11/29/movie-magic-in-the-alabama-hills/.

Grant, Bruce. 1964. "Grant On Golf." *San Bernardino County Sun*, September 5, 1964.

Gregory, Alice. 2018. "Lessons from the Last Swiss Finishing School." *The New Yorker*, October 1, 2018.

Handler, David. 1972. "Local Media rebuke Minier, Capello, UC actions." *Daily Nexus*, 1972.

Inyo Register. 2022. "Judge dismisses $20 million lawsuit filed against county, county official by former Inyo County Sheriff Hollowell," March 17, 2022, https://www.inyoregister.com/news/judge-dismisses-20-million-lawsuit-filed-against-county-county-official-by-former-inyo-county-sheriff/article_e1850b9e-a619-11ec-bfaf-eb4f8641a32e.html.

Japenga, Ann. 1986. "A Couple Disappear in Bermuda Triangle of Death Valley." *Los Angeles Times*, December 21, 1986, https://www.latimes.com/archives/la-xpm-1986-12-21-vw-3821-story.html.

Jensen, Anthony, and Aun Pheap. 2016. "Cambodia Perceived as Most Corrupt in Region." *Cambodia Daily*, January 28, 2016, https://english.cambodiadaily.com/news/cambodia-perceived-as-most-corrupt-in-region-106639/.

Johnson, Akemi. 2018. "Ladies' Night: Circling the Bases on Okinawa." *Kyoto Journal*, March 14, 2018, https://www.kyotojournal.org/society/ladies-night-circling-the-bases-on-okinawa/.

Kaplan, Tracey. 1989. "Once-remote Box Canyon Being Pried Open." *Los Angeles Times*, March 19, 1989, https://www.latimes.com/archives/la-xpm-1989-03-19-me-440-story.html.

Kari, Doug. 2015. "Double Murder in the Mojave." *LA Weekly*, March 10, 2015, https://www.laweekly.com/a-1986-double-murder-cold-case-in-the-mojave-desert-is-finally-unraveling/.

————. 2017. "The Dawn of Desert Survivors." *The Survivor*, Spring 2017, https://desert-survivors.org/wp-content/uploads/2020/11/The-Survivor-Spring-2017-.pdf.

————. 2018. "Suspect in unsolved murders set to be freed." *Inyo Register*, July 17, 2018

————. 2018. "Berman murders: Press charges or open files." *Inyo Register*, May 3, 2018.

————. 2018. "Appellate Court Reverses Sex Crimes Conviction of Double-Murder Suspect." *LA Weekly*, July 23, 2018, https://www.laweekly.com/appellate-court-reverses-sex-crimes-conviction-of-double-murder-suspect/.

————. 2018. "High court should hear child rape case." *SF Daily Journal* and *LA Daily Journal*, November 1, 2018.

————. 2021. "Retrial begins for ex-Marine accused of sex crimes in Cambodia." *Long Beach Post*, August 6, 2021, https://lbpost.com/news/michael-pepe-cambodia-retrail-marines#:~:text=Charles%20Brown%2C%20one%20of%20Michael,where%20he%20sexually%20abused%20girls.

———. 2021. "Jury finds former U.S. Marine guilty of molesting girls in Cambodia." *Long Beach Post*, August 12, 2021, https://lbpost.com/news/jury-finds-former-u-s -marine-guilty-of-molesting-girls-in-cambodia/#:~:text=The%20federal%20court %20jury%20found,illicit%20sexual%20conduct%20with%20minors.

———. 2022. "Former professor sentenced to 210 years in Cambodia sex crimes case." *Long Beach Post*, February 14, 2022, https://lbpost.com/news/crime/michael-pepe -cambodia-sex-crimes-sentence#:~:text=A%20judge%20in%20Los%20Angeles ,sentence%20would%20be%20unduly%20harsh.

———. 2023. "New clue emerges in veteran's Death Valley disappearance." *Las Vegas Review-Journal*, March 27, 2023, https://www.reviewjournal.com/local/local -nevada/new-clue-emerges-in-veterans-death-valley-disappearance-2751732/.

Kendall, John. 1998. "Remains of Long-Missing Couple Found in Desert." *Los Angeles Times*, November 16, 1998, https://www.latimes.com/archives/la-xpm-1988-11-16 -mn-305-story.html.

Kennedy, Sheila. 1987. "Puzzle of Missing Family Remains Unsolved." *Santa Barbara News-Press*, July 19, 1987.

Kessler, Bennett. 1996. "Sentence of Ex-Sheriff Fuels Anger." *Los Angeles Times*, April 9, 1996, https://www.latimes.com/archives/la-xpm-1996-04-09-mn-56457-story .html.

Kim, Victoria. 2014. "Ex-Marine convicted of sex acts with young girls in Cambodia gets life." *Los Angeles Times*, February 28, 2014, https://www.latimes.com/local/lanow/la -xpm-2014-feb-28-la-me-ln-cambodia-child-sex-sentence-20140228-story.html.

Kozlowski, Kim. 2018. "Larry Nassar now housed in Arizona prison." *Detroit News*, February 11, 2018, https://www.detroitnews.com/story/news/local/michigan/2018/02 /09/larry-nassar-milan/110251634/.

Kragen, Pam. 1988. "Green Valley developer has interests beyond housing." *Escondido Times-Advocate*, May 25, 1988.

Krikorian, Greg 2007. "Ex-Marine to face U.S. charges in Cambodian child-rape case." *Los Angeles Times*, February 10, 2007, https://www.latimes.com/archives/la-xpm -2007-feb-10-me-marine10-story.html.

LA Daily News. 2022. "Jill Stewart joins Los Angeles Daily News as city editor," April 14, 2022, https://www.dailynews.com/2022/04/14/stewart-joins-los-angeles-daily -news-as-city-editor/.

Langmuir, Molly. 2018. "Mia Farrow Takes an Unflinching Look at Her Past in the Wake of the #MeToo Movement." *Elle*, October 10, 2018, https://www.elle.com/culture/ movies-tv/a23653929/mia-farrow-women-in-hollywood-me-too/.

Love, Mike. 2018. "The Ashram Where the Beatles Sought Enlightenment." *Smithsonian*, January 2018, https://www.smithsonianmag.com/travel/beatles-ashram-sought -enlightenment-180967494/.

McCarthy, Clare. 1991. "Brad Pitt's $5.5million California beach house is under a 'threat to life' evacuation warning as Alisal wildfire rages across 15,360 acres and is only 5% contained." *Daily Mail*, October 16, 1991, https://www.dailymail.co.uk/news/arti- cle-10091243/Brad-Pitts-5-5million-California-beach-house-evacuation-warning -Alisal-wildfire-rages.html.

Mostrom, Tony. 2016. "1960s Canyon Culture Has Been Preserved in Amber in a Little Foothills Spot." *LA Weekly*, April 9, 2016, https://www.laweekly.com/1960s-canyon -culture-has-been-preserved-in-amber-in-a-little-foothills-spot/.

Mydans, Seth. 2004. "Abdication by Cambodia's King Throws His Nation Into Confusion." *New York Times*, October 8, 2004, https://www.nytimes.com/2004/10 /08/world/asia/abdication-by-cambodias-king-throws-his-nation-into-confusion .html.

Oliver, Myrna. 1998. "J. Berman; 'Mr. Kahlua' Was Developer, Donor." *Los Angeles Times*, July 22, 1998, https://www.latimes.com/archives/la-xpm-1998-jul-22-mn-6063 -story.html.

Overaker, Ken. 1970. "Fight to Preserve Nature May Land Her in Jail." *Charlotte Observer*, November 20, 1970.

Patterson, Troy. 2018. "'Wild Wild Country' Is a Tabloid Epic of the American Frontier." *New Yorker*, April 11, 2018, https://www.newyorker.com/culture/on-television/wild -wild-country-is-a-tabloid-epic-of-the-american-frontier.

Phnom Penh Post. 2013. "Pedo's accomplice says she's 'learned lesson,'" September 20, 2013, https://www.phnompenhpost.com/national/pedo%E2%80%99s-accomplice -says-she%E2%80%99s-%E2%80%98learned-lesson%E2%80%99.

Power, Samantha. 2009. "The Enforcer – A Christian lawyer's global crusade." *New Yorker*, January 19, 2009.

Rasmussen, Cecilia. 2003. "Mountain Retreats Evolved From Reservoirs to Playgrounds." *Los Angeles Times*, November 9, 2003, https://www.latimes.com/archives/la-xpm -2003-nov-09-me-then9-story.html.

Rogers, Melinda. 2011. "Elizabeth Smart kidnapper booked at federal prison in Arizona." *Salt Lake Tribune*, September 15, 2011, https://archive.sltrib.com/article.php?id =52500560&itype=CMSID.

Ross, Alex. 2016. "The Timbisha Shoshone of Death Valley and the Shadow of Trump." *New Yorker*, November 15, 2016, https://www.newyorker.com/culture/culture-desk /the-timbisha-shoshone-of-death-valley-and-the-shadow-of-trump.

Saner, Emine. 2016. "Poor little rich kids-the perils of inheriting vast wealth." *The Guardian*, August 12, 2016, https://www.theguardian.com/money/2016/aug/12 /poor-little-rich-kids-the-perils-of-inheriting-vast-wealth-hugh-grosvenor-duke -of-westminster.

Schrader, Jessica. 2021. "The Personality Disorder We Don't Hear Enough About." *Psychology Today*, June 21, 2021, https://www.psychologytoday.com/us/blog/and -running/202106/the-personality-disorder-we-dont-hear-enough-about.

Schroeder, Laurie Mason and Peter Hall. 2015. "'Violent' sex trafficker gets 24-plus years in federal prison." *Morning Call*, February 6, 2015, https://www.mcall.com/2015 /02/06/violent-sex-trafficker-gets-24-plus-years-in-federal-prison/.

Sharma, Manraj Grewal and Prabha Raghavan. 2019. "The dera by the Beas." *Indian Express*, December 8, 2019, https://indianexpress.com/article/india/the-dera-by -the-beas-6155961/.

Sloane, Leonard. 1981. "Jules Berman Returns to Liquor Business." *New York Times*, December 29, 1981.

Stall, Bill. 1967. "Cassius Clay Says He Wants to Fight One More Time." *Santa Cruz Sentinel,* July 13, 1967

UPI. 1970. "Foes Block $60 Million Development on Ranch." *Fresno Bee,* August 30, 1970.

———. 1967. "State Commissioners turn down Clay license." *Redlands Daily Facts,* July 13, 1967.

Wall, Deborah. 2021. "Eureka Dunes in Death Valley National Park perfect for adventurers." *Las Vegas Review-Journal,* February 18, 2021, https://www.reviewjournal.com /local/local-columns/deborah-wall/eureka-dunes-in-death-valley-national-park -perfect-for-adventurers-2283508/.

Wang, K. S. 2008. "Celebrity Drive: Voice of the Beach Boys Mike Love Loves His Cars - Especially British Ones." *Motortrend,* May 31, 2008, https://www.motortrend.com/ features/mike-love-celebrity-drive/.

Welsh, James, and Pin Sisovann. 2007. "Svay Pak Child-Sex Trade Back in Business – Again." *Cambodia Daily,* May 14, 2007, https://english.cambodiadaily.com/news/ svay-pak-child-sex-trade-back-in-business-again-1197/.

Welsh, James. 2008. "Officials Defend Testimonies in US on Behalf of Pedophile." *Cambodia Daily,* June 26, 2008, https://english.cambodiadaily.com/news/officials -defend-testimonies-in-us-on-behalf-of-pedophile-58244/.

Wilson, Audrey. 2016. "Goodbye to Phnom Penh's 'sleaziest bar.'" *Phnom Penh Post,* May 6, 2016, https://www.phnompenhpost.com/post-weekend/goodbye-phnom-penhs -sleaziest-bar.

Zimmerman, Rick 2021. "History of Lake Arrowhead Country Club." *Mountain News,* June 30, 2021, https://mountain-news.com/news/40599/history-of-lake-arrow-head-country-club/#:~:text=The%20original%20Clubhouse%20was%20con-structed,when%20it%20went%20into%20receivership.

WEBSITES

ABTL (n.d.). "Federal District Court Judge Dale Fischer," https://abtl.org/profiles/ fischer.pdf.

AIM (n.d.). https://aimfree.org/.

Archuleta County, CO. (n.d.). "History of Archuleta County," https://www.archule-tacounty.org/101/History-of-Archuleta-County.

ASVAB. (n.d.). "What's the Difference? Enlisted vs. Officer," https://www.asvabprogram .com/media-center-article/66.

Basin and Range. 2020. "Desert Pavement: It's Natural." August 14, 2020, https://www .basinandrangewatch.org/DesertPavement.html.

Beverly Hills High School. (n.d.). "Class of 1968," https://www.bhhs1968.com/class _profile.cfm?member_id=383751.

Burning Man. (n.d.). "Historical timeline," https://burningman.org/timeline/.

CA.gov. (n.d.). "Red Rock Canyon State Park," https://www.parks.ca.gov/?page_id=631.

Camp Lejuene. (n.d.) https://www.lejeune.marines.mil/.

Captain History. 2018. "1914 Las Vegas Post Card – Clark County Court House-De-Longchamps," January 17, 2018, http://captainhistory.com/wordpress1/2018/01/17/337/.

Chamings, Andrew. 2021. "Five months after an 'unusual death,' another man is missing at unique Death Valley hot springs." SF Gate, May 13, 2021, https://www.sfgate.com/bayarea/article/california-death-valley-missing-person-hot-springs-016174964.php#:~:text=in%20the%20US-,Five%20months%20after%20an%20'unusual%20death%2C'%20another%20man%20is,unique%20Death%20Valley%20hot%20springs&text=The%20body%20of%20Donald%20Vanneman,currently%20missing%20from%20the%20area.

Char Margolis. (n.d.). https://www.char.net/about.

City of Solvang. (n.d.). "Official Visitor Guide," https://www.solvangusa.com/.

Corfield, Justin. (n.d.). "eMelbourne the city past & present," https://www.emelbourne.net.au/biogs/EM00283b.htm.

Cornell Law School. (n.d.). "Motion to suppress," https://www.law.cornell.edu/wex/motion_to_suppress#:~:text=The%20concept%20of%20a%20motion,from%20unlawful%20searches%20and%20seizures.

Criminal Law Notebook. (n.d.). "Chapter 7: Circumstantial Evidence," http://criminalnotebook.ca/index.php/Circumstantial_Evidence.

Cross, Alan. 2016. "Where Did the Phrase 'Sex, Drugs and Rock'n'Roll' Actually Come From?" A Journal of Musical Things, April 6, 2016, https://www.ajournalofmusicalthings.com/phrase-sex-drugs-rocknroll-actually-come/.

Crothers, Lauren. 2015. "Cambodia's judicial system among the most corrupt." Anadolu Agency, September 17, 2015, https://www.aa.com.tr/en/world/cambodia-s-judicial-system-among-most-corrupt/123628.

———. 2014. "Corruption in Cambodian courts endemic, says new report." Anadolu Agency, September 9, 2014, https://www.aa.com.tr/en/world/corruption-in-cambodian-courts-endemic-says-new-report/119302.

DangerousRoads.com. (n.d.). "Lippincott Mine Road in CA is only for experienced 4WD drivers and vehicles," https://www.dangerousroads.org/north-america/usa/998-lippincott-mine-road-usa.html.

DeathValley.com. (n.d.). "Steel Pass," https://www.deathvalley.com/index.php/exploring-death-valley-backcountry-4x4/326-steel-pass.

Desert Survivors. (n.d.). https://www.desert-survivors.org/.

Digital Desert. (n.d.). "Desert Flash Floods," https://digital-desert.com/flash-floods/.

Dr. Koplin. (n.d.). "Biography," https://www.drkoplin.com/about-dr-koplin/.

Fabricant, Danny. 2013. "The Federal Prison System and the Tucson Penitentiary," February 14, 2013, https://fastandfuriousandfabricant.wordpress.com/2013/02/14/the-federal-prison-system-and-the-tucson-penitentiary/.

Facebook. (n.d.). "Dwayne's Friendly Pharmacy," https://www.facebook.com/dwaynes-pharmacy/.

Famous-Trials.com. (n.d.). "Testimony by Dr. Michael Maloney," https://www.famous-trials.com/mcmartin/917-maloneytestimony.

Faraway Medicine. (n.d.). "Dr. Laura Watson," https://www.farawaymedicine.com/dr
-laura-watson.

F. D. Sweet & Son. 2017. "Obituary for Loth Westerman Jr.," November 15, 2017, https://
www.obituary-assistant.com/obituaries/fd-sweet-son/loth-westerman-jr-obituary.
———. (n.d.). "St. Joseph Catholic Church Phnom Penh," https://m.facebook.com/
profile.php?id=315895185098074.

Fitch, Brian. 2014. "The Truth About Lying: What Investigators Need to Know," Law
Enforcement Bulletin, June 10, 2014. https://leb.fbi.gov/articles/featured-articles/
the-truth-about-lying-what-investigators-need-to-know.

Forgotten Roller Rinks. (n.d.). "Rollerbowl," https://forgottenrollerrinksofthepast.com/
Hollywood%20CA.html.

Frenzel, Lou. 2020. "Heathkit: An Employee's Look Back," Electronic Design, November
30, 2020. https://www.electronicdesign.com/blogs/contributed-blogs/archive/com-
muniqu/article/21148923/electronic-design-heathkit-an-employees-look-back.

Ganner, Tom. (multiple dates). "The Saline Valley Chronicles." https://timenspace.net/
saline-valley-chronicles/.

Geberth, Vernon J. 1996. "The Classification of Sex-Related Homicides," http://practi-
calhomicide.com/articles/sexrelatedhomicides.htm.

Glass, Andrew. 2019. "U.S. planes bomb Libya, April 15, 1986." Politico, April 15, 2019,
https://www.politico.com/story/2019/04/15/reagan-bomb-libya-april-15-1986
-1272788.

GlobalSecurity.org. (n.d.). "Marine Corps Logistics Base, Barstow," https://www.milita-
rymuseum.org/MCLBB.html.

Gregoire, Carolyn. 2014. "How Money Changes The Way We Think and Behave."
Huffington Post, January 6, 2014, https://www.huffpost.com/entry/psychology
-of-wealth_n_4531905#:~:text=Wealth%20can%20cloud%20moral%20judg-
ment.&text=Another%20study%20suggested%20that%20merely,exposed%20to
%20money%2Drelated%20words.

Harrell, Ashley. 2021. "San Francisco man's unusual death in Death Valley thermal pool
alarms hot springs community." SF Gate, January 21, 2021, https://www.sfgate
.com/california-parks/article/san-francisco-death-valley-saline-warm-springs
-15886069.php.

Henshaw, David. 2011. "The US agents tracking down sex tourists in Cambodia." BBC,
January 20, 2011, https://www.bbc.com/news/world-us-canada-12298870.

Hirst, K. Kris. 2020. "Angkor Civilization: The Ancient Empire in Southeast Asia."
ThoughtCo., April 5, 2020, https://www.thoughtco.com/angkor-civilization
-ancient-khmer-empire-169557.

History.com. (n.d.). "Mass suicide at Jonestown," https://www.history.com/this-day-in
-history/mass-suicide-at-jonestown.

Hughes, Matthew. 2020. "Can Law Enforcement Really Recover Files You've Deleted?"
How-To Geek, June 22, 2020, https://www.howtogeek.com/675784/can-law
-enforcement-really-recover-files-you%E2%80%99ve-deleted/.

ICE. (n.d.). "Role of ICE," https://www.ice.gov/features/human-trafficking#:~:text
=training%20and%20awareness.-,Role%20of%20ICE,national%20security
%20and%20public%20safety.

IMDB. (n.d.). *12 Angry Men* (1957), https://www.imdb.com/title/tt0050083/.

Inyo County. (n.d.). "A Brief History of the Inyo County Sheriff's Office," https://www
.inyocounty.us/services/sheriff.

———. (n.d.). "Thomas L. Hardy-District Attorney," https://www.inyocounty.us/ser-
vices/district-attorney/district-attorney-staff.

Inyo SAR. (n.d.). https://inyosar.com/.

Kemp, Sam. 2022. "Barker Ranch: The abandoned gold mine that became Charles Manson's hideout." Far Out, June 19, 2022, https://faroutmagazine.co.uk/barker-ranch
-charles-mansons-hideout/.

KI-Media. 2006. "US Citizen arrested for having sex with young girls in Cambodia," June
2, 2006, http://ki-media.blogspot.com/2006/06/us-citizen-arrested-for-having-sex
.html.

L.A. Conservancy. (n.d.). "Belmont High School," https://www.laconservancy.org/loca-
tions/belmont-high-school.

LADWP. (n.d.). "St. Francis Dam Disaster," https://waterandpower.org/museum/St.
%20Francis%20Dam%20Disaster.html.

Legacy.com. 2020. "Dennis Ferrel Carpenter," February 9, 2020, https://www.legacy.com/
us/obituaries/venturacountystar/name/dennis-carpenter-obituary?id=2047834.

Life of Sailing. (n.d.). "How To Sail From California To New Zealand," https://www
.lifeofsailing.com/post/how-to-sail-from-california-to-new-zealand.

Linder, Douglas. (n.d.). "The McMartin Preschool Abuse Trial: An Account," https://
famous-trials.com/mcmartin/902-home.

LinkedIn (n.d.). "Cody Hoffman," https://www.linkedin.com/in/cody-hoffman
-172a39199.

Lutz, Ashley. 2012. "Former Detective Reveals How to Tell When Suspects Are Lying."
Business Insider, April 5, 2012, https://www.businessinsider.com/police-detective
-reveals-how-she-can-tell-suspects-are-lying-2012-4.

Macrotrends. (n.d.). "Phnom Penh, Cambodia Metro Area Population 1950-2023,"
https://www.macrotrends.net/cities/20357/phnom-penh/population.

The Marshall Project. 2017. "Prison is a Real-Life Example of the World White Supremacists Want," August 24, 2017, https://www.themarshallproject.org/2017/08/24/
prison-is-a-real-life-example-of-the-world-white-supremacists-want.

Mattern, Jim. 2015. "Ko'onzi Village – Saline Valley," March 24, 2015, http://deathvalley-
jim.com/koonzi-village-saline-valley/.

———. 2014. "Saline Valley Salt Tram," May 6, 2014, http://deathvalleyjim.com/saline
-valley-salt-tram/.

Matthews, Dylan. 2018. "How the 9th Circuit became conservatives' least favorite
court." Vox, January 10, 2018, https://www.vox.com/policy-and-politics/2018/1/10
/16873718/ninth-circuit-court-appeals-liberal-conservative-trump-tweet.

Military Installations. (n.d.). "Naval Base Ventura County-Point Mugu/Port Hueneme-In-depth Overview," https://installations.militaryonesource.mil/in-depth-overview/naval-base-ventura-county-point-mugu-port-hueneme.

MotorcycleSpecs. (n.d.). "Yamaha IT 175," https://www.motorcyclespecs.co.za/model/yamaha/yamaha_it175d.htm.

———. (n.d.). "Yamaha IT 200," https://www.motorcyclespecs.co.za/model/yamaha/yamaha_it200%2084.htm.

Mule Days. (n.d.). https://muledays.org/.

NGOsource. (n.d.). "What is an NGO?" https://www.ngosource.org/what-is-an-ngo#:~:text=NGO%20stands%20for%20non%2Dgovernmental,all%20parts%20of%20the%20world.

NotreHistoire. (n.d.). "Les Fougères," https://notrehistoire.ch/entries/KgQYAml2Ywv.

NPS. 1970. "History of the Charcoal Kilns - Excerpt from "Charcoal Kilns Historic Structures Report 1970," https://www.nps.gov/deva/learn/historyculture/charcoalkilns.htm.

———. (n.d.). "Eureka Dunes," https://www.nps.gov/deva/planyourvisit/eureka-dunes.htm.

———. (n.d.). "Scotty's Castle," https://www.nps.gov/deva/learn/historyculture/scottys-castle.htm.

———. (n.d.). "The Racetrack," https://www.nps.gov/deva/planyourvisit/the-racetrack.htm.

Oberlin. n.d. "Kodak Instamatic camera 304," https://ohio5.contentdm.oclc.org/digital/collection/artifacts/id/575/.

OJP. (n.d.) "Commanding Officer's Guide to the NCIS (Naval Criminal Investigative Service)," https://www.ojp.gov/ncjrs/virtual-library/abstracts/commanding-officers-guide-ncis-naval-criminal-investigative-service#:~:text=The%20NCIS%20was%20formerly%20known,General%20Counsel%20of%20the%20Navy.

Paññāsāstra University of Cambodia, http://www.puc.edu.kh/.

PBS. (n.d.). "Learning from Skeletons," https://www.pbs.org/opb/historydetectives/technique/learning-from-skeletons/index.html.

Perrotta, Giulio. 2020. "Pedophilia: Definition, classifications criminological and neurobiological profiles, and clinical treatments." Peerteckz, 2020, https://www.peertechzpublications.com/articles/OJPCH-5-126.php.

Psychcentral. (n.d.) "What Is Polarity Therapy?" https://psychcentral.com/health/polarity-therapy.

Quote Investigator. 2017. An Army Marches On Its Stomach, https://quoteinvestigator.com/2017/10/15/army/

Radar. 2013. "Neighbors From Hell: Furious Locals Accuse Brad Pitt and Angelina Jolie of Destroying Fragile Californian Coastline," April 26, 2013, https://radaronline.com/exclusives/2013/04/brad-pitt-and-angelina-jolie-accused-of-destroying-worlds-most-fragile-coastline/.

Radio Free Asia. 2014. "Ethnic Vietnamese in Cambodia Left in Limbo Without Citizenship," May 19, 2014, https://www.rfa.org/english/news/cambodia/vietnamese-03192014205359.html.

Reagan Foundation. 1986. "White House Diaries." Ronald Reagan Presidential Foundation & Institute, January 3, 1986, https://www.reaganfoundation.org/ronald-reagan/white-house-diaries/diary-entry-01031986/.

Reagan Ranch. (n.d.). https://reaganranch.yaf.org/rancho-del-cielo/.

Ross, Phil. 2004. "Cambodia-The Wild West of Asia." Stickman Bankok, April 15, 2004, https://www.stickmanbangkok.com/readers-submissions/2004/04/cambodia-the-wild-west-of-asia/.

Roy, Sandip. 2018. "50 years in, India is celebrating the Beatles' infamous trip to the country." TheWorld, March 5, 2018, https://theworld.org/stories/2018-03-05/50-years-india-celebrating-beatles-infamous-trip-country.

RSSB.org. (n.d.). https://rssb.org/overview.html.

RSSB. n.d. "A Brief Biography of Maharaj Charan Singh," https://rssb.org/Maharaj_Charan_Singh.html.

Saline Preservation Association. (n.d.). https://salinepreservation.org/.

Schat's Bakery. (n.d.). https://schatsbakery.com/wp/shipping/.

ScotchWhiskey.com. (n.d.). "Schenley Industries," https://scotchwhisky.com/whiskypedia/5996/schenley-industries/.

Singh, Nandita. 2019. "Gurinder Singh Dhillon — the music & film-loving Radha Soami head at heart of Fortis crisis." ThePrint, November 16, 2019, https://theprint.in/india/gurinder-singh-dhillon-the-music-film-loving-radha-soami-head-at-heart-of-fortis-crisis/321764/.

Sip Awards. (n.d.). "A Brief History of Kahlua," https://sipawards.com/cocktail-knowledge/a-brief-history-of-kahlua/.

SpruceEats. 2022. "What Is Paan? A Guide to Paan and Its Use in Indian Cuisine." SpruceEats, September 7, 2022, https://www.thespruceeats.com/definition-of-paan-1957541.

Stringfellow, Kim. 2015. "Holes in the Desert: A Mojave Crime Compendium." KCET, November 30, 2105, https://www.kcet.org/shows/artbound/holes-in-the-desert-a-mojave-crime-compendium.

SummitPost.org. (n.d.). "Dry Mountain," https://www.summitpost.org/dry-mountain/764192.

Swendson, Paul. 2022. "The Ultimate Generation Gap of the 1960s." Soapboxie, October 19, 2022, https://soapboxie.com/social-issues/The-Ultimate-Generation-Gap-of-the-1960s.

The Tempel Lipizzans. (n.d.). "The History of the Lipizzan Breed, https://www.tempelfarms.com/the-history-of-the-lipizzan.html#:~:text=The%20breed%20got%20its%20start,the%20court%20stud%20at%20Kladrub.

Tha, Thai. 2017. "Cambodia's Prey Sar Prison Like Being 'in Hell' Former Inmate Says." Radio Free Asia, March 3, 2017, https://www.rfa.org/english/news/cambodia/prison-03032017132739.html#:~:text=Confinement%20in%20Cambodia's%20notorious%20Prey,%2C%2025%2C%20said%20on%20Feb.

TopGear. 2013. "History lesson: The Datsun name," July 16, 2013, https://www.topgear.com/car-news/classic/history-lesson-datsun-name.

Trailmaster. (n.d.). "Runyon Canyon Park," https://www.thetrailmaster.com/trails/griffith -park-runyon-canyon-park-south/.

Trip Advisor. (n.d.) "Sharky Bar and Restaurant," https://www.tripadvisor.com/Attraction_Review-g293940-d324074-Reviews-Sharky_Bar_and_Restaurant-Phnom _Penh.html.

University of British Columbia. (n.d.). "The Timbisha Shoshone Indigenous People and Death Valley National Monument, USA," https://cases.open.ubc.ca/w17t2cons200 -36/.

University of Minnesota. (n.d.). "Holocaust and Genocide Studies, Cambodia," https:// cla.umn.edu/chgs/holocaust-genocide-education/resource-guides/cambodia.

U.S. Courts. (n.d.) "About the Supreme Court," https://www.uscourts.gov/about-federal-courts/educational-resources/about-educational-outreach/activity-resources/ about#:~:text=The%20Supreme%20Court%20agrees%20to,asked%20to%20review %20each%20year.

USMC. (n.d.). "MCB Camp Pendleton," https://www.pendleton.marines.mil/Main -Menu/History-and-Museums/.

———. (n.d.). "MCAS Iwakuni, Japan," https://www.mcasiwakuni.marines.mil/.

———. (n.d.). "Origins of the Ka-Bar Knife," https://www.mcl567.com/kabar-1a.

U.S. Navy. (n.d.). "Naval Air Weapons Station China Lake," https://cnrsw.cnic.navy.mil/ Installations/NAWS-China-Lake/.

VAWnet. (n.d.). "The Scope of the Problem: Intimate Partner Homicide Statistics," https: //vawnet.org/sc/scope-problem-intimate-partner-homicide-statistics.

Walters, F.E., Jr. 2010. Vantage Point, November 13, 2010, https://news.va.gov/534/my -experience-at-usmc-boot-camp-parris-island-1971/.

Wikipedia (n.d.). "Andrew Kleinfeld," https://en.wikipedia.org/wiki/Andrew_Kleinfeld.

———. (n.d.). "Edward R. Roybal Federal Building," https://en.wikipedia.org/wiki/ Edward_R._Roybal_Federal_Building_and_United_States_Courthouse.

———. (n.d.). "FUNCINPEC," https://en.wikipedia.org/wiki/FUNCINPEC.

———. (n.d.). "Jacqueline Nguyen," https://en.wikipedia.org/wiki/Jacqueline_Nguyen.

———. (n.d.). "Kenny Roberts Jr.," https://en.wikipedia.org/wiki/Kenny_Roberts_Jr.

———. (n.d.). "Luke Hunt," htttps://en.wikipedia.org/wiki/Luke_Hunt.

———. (n.d.). "Robert William Prescott," https://en.wikipedia.org/wiki/Robert_William_Prescott.

———. (n.d.). "Sidney Thomas," https://en.wikipedia.org/wiki/Sidney_R._Thomas.

———. (n.d.). "Universal Life Church," https://en.wikipedia.org/wiki/Universal_Life _Church.

Willett-Wei, Megan. 2016. "Here are all the luxurious properties at stake in the Brangelina divorce." Insider, September 21, 2016, https://www.insider.com/brad-pitt -angelina-jolie-divorce-who-gets-what-2016-9.

Wilkerson, George T. 2018. "It's Surprisingly Tough to Avoid Snitching in Prison." The Marshall Project, July 19, 2018, https://www.themarshallproject.org/2018/07/19/it -s-surprisingly-tough-to-avoid-snitching-in-prison.

Wisdom Retreats. (n.d.). "Mary Sullivan biography," https://www.wisdomretreats.us/ mary.

Woodruff, Bob, John Kapetaneas, Geoff Martz, and Karson You. 2017. "Inside the world of Cambodia's child sex trade, as told through the eyes of a survivor." ABC News, March 8, 2017, https://abcnews.go.com/International/inside-world-cambodias -child-sex-trade-told-eyes/story?id=45990734.

World Bank Group (n.d.). "Climatology – Cambodia," https://climateknowledgeportal .worldbank.org/country/cambodia/climate-data-historical.

World Hope International. (n.d.). https://worldhope.org/.

YouTube. (n.d.). "Jimi Hendrix Sets Guitar On Fire at Monterey Pop Festival. 1967," https://www.youtube.com/watch?v=1ZiFUN8cIuo.

Zoukis Consulting Group. (n.d.). "Corrlinks.com Inmate Email/TRULINCS Federal Prison Email," https://federalcriminaldefenseattorney.com/prison-life/corrlinks -inmate-email-trulincs/.

———. (n.d.). "MDC Los Angeles - Metropolitan Detention Center Los Angeles," https://federalcriminaldefenseattorney.com/federal-bureau-prisons/mdc-los-ange- les/.

OTHER

18 USC § 2241(c).

18 USC § 2423(b).

California Superior Court, San Diego. 1976. Case #D101882, Carol Ann Pepe v. Michael Joseph Pepe, March 3, 1976.

Catrone, Kristin M. 2020. "Divorce as Liberation: Marital Expectations Among the Working Class in the 1950s." Dissertation, City College of New York, 2020, https:// academicworks.cuny.edu/cgi/viewcontent.cgi?article=1633&context=hc_sas_etds.

Hawley, Dean. 1992. "Death by Strangulation," http://www.markwynn.com/wp-content/ uploads/death-by-strangulation.pdf.

ICE. 2014. "Ex-Marine receives 210-year federal prison term for drugging and rap- ing girls in Cambodia," February 28, 2014, https://www.ice.gov/news/releases /ex-marine-receives-210-year-federal-prison-term-drugging-and-raping-girls -cambodia.

Last Management. 2008. "Runyon Canyon Park." Privately published, c. 2008.

Poster, Marc. (n.d.). "Taking It To the Banc," https://www.gmsr.com/wp-content/uploads /2016/06/Taking-it-to-the-Banc.pdf.

PROTECT Act (2003). Pub. L. No. 108-21, 117 Stat. 650.

Renta, Mike. 1987. "Operations Reports." China Lake Mountain Rescue Group, https:// www.clmrg.org/taluspile/tp%20071.pdf.

———. 1986. "Operation Reports." China Lake Mountain Rescue Group, https://www .clmrg.org/taluspile/tp%20065.pdf.

Rostker, Bernard D., Harry J. Thie, James L. Lacy, Jennifer H. Kawata, and Susanna W. Purnell. 1993. "The Defense Officer Personnel Management Act of 1980: A Retrospective Assessment." RAND, https://www.rand.org/pubs/reports/R4246 .html.

Shultz, Hazel. (n.d.). "B24 Crash Lands in Saline Valley," http://www.owensvalleyhistory .com/stories/b24_crash_in_saline_valley.pdf

Simmons, Phillip. 2012. "Metal Finishes – Barry Berman, Goleta." March–April 2012. Privately Published.

United States v. Clark, 435 F.3d 1100 (9th Cir. 2006).

United States v. Pepe. 2017. "USA v. Michael Pepe." (The hearing video can be viewed by entering Case #14-50095), https://www.ca9.uscourts.gov/media/.

United States v. Pepe, 895 F.3d 679 (9th Cir. 2018).

University of California, Los Angeles. 1996. "Interview of Jules Berman." Entrepreneurs of the West, UCLA Oral History Program, Center for Oral History Research, Charles E. Young Research Library, https://oralhistory.library.ucla.edu/.

Unrau, Harlan D. 1997. "A History of the Lands Added to Death Valley National Monument by the California Desert Protection Act of 1994." Death Valley National Park Special History Study.

U.S. Army Criminal Investigation Division. (n.d.). "U.S. Army Criminal Investigation Command," https://irp.cdn-website.com/cadac795/files/uploaded/CIDBrochure.pdf.

U.S. Constitution, Article I, Section 8, Clause 3.

U.S. Court of Appeals 9th Cir. 2014. Case #14-50095, USA v. Michael Joseph Pepe. 2022. Case #22-50024, USA v. Michael Joseph Pepe.

U.S. Department of Justice. 2003. "Fact Sheet Protect Act," April 30, 2003.

———. 2008. "Ex-Marine Guilty of Using Drugs and Force to Have Sex With Young Girls in Cambodia," May 29, 2008, https://www.justice.gov/archive/usao/cac/Pressroom/pr2008/074.html.

———. 2009. "Attorney General Holder Recognizes Department Employees and Others for Their Service at Annual Awards Ceremony," October 21, 2009, https://www.justice.gov/opa/pr/attorney-general-holder-recognizes-department-employees-and-others-their-service-annual.

U.S. Department of the Navy. 1992. "MCO 1560.24D Broadened Opportunity for Officer Selection and Training (BOOST) Program," August 9, 1992, https://www.marines.mil/Portals/1/Publications/MCO%201560.24D.pdf.

U.S. District Court, Central District of California. 2007. Case #2:06-mj-01717-DUTY, USA v. Michael Joseph Pepe.

———. 2007. Case #CR-07-168 DSF, USA v. Michael Joseph Pepe.

U.S. District Court, Northern District of Texas. 2006. Case #3:06-CR-262-N(02), USA v. Quincy Lamon Walters.

U.S. Marine Corps. 2018. "Marine Corps Uniform Regulations." May 1, 2018, https://www.marines.mil/portals/1/Publications/MCO%201020.34H%20v2.pdf?ver=2018-06-26-094038-137.

———. (n.d.). "Cadences," https://www.usmcu.edu/Portals/218/Quantico-%20Crossroads%20Of%20The%20Marine%20Corps.pdf.

U.S. Marine Corps. (n.d.). "Quantico: Crossroads of the Marine Corps. History of Museum Division, Headquarters, US Marine Corp, https://www.usmcu.edu/Portals/218/Quantico-%20Crossroads%20Of%20The%20Marine%20Corps.pdf.

INDEX

Note: Photo insert images between pages 90 and 91 are indicated by *p1*, *p2*, *p3*, etc.

About the Author

Doug Kari is an investigative journalist and attorney who focuses on true crime. Besides writing about the Berman case, Doug has covered stories ranging from the cartel's slaughter of Mormon moms and children in Mexico, to the baffling disappearance of a teenage girl from alongside a rural highway in eastern California. His articles have been featured in the *Las Vegas Review-Journal*, *LA Weekly*, *San Diego Union-Tribune*, the *LA Times*, and many other outlets.

While majoring in English at UC Berkeley, Doug studied creative writing under Leonard Michaels (*Sylvia*, *The Men's Club*). After graduating magna cum laude from UC Law SF, Doug spent seventeen years as a litigation attorney for Orrick, an international law firm, and then became chief legal officer of Arbitech, a technology company.

An avid outdoorsman, Doug cofounded the conservation group Desert Survivors. As chronicled in Frank Wheat's book *California Desert Miracle*, Doug took a lead role in fighting to protect the remote wilderness where the Bermans disappeared.